The
Fast Forward
MBA in Business

The Fast Forward MBA in Business

VIRGINIA O'BRIEN

John Wiley & Sons, Inc.

New York • Chichester • Brisbane • Toronto • Singapore

ISBN-0-471-14660-9

Printed in the United States of America

10 9 8 7 6 5 4 3 2 1

for
Seana and Buzz

VIRGINIA O'BRIEN

Virginia O'Brien's professional experience includes working as the director of communication for organizations in both the business and nonprofit sectors. She has also freelanced as a writer, ghostwriter, and editor. Her articles on business intelligence have been published in the United States and the European business press, and she was a contributing author to *Winning in the New Europe: Taking Advantage of the Single Market,* ed. Liam Fahey (Englewood Cliffs, N.J.: Prentice Hall, 1992). Ms. O'Brien has designed and taught organizational communication courses on the college level, and developed and presented seminars on business intelligence to *Fortune* 500 executives. She has a B.A. in psychology and holds a Master of Science degree from Boston University's College of Communication.

ACKNOWLEDGMENTS

I offer my acknowledgments in a chronological fashion, following the path along which this project unfolded. First, I am thankful to Art Kleiner, a writer whom I met while working on a project at MIT. We all need someone to open doors for us and he opened an important door for me. I am truly grateful to Janet Coleman, my editor, who invited me in and gave me the opportunity to work on this project, and I thank her for helping me to shape it and breathe life into it. Thanks also go to all the scholars, academics, journalists, business researchers, and corporate people whose work forms the foundation of this book. It is their ideas, their research, and their experience that is reflected within these pages. I sincerely appreciate the valuable suggestions Stuart Robinson provided for Section 2. And finally, I am deeply grateful to my husband, Buzz Jenney, for all his loving and patient support. Along with the great shoulder massages he gave me as I sat over my computer, he offered keen editorial guidance on the entire manuscript. His eye for detail and his suggestions were invaluable to me.

CONTENTS

CHAPTER FOUR—NEW RELATIONSHIPS: TEAMWORK AND THE CUSTOMER CONNECTION

CHAPTER SEVEN—THE MACRO AND MICRO OF ECONOMICS

SECTION THREE
FUNCTIONS AND STRATEGIES: MAKING BUSINESS WORK

CHAPTER EIGHT—INFORMATION TECHNOLOGY: THE NEW ENGINE OF BUSINESS

CHAPTER NINE—M&M: MANUFACTURING AND MARKETING

CHAPTER TEN—STRATEGIC THINKING: IT'S ALL ABOUT MOVES

INTRODUCTION

Knowledge is the key to the future. Managers who demonstrate their understanding of key business concepts and who integrate that understanding into successful business performance are highly valued in the workplace.

The Fast Forward MBA in Business is designed to give those aspiring to executive-level positions a means of quickly garnering knowledge of basic business principles as well as cutting-edge thinking. In easy-to-read format, this latest edition of our popular MBA series presents the key fundamentals spanning topics from human resource performance appraisal methods to flexible manufacturing operations to reengineering business processes to global strategies for large and small companies.

Reflecting the transition going on in the business world, this latest edition breaks away from the series' traditional format and presents a new approach. *The Fast Forward MBA in Business* provides a balanced framework that examines both the soft and hard issues facing managers as the twenty-first century approaches. In addition to key business concepts that are drawn from the works of scholars, academicians, and business researchers, it provides practical tips for implementing theories presented and offers warnings about practices to be avoided. Its stories and profiles highlight successful companies and their leaders. Through real-life examples, the reader sees the results of putting ideas into action.

Throughout *The Fast Forward MBA in Business*, emphasis is placed on the significance of integrating the softer issues of people and values with the harder disciplines of accountability and responsibility. Separated into three sections, *The Fast Forward MBA in Business* opens by focusing on the people end of business. The first chapter examines leadership and management—every company needs men and women at all levels of the organization who can lead their people through the changes required to succeed in the twenty-first century. And, as Chapter 2 reveals, every company also needs to understand the significance of its corporate culture—how the company's values and beliefs influence the people within it. Without that understanding, managers will not be able to guide their workers through the change that is demanded by the forces of a global, competitive market.

The first section continues to examine the significance of people and purpose as it discusses the evolving role of human resource management and the newly emerging relationships being created by teamwork and by partnering with customers, as companies strive to give customers the value they want and deserve.

Section 2 deals with the fundamental issues of the bottom line, providing the reader with the ability to understand the basics of accounting and the value of financial statements. By explaining how to analyze operations and interpret numbers in relation to organizational practices, the reader gains insight into the process of making sound business and investment decisions. And because the emphasis today is on a systems approach, this section also includes economic principles, informing the reader of ways to evaluate and factor in the macro and micro environment when deciding on business opportunities. No company, no industry, no nation operates in isolation; each is inextricably linked with the other. Although the connections might at first glance seem indiscernible, each touches the other, influencing outcomes.

The latest cutting-edge issues are handled in Section 3. It opens with a review of the enormous impact of information technology on business life—how it revs the corporate engine and how it can be strategically used to drive the company into the future. Manufacturing and marketing form an unusual alliance in Chapter 9, as progressive thinking is examined. Company stories illustrate the benefits that are derived when functions in a flattened, team-oriented organization span traditional boundaries, and marketing's focus on the customer is embraced by manufacturing and R&D. And the last chapter in *The Fast Forward MBA in Business* discusses the latest business strategies companies are using to regenerate themselves, predict the future, and gain competitive advantage. Topics examined as possible strategic moves include innovation, growth, the development of core competencies, and reengineering.

We hope our new edition enlightens and informs you—that you will learn from it and that you will be able to apply what you learn in your own business life to improve performance in some discernible way.

The
Fast Forward
MBA in Business

The New, Softer Side of Business

If our souls aren't on the journey, if our quest is only about figuring our economic worth, it will be just another strategy, just another plan, just another game.

Tom Chappell

Leadership and Management

Today's chaotic and competitive business environment desperately calls for excellence in leadership and management.

Business is becoming more complex and global. The scope of operations is widening, as is the diversity of customers, suppliers, and investors. Managers are being challenged to demonstrate leadership—to foresee future challenges and opportunities, to energize their organizations, and to direct them forward with vision and wisdom.

Traditional management skills—the ability to plan strategy, organize staff, set budgets, and problem solve on a day-to-day basis—are still essential. Yet the emphasis is shifting. As corporations vie for competitive position in a vastly changed market, more and more significance is being placed on the manager's ability to lead the organization's people through these turbulent times.

This chapter examines the competencies, mastery, and talent required of today's organizational leaders as companies evolve to new states of being.

KEY CONCEPT

PEOPLE AND PURPOSE: A NEW CORPORATE STRATEGY

Today's corporate leaders share a consistent philosophy. Rather than emphasizing planning and strategy, executives emphasize corporate purpose. Rather than focusing on formal structural design, they focus on effective management processes. Rather than being concerned with controlling their employees, they are more concerned with developing the capabilities and skills of the people who work for them.[1]

Top management today sees its main responsibilities as shaping, defining, and articulating purpose, while guiding people through organizational processes. People have always been important, but in today's highly competitive and turbulent world, managers are focusing on people in a new way. Recent studies on management practices in 20 large companies, including Canon, 3M, Intel, Corning, AT&T, and ABB, reveal management's focus on "purpose, process, and people." In contrast to the traditional management model, which called for managers to distribute resources, delegate responsibilities, and direct subordinates, the new approach calls for managers "to shape the behaviors of people and create an environment that enables them to take initiative, to cooperate, and to learn."[2]

Successful senior managers, like good parents, understand the importance of nurturing their employees, providing both support and discipline. Control and reward systems are still needed, as are discipline and performance standards, but companies are realizing that frontline managers, subordinates, and employees across the organization can contribute more to the work environment and to the productivity of the organization if they have more of a role in setting goals for themselves.

KEY CONCEPT — BLENDING THE ART OF LEADERSHIP WITH THE SKILL OF MANAGEMENT

The primary function of management, and the reason it was created, is to keep complex organizations on time and on budget. Management's role is to maintain homeostasis and control so that the organization can meet its goals.[3] Complex organizations obviously have a need for controls—they must remain within budget, maintain profitability, and achieve objectives within set time frames. Order and control are necessary for everyday functioning. People also need consistency; they need to know what is expected of them and what they can expect. An organized approach is essential. Companies cannot function effectively without managers who possess these abilities.

However, traditional management skills need to be blended with the art of leadership. Honesty and integrity, determination and daring, collaboration and coordination, flexibility and adaptability are characteristics required in today's business world. Today's managers must be role models and coaches as well as great team players. In order to align, motivate, and inspire employees, managers must possess intelligence, energy, and stamina.

Organizations need executives who have the experience and the proficiency to combine management skills with the art of leadership. (See Table 1.1.) In fact, some experts claim "it is no longer valid even to draw a distinction between management and leadership. All managers, from the frontline to the CEO, must now exhibit leadership qualities."[4]

TABLE 1.1 SEVEN STEPS: MANAGING AND LEADING FOR THE LONG RUN

1

Build a positive work environment and set high standards by establishing the organization's values and by instituting business policies, concepts, goals, and performance standards that are consistent with those values. By creating a positive environment along with goals and guidelines, the manager provides direction and influences the behaviors in the culture.

2

Establish strategic direction by determining which processes will be employed to develop, review, and implement strategy. The manager needs to have an understanding of the operational aspects of the business as well as "bold, innovative ideas that provide a new vision for the business rather than a slight alteration of existing strategy."

3

Mobilize resources by having a combined knowledge base of hard resources (cash, plant, and equipment) and soft resources (people and technology). The manager must take responsibility for "marshaling and allocating" these resources.

4

Upgrade the quality of management at all levels across the organization by making sure that work challenges employees, utilizes their skills, and is properly rewarded.

5

Design the organizational structure to support success in a competitive environment—that means defining functional areas, reporting structures, interfunctional relationships, and the role of measurements, controls, and policies.

6

Create excellence by influencing the day-to-day operations of the organization through coordination and planning.

7

Maintain a broad perspective by constantly questioning the fundamental premises on which actions and strategies are based. Ask: "Why?", "What if?", and "What will it take?".

Adapted from: *Leonard A. Schlesinger, "How to Think Like An Executive: The Art of Managing for the Long Run," in* The New Portable MBA, *eds. Eliza G. C. Collins and Mary Anne Devanna (New York: John Wiley & Sons, 1994), pp. 15–29.*

ONE WITHOUT THE OTHER WON'T WORK

Leadership by itself never keeps an operation on time and on budget year after year. And management by itself never creates significant useful change. . . . Strong management without much

leadership can turn bureaucratic and stifling, producing order for order's sake. Strong leadership without much management can become messianic and cult-like, producing change for change's sake.[5]

WOMEN AS LEADERS

The leadership skills needed for the future have been identified by some experts as skills inherent in women's ways of leading. Women's style of leadership, whether natural or due to social programming, has focused on relationship and on meeting the needs of others. Parenthood, but most particularly motherhood, calls for guiding, leading, teaching, decision making, having supreme organizational skills, and handling conflict between valued constituents.

Janet Wylie, operations vice president of a *Fortune* 500 computer services corporation and author of *Chances and Choices: How Women Can Succeed in Today's Knowledge-Based Business,* has spent over 18 years working in the information services sector. She claims, "the unique way women gather and process information can be used to our advantage in business . . . women in business have the potential to be better verbal and written communicators, more adept at managing multiple facets in a changing business, more in tune with customers, and better managers of people—exactly the skills needed to be highly successful in the information age."[6]

In her book, *The Female Advantage: Women's Ways of Leadership,* author Sally Helgesen contrasted the leadership styles of four women with traditional leadership styles of men. Following the format of management scientist Henry Mintzberg's classic diary studies, she followed the daily activities of four dynamic women leaders. Although there is a significant time lapse between the findings (Mintzberg's studies were conducted in the late '60s and Helgesen's in the late '80s), they are worth noting. The emphasis today is being placed on the need for these "female" characteristics in what is, for the most part, still a male-dominated business world. (See Table 1.2.) If women in the diary studies are reflective of the larger population, then perhaps women do have a leadership advantage "in their ability to communicate, to prioritize, to see the broad picture."[7]

More recently, Dr. Lawrence A. Pfaff, a psychologist and human resource consultant, conducted a 14-month study in which he assessed the interpersonal, management, and leadership styles of 1,059 managers at all levels in 211 organizations across 10 states. The findings, Pfaff says, provide "evidence that women may be more effective managers of people." Using a 360-degree feedback inventory completed by the managers, their employees, and their bosses, the study examined 20 skill areas. Employees rated female managers higher in all 20 areas. Bosses rated females higher in 19 areas. And when managers assessed themselves, women scored higher in 15 areas. "The statistical significance of this data is dramatic," Pfaff says. Women not only out-ranked men in communication and teamwork, but also in areas such as planning and decisiveness.[8]

Additionally, the National Foundation for Women Business Owners conducted a study on gender differ-ences in management styles that examined the ways men and women business owners processed informa-tion, managed their businesses, and defined success. These results, like Pfaff's, cause one to pause and won-der what they imply for the future. Two interesting findings in the NFWBO study indicate women seem to have the traits that are being viewed as essential for success in the future:

- Women derive satisfaction and success from build-ing relationships, while men describe success as achieving goals.

- Women business owners typically speak of their businesses as a connected network, whereas many men business owners speak in hierarchical terms.[9]

Not only are women demonstrating leadership, but their businesses are growing in number. Businesses

TABLE 1.2

Mintzberg's Men	Helgesen's Women
Worked at an unrelenting pace with no breaks	Worked at steady pace with small breaks
Had interrupted, fragmented work days	Incorporated interruptions as part of the flow of work days
Focused on work-related activities	Made time for non-work-related activity
Preferred personal communication; left written work for secretaries	Preferred personal communication but also took careful time with correspondence
Maintained complex network of relationships outside company	Maintained complex network of relationships outside company
Lacked time for reflection	Focused on big picture and saw self as part of society
Identified with jobs	Had complex and multifaceted identities
Had difficulty sharing information	Scheduled time to share information

Source: From The Female Advantage: Women's Ways of Leadership by Sally Helgesen. Copy-right © 1990 by Sally Helgesen. Used by permission of Doubleday, a division of Bantam Dou-bleday Dell Publishing Group, Inc.

owned by women employ over 11 million people and are growing at double the rate of other businesses.[10]

THE WEB: A NEW ORGANIZATIONAL STRUCTURE

Management experts are recognizing the need for a circular or weblike structure in which leadership flows from the center rather than from the top down. Women almost intuitively work out from the center. Helgesen discovered the women in her study used weblike systems in structuring their work lives. Frances Hesselbein, who was the national executive director of the Girl Scouts of the USA and is now president of the Peter Drucker Foundation for Nonprofit Management, created a circular management chart in which staff jobs rotated. Nancy Badore, executive director of Ford's Executive Development Center, put herself at the center of the management chart, with program heads branching out from her position.[11]

Information in a web flows in all directions, while at the same time enabling the center of web to directly send and receive information to numerous points. The nodes, the places where strands intersect, provide connection and support for the web, demonstrating the significance of interrelationships.

In the circularity of a web, "authority comes from connection to the people around rather than distance from those below; this in itself helps to foster a team approach . . . the strategy of the web is guided by opportunity, proceeds by the use of intuition, and is characterized by a patience that comes of waiting to see what comes next."[12] Tom's of Maine uses a circular organizational chart (see Figure 1.1). The circle, representing wholeness and completion, offers an egalitarian, respectful, and open method for conducting business.[13]

LEADERS MUST LEARN TO LISTEN

Listen. Listen. Listen. And listen some more. In order to achieve effective results, managers and leaders must learn to listen to their constituencies. *Active listening* is one of the most important skills of management; it carries with it the intention to understand and learn. It empowers people because it sends a caring message: It tells the person speaking that he or she is being acknowledged and respected without being judged.

Effective listening enables managers to determine what's really happening in their organizations. Bill Hewlett and Dave Packard were known for their "management-by-walking-around," listening and talking to employees at all levels of the organization.[14]

Lawrence Bossidy, CEO and chairman of AlliedSignal, spent his first 60 days on the job talking to 5,000 employees.

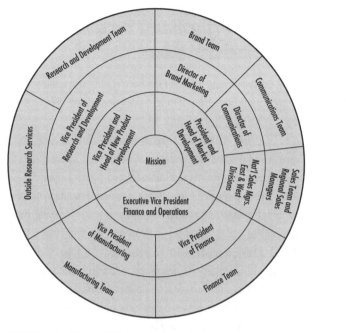

FIGURE 1.1 *Tom's of Maine organizational chart.*

We talked about what was wrong and what we should do about it. . . . It's really remarkable how many people know what's really going on in their company. I think it's important to try to get effective interaction with everybody in the company, to involve everyone. . . . I think the combination of talking to a lot of people in an interactive setting and doing skip-levels and conducting periodic attitude surveys gives you a pretty good handle on how people think about things.[15]

Percy Barnevik, CEO (see Stellar Performer) of Asea Brown Boveri (ABB), believes leaders must meet directly with staff members and "not hide up there in an ivory tower." ABB is a large global company; it would be easy for Barnevik to cut himself off, but he meets with thousands of people each year, and he makes sure his senior managers do, too.[16]

Listening also helps clarify assumptions and uncovers interpretations that can be harmful. Effective listening skills guide managers by enabling them to know the type of direction and guidance to give. Good listening focuses on people and goes hand in hand with good management.

DARTH VADER WAS A LEADER, TOO

DANGER!

There is a dark side to visionary leadership. Its strengths can become its weakness. Vision is a passionate and personal concept; when it is attached to a strong ego, it can sometimes cause problems. When a

Stellar Performer: Percy Barnevik
European Star

Percy Barnevik, CEO of Asea Brown Boveri (ABB), who combines management skills and the art of leadership, was named 1994's most admired chief executive in Europe.

In interviews with over 100 executives and financial analysts, Barnevik was described as "professional, determined, humane, close to his employees, an excellent communicator, and a good decision maker." He emphasizes the importance of corporate culture in his work and takes the time to know what his employees value. Each year, he meets with several thousand people throughout the organization. In addition to being a good listener, he understands the power of persuasion and, when necessary, he flies people to foreign locations to have them see firsthand the point he is trying to make. He also knows that managing change takes time and says that managers create problems if they don't take the time to convince people.

Since he took over as head of ABB in 1988, he has been acknowledged for his ability to save the $30 billion electrical engineering company through bold strategic moves and lean management: He radically decentralized the head office, by cutting staff from 2,000 to 200. When he came on board, he implemented a global matrix management system: Workers report to local country managers, who report to international business segments that report to super regions. The matrix captures the paradoxes the company has to manage as a global company operating with local units. He also instituted the T-50 program, which is designed to improve customer service, reducing lead times by 50 percent. Under Barnevik, ABB exemplifies duality at work: It is "global and local, big and small, decentralized and centralized."

Barnevik's objective in decentralizing was "to modify behavior and transform values." Working with his senior management team, it took him five years to build entrepreneurial processes and "to integrate and leverage resources and capabilities." He reconstructed the business into 1,300 separate companies operating in national markets worldwide. These frontline units are ABB's "basic building blocks" and "the unit managers act as entrepreneurial champions."

Barnevik is committed to a continual renewal process, and his colleagues in Europe admire him for it.

Sources: A. Brown, "Top of the Bosses," International Management (April 1994), pp. 26–29; C. Bartlett and S. Ghoshal, "Changing the Role of Top Management: Beyond Strategy to Purpose," Harvard Business Review (November/December 1994), pp. 79–88; C. Bartlett and S. Ghoshal, "Changing the Role of Top Management: Beyond Structure to Process," Harvard Business Review (January/February 1995), pp. 86–96; C. Bartlett and S. Ghoshal, "Changing the Role of Top Management: Beyond Systems to People," Harvard Business Review (May/June 1995), pp. 132–142.

leader invests so much personal vision into the organization there is a danger that he or she can develop a blind spot. Leaders, driven by ego, can become unable to see a problem or other points of view. And they can develop distorted perceptions of opportunities or threats.[17]

A good example is Canadian Robert Campeau. Once a successful real estate developer, he envisioned building an empire, combining his commercial land development expertise with large retail operations. He spent $13.4 billion chasing his dream, but a drop in retail sales, a glut of shopping malls, inefficient operations, and junk-bond debt, combined with his blind ambition, killed his vision and his fortune.[18]

Peter Drucker warns of the danger of charismatic leaders. Charisma, he claims, can make leaders "inflexible, convinced of their own infallibility, and unable to change." He points out that Abraham Lincoln, Dwight Eisenhower, and Harry Truman were all effective leaders, but none had charisma, while Stalin, Hitler, and Mao were strong charismatic leaders who led their countries down chaotic paths.[19]

GOOD LEADERS GROOM OTHERS FOR LEADERSHIP

Good leaders mentor and develop those who work with them. Leadership and vision are directed toward the future. The point of leadership is to preserve the vision and the organization long after the leader has stepped down. A leader focused solely on himself can be dangerous. In 1991, GE CEO Jack Welch announced he would devote a part of every working day to a succession plan, yet he is not due to retire until the year 2000. This is a tribute to Welch's leadership qualities, but it also reflects one of GE's values: to build excellent leaders. All GE's CEOs have come from inside the organization; managers have been trained and prepped for leadership positions. In 1974, then-CEO Reginald Jones created "A Road Map for CEO Succession" in preparation for his own departure even though he did not step down until seven years later when Jack Welch took over.[20]

KEY CONCEPT LET THE FORCE BE WITH YOU

In the new decentralized organizations, more people are being given the power to determine how work will be done and the authority to make final decisions. There is a difference between power and authority. Authority is the right to make decisions, while power is the ability to influence others. Both power and authority require levels of trust, responsibility, and accountability.

Effective leaders are compromisers who "are painfully aware that they are not in control of the universe." The effective leader, writes Peter Drucker, does what is "right and desirable," and sees "leadership as a responsibility." Drucker emphasizes the leader's need to be aware of his or her responsibility to co-workers. Effective leaders want others to be strong. They encourage and nurture growth and ultimately hold themselves "responsible for mistakes of associates and subordinates."[21]

Twenty years ago, David McClelland examined these same issues of leadership and management. He wrote:

> *A good manager is one who, among other things, helps subordinates feel strong and responsible, rewards them properly for good performance, and sees that things are organized so that subordinates feel they know what they should be doing. Above all, managers should foster among subordinates a strong sense of team spirit, of pride in working as part of a team.*[22]

McClelland examined the difference between managers who wanted to achieve and managers who wanted power. Achievers were self-focused, wanting to improve themselves and be liked, while those who strove for power wanted to have an impact on the organization and to influence others, motivating them to achieve. The desire for power, however, wasn't dictatorial; it was disciplined with a desire to serve the organization. This kind of power contains a great sense of responsibility and team spirit. Power-motivated managers make their subordinates feel strong rather than weak. They coach rather than rule. Good managers "must be interested in playing the influence game in a controlled way." Successful managers in McClelland's studies shared the same general characteristics. They liked to work and had a longer-range view and a keen sense of justice. They were:

- Willing to sacrifice
- Emotionally mature
- Less egotistic
- Less defensive
- Willing to seek advice
- Not preoccupied with personal possessions[23]

McClelland's original work was conducted in large, hierarchical organizations, but he has continued to study managers in both centralized and decentralized companies, and says that the aforementioned characteristics "continually emerge as what separates world-class managers from mediocre ones."[24]

Tom Chappell (see Stellar Performer) is a leader driven by a sense of responsibility and social consciousness. Tom's of Maine reflects his own personal journey. In his desire to balance profit and purpose, he leads the company in building vision and soul, while keeping it grounded with sound, responsible management techniques.

KEY CONCEPT: IT TAKES A LEADER TO CHANGE A CULTURE

As organizations adapt themselves to the new competitive environment, managers are learning how to lead organizations undergoing change processes. Implementing change is difficult. It has been reported that 70 percent of the big change efforts in corporations in the United States have failed.[25]

The invisible rules of the culture—the below-the-waterline norms, values, and beliefs—require attention because they are the prime motivators of the behaviors that determine performance. Cultural change messages must come from senior managers, who understand the content and strength of the culture, and the commitment and cooperation necessary for success. Leaders who can foresee future problems and develop communication plans will be more successful in motivating employees to embrace the change effort, helping them to shift their values and beliefs in order to alter their behaviors.

In the late '80s, Tetsuya Kataday, president of Komatsu, realized his company was in danger due to its myopic vision. The culture had been focused so long on competing with Caterpillar that it had developed tunnel vision. In order to broaden focus, stimulate growth, and get people thinking creatively, he led in the development and implementation of a cultural change process under the banner, "Growth, Global, Group-wide." Not only did he change the culture, softening his top-down, systems-driven management, but the change impacted construction sales: In four years it increased from 27 percent to 37 percent of total sales.[26]

Perhaps the most widely known change leader of recent years is GE's Jack Welch, who motivated GE's workforce to operate with "speed, simplicity, and self-confidence." Under his leadership, bureaucracy was decreased, while leadership across the organization was increased. The corporate culture became less control-oriented and more centered on individual initiative and decision making.[27]

Ingvar Kamprad, founder of IKEA, the huge home furnishings manufacturer, started a personal communication network in 1980 to get his message out. He conducted training sessions on IKEA's history, values, and beliefs, and, by the '90s, approximately 300 cultural ambassadors were operating in a personal global network covering 20 countries, collecting and disseminating information and communicating IKEA's values and beliefs across the organization.[28]

Stellar Performer: Tom Chappell
Soul Manager

Founded by Tom and Kate Chappell in 1970, Tom's of Maine is the leading manufacturer of natural personal care products. Tom's was the first company in the United States to produce a nonpolluting, liquid laundry detergent. From the beginning, the company's business strategy centered on respect for human dignity. Its mission was to manufacture only natural products, and its vision was to become a leader in natural personal care products. Tom's was committed to respect for humans, the natural world, and the community. Chappell attributes his company's success to the couple's intuitive instincts and their ability to establish an "I-Thou" relationship with customers and employees.

In 1975, the company produced the first natural toothpaste. By 1981, sales were $1.5 million and, in pursuit of its vision, the company undertook an aggressive five-year growth plan. By 1986, sales grew to $5 million. But even with his success, Chappell felt something was missing. Looking for a higher and loftier mission, he went to Harvard Divinity School where he tackled philosophy and ethics. In the course of his studies, he began to understand some of the tension that existed between him and the MBAs who were helping to run the company—they focused on numbers and he focused on soul.

In an attempt to reconcile the conflict between hard numbers and soft feelings, Chappell gathered his senior management team together and they hammered out their beliefs and mission. They came to agree the company could "be financially successful while behaving in a socially responsible and environmentally sensitive manner."

In the first year after the mission was implemented, however, it became evident that the male-dominated, competitive culture of the company was in conflict with the new mission. Employees were tentative and fearful. Without the proper communication structure in place, Chappell was unable to hear what they had to say; he was unaware of many of the employees' feelings. It took one of his new female managers to convince him that he needed "to be an ear."

Chappell initiated group meetings and, in response to what he heard, he began to institutionalize the mission, embodying it with his actions: He tarred the road to protect employees' cars from potholes, developed a company newsletter, cleaned up the building, and provided assistance with childcare. Eventually, employees began to implement the mission themselves, but it took two to three years to really take hold. And during that process, Chappell realized he needed to have a great deal of faith in his managers and trust in their decisions.

(Continued)

(Continued)

The company's new, clear identity and mission helped it flourish financially. By 1992, sales increased by 31 percent; profits increased by 40 percent. The company entered new markets, increased its share in old markets, and had strong balance sheets. By 1995, it had a record-breaking year of profitability with sales approaching $20 million, of which it tithed 10 percent of pretax profits to nonprofit groups serving the community.

Ever conscious of its soul, Tom's has introduced companywide retirement savings and profit-sharing plans, and provided educational support, childcare benefits, and parental leave. The company uses recycled packaging and doesn't use animals for testing. Its values have reinforced and sharpened its competitive edge. Rather than being driven by the market, the company continues to create products by identifying with, and relating to, its customers. In 1995, it received the Seal of Acceptance for its three most popular toothpastes from the American Dental Association—a breakthrough for the natural products industry. Tom's applied for the seal because of its importance to customers and dentists.

Chappell claims his vision helps his employees make products come to life, but vision, he warns, can't become real without thought and rational discussion. Structures and plans are required. Without the mission in place, the management team would never have come up with the information it needed to create effective strategy. He is a great believer in the power of intuition and creativity. But he also believes that holding creativity accountable has been the key to the company's success. The company can live with honest mistakes, but employees are expected to be competent.

Chappell also believes in the power of the circle as an organizational structure, claiming its egalitarian nature supports wholeness, completion, openness, and learning. He uses it in a variety of ways in the work setting. Additionally, Chappell has discovered the benefits of operating with duality: Tom's of Maine doesn't have "to be all analysis or all intuition. It can be both."

Sources: Tom Chappell, The Soul of a Business: Managing for Profit and the Common Good *(New York: Bantam Books, 1994); Michele Galen and Karen West, "Companies Hit the Road Less Traveled,"* Business Week, *5 June 1995 (America Online; McGraw-Hill, 1995); Tom's of Maine corporate material.*

COMMUNICATION IS KEY

Communication is one of the most important tools managers can use in the cultural change process. Its significance cannot be overemphasized. Like satellite dishes in space, effective, targeted communication sends powerful signals, which can make the difference between energized life or the slow death of the organization. Communication can be effective only if people hear and understand the message. In a change process, communication has to be shaped and delivered in a way that fosters belief and deepens trust, because only then will it influence values and beliefs and change behaviors.

In order to understand and accept the values of a new culture, or to reinforce and sustain core values of existing cultures, management must persuade employees by developing and implementing a thorough, clear, and consistent communications plan, which should be continually transmitted throughout the organization.

ANITA RODDICK: FEMININE POWER

Anyone listening to Anita Roddick, CEO of The Body Shop, will be caught by her words. They are earthy and strong, and they pack tremendous power. A funny, engaging storyteller, she travels the globe (her company has approximately 700 locations in 40 countries), visiting her stores and speaking to large groups. Roddick continually provides clear, consistent communications, espousing her company's commitment to social and environmental causes.[29] Preferring informal to formal systems, her company has developed videos that educate the viewer on the differences in the way women's beauty is valued in cultures around the world—at the same time, the video demonstrates the lengths to which The Body Shop goes in its search for natural ingredients for its products.

The organization's delivery trucks are other vehicles Roddick uses to carry a variety of messages communicating the social consciousness and empowerment that are the heart of The Body Shops.

If you think you're too small to be effective, you've never been in bed with a mosquito!

Not only is Roddick a powerful speaker, but she is also a great listener: Through her Department of Damned Good Ideas, she and senior management listen to suggestions from employees.[30]

Roddick is also an energetic and enthusiastic leader who believes in developing her employees: She created an education center that offers sociology courses as well as training for her employees. And she develops networks of women around the world to communicate her message and deep belief that business can and should be a major force of social change. Her Values and Vision Network offers lectures on spirituality and service, corporate responsibility, and women in business.[31]

TIP PRACTICE WHAT YOU PREACH

Actions speak louder than words. Senior managers are models for the changes they are professing: Their behaviors must match their proclamations. Words without actions create cynical, dissatisfied employees and customers. Rhetoric has to be backed with action that focuses on outcomes. Everything managers do on a day-to-day basis must be in concert with the new cultural and strategic direction the company is aiming towards.

CHUCK MITCHELL: SMALL COMPANY, BIG LEADER

Star

In 1993, when Chuck Mitchell took over GTO, Inc., $4 million manufacturer of automatic gate openers in Tallahassee, Florida, the company was in dismal shape. Morale and credit were both extremely low. Suppliers operated on a COD basis. And GTO had a Dun & Bradstreet credit rating of 32 (versus 75 for the industry).

But Mitchell is a leader with vision, inner values, and an ability to help people help themselves. He firmly believes in cooperation, interaction, and a team approach. Rather than slashing staff, he set out to transform the culture, and he succeeded. In a year, net profit went from a negative $311,000 to a positive $475,000. Overdue accounts receivable dropped from 50 percent to 30 percent, sales increased 10 percent, and returns dropped from 5 percent to 1 percent. The employee turnover rate dropped to 5 percent from 25 percent. And the company's D&B rating is now 80.[32]

GTO's performance improved because Mitchell paid attention to his employees. In his first three weeks on the job, he met with each of GTO's 50 employees, asking for suggestions from everyone. Mitchell says he knew he had a "resourceful, talented group of people who had a lot of the answers, whether they knew it or not." His job, he says, was to elicit "good ideas, thoughts, and suggestions" from them because they had been working with the issues and problems. "You tell me what we can do to improve processes," he said to them. Mitchell believes "everyone is a resourceful person if you can get them to feel like they can make a contribution." By the end of his meetings, he had a master list of items that were impeding profitability.

When management pays attention to employees, Mitchell claims it demonstrates a level of caring that translates into better business all the way around. He understands the importance of communication. He advises other managers to "Listen to your folks, really listen to them. Talk to them. Let down your guard. Share ideas." Mitchell also suggests being vulnerable: "Don't be afraid to be wrong. Don't let it inhibit you from trying things." And he believes in sharing the rewards that effort and teamwork reap. When employees have a stake in the company's success, he thinks they will pull together and work hard to achieve superior results. He allocated 5 percent of net profits for an employee profit-sharing plan, created a bonus system, and changed health and disability insurance to provide workers with better coverage. He took care of little everyday things, too, like making sure the vending machines and coffee supplies were kept fully stocked. And on weekends, he gave employees keys to the building and let them use equipment to make repairs to their own cars. Gradually, he built a trusting environment.

He communicated his vision in his words and, more important, in his everyday actions. Along with tightening up procedures to reduce waste, he purchased new equipment and expanded the product line. The result is a company growing in size and prosperity. GTO moved into a beautiful new building in January of 1995—a building employees helped to design. Mitchell firmly believes, "People are the reason things turned around."[33]

END POINT

Competitive advantage in the new millennium will require managers to have practical business abilities as well as creative, motivational skills. Duality is in. Head *and* heart now count. Both soft and hard issues matter.

In the business world, women have been emulating men for a long time; now it's time for men to emulate women. Skills that have traditionally been considered feminine are now being recognized for their value: The organization of the twenty-first century will draw from both the masculine and the feminine. In order for organizations to be effective, managers will have to learn how to nurture, develop, and teach others. This will require people who understand the value of building trust over time. And it will require people who are willing to give the effort and the energy essential for building long-term, mutually beneficial relationships.

As managers hone their intuitive abilities, they will begin to alter the way they think and behave. The bottom line will always count, but now it won't be the only line that's important. The invisible lines of communication that draw people ever closer into webs of relationship will gain more relevance. Better interpersonal communication skills will be a requisite for everyone.

The landscape is shifting and it's changing the context of organizations as we know them. Although this change seems frightening to many, if companies are paying attention to both ends of a continuum and if they continue to develop soul looking for right action, while being fiscally responsible to all stakeholders, then performance will be enhanced and the organization will be able to fulfill its purpose, while taking care of its people.

Managing culture, as well as planning and implementing strategy, have been recognized as important parts of the new leader's job. The next chapter points out the significance of understanding corporate culture as managers seek to implement change in their organizations.

MORE READING

Argyris, Chris. *Interpersonal Competence and Organizational Effectiveness.* Homewood, Ill.: Irwin Dorsey Press, 1962.

Beckhard, Richard, and Rubin T. Harris. *Organizational Transitions: Managing Complex Change.* 2d ed. Reading, Mass.: Addison-Wesley, 1987.

Bennis, Warren G., and B. Nanus. *Leadership.* New York: Harper & Row, 1985.

Bradford, David L., and Allan R. Cohen. *Managing for Excellence: The Guide to Developing High Performance in Contemporary Organizations.* New York: John Wiley, 1988.

Chappell, Thomas, M. *The Soul of Business: Managing for Profit and the Common Good.* New York: Bantam Books, 1994.

Cohen, Allan R., and David L. Bradford. *Influence Without Authority.* New York: John Wiley, 1990.

Collins, James C., and Jerry I. Porras. *Built to Last: Successful Habits of Visionary Companies.* New York: Harper-Business, 1994.

Conger, J. A. *The Charismatic Leader.* San Francisco: Jossey-Bass, 1989.

———. *Learning to Lead.* San Francisco: Jossey-Bass, 1992.

Conrad, Charles. *Strategic Organizational Communication: An Integrated Perspective.* Fort Worth: Harcourt Brace Jovanovich, 1990.

Davis, Keith, and John W. Newstrom. *Human Behavior at Work: Organizational Behavior.* New York: McGraw-Hill, 1985.

Drucker, Peter. *Management: Tasks, Responsibilities, Practices.* New York: Harper & Row, 1974.

———. *Managing for the Future: The 1990s and Beyond.* New York: Truman Talley Books/Plume, 1993.

Fiedler, Fred. *A Theory of Leadership Effectiveness.* New York: McGraw-Hill, 1967.

Graham, Pauline. *Mary Parket Follett—Prophet of Management.* Boston: Harvard Business School Press, 1995.

Guillen, M. F. *Models of Management: Work, Authority, and Organization in a Comparative Perspective.* Chicago: University of Chicago Press, 1994.

Hampden-Turner, Charles. *Charting the Corporate Mind.* Oxford: Blackwell Publishing, 1994.

Kanter, Rosabeth M. *The Change Masters: Innovation for Productivity in the American Corporation.* New York: Simon & Schuster, 1983.

———. *Men and Women of the Corporation.* New York: Basic Books, 1977.

Kanter, Rosabeth M., Barry Stein, and Todd Jick. *The Challenge of Change.* New York: The Free Press, 1992.

Kotter, John P. *A Force for Change: How Leadership Differs from Management.* New York: The Free Press, 1990.

————. *The Leadership Factor.* New York: The Free Press, 1988.

————. *Power and Influence.* New York: The Free Press, 1985.

Likert, Rensis. *The Human Organization.* New York: McGraw-Hill, 1967.

Mintzberg, Henry. *The Nature of Managerial Work.* New York: Harper & Row, 1973.

Nhria, Nitin, James D. Berkley, and Robert G. Eccles. *Beyond the Hype: Rediscovering the Essence of Management.* Boston: Harvard Business School Press, 1992.

Ouchi, William. *Theory Z.* Reading, Mass.: Addison-Wesley, 1981.

Pascale, R. T. *Managing on the Edge.* New York: Simon & Schuster, 1990.

Pascale, Richard T., and Anthony G. Athos. *The Art of Japanese Management.* New York: Simon & Schuster, 1981.

Peters, Tom, and Nancy Austin. *A Passion for Excellence: The Leadership Difference.* New York: Random House, 1985.

Peters, Tom, and R. W. Waterman. *In Search of Excellence.* New York: Harper & Row, 1982.

Sathe, Vijay. *Culture and Related Corporate Realities.* Homework, Ill.: Richard D. Irwin, 1985.

Schein, Edgar H. *Organizational Culture and Leadership.* San Francisco: Jossey-Bass, 1985.

————. *Organizational Psychology.* Englewood Cliffs, N.J.: Prentice-Hall, 1988.

Spears, Larry C. (ed.). *Reflections on Leadership: How Robert K. Greenleaf's Theory of Servant-Leadership Influenced Today's Top Management Thinkers.* New York: John Wiley & Sons, 1995.

Tichy, Noel M., and Mary Anne Devanna. *Transformational Leaders: Molding Tomorrow's Corporate Winners.* New York: John Wiley & Sons, 1986.

Tichy, Noel M., and Stratford Sherman. *Control Your Destiny or Someone Else Will.* New York: Doubleday/Currency, 1993.

Vroom, V., and P. Yetton. *Leadership and Decision Making.* Pittsburgh: University of Pittsburgh Press, 1973.

2

Culture:
Intangible, Untouchable,
But Oh So Important

The world is at a turning point. All the old ideas about business organizations—what they are, why they prosper, who they serve—seem oddly inaccurate. No longer seen as static institutions, companies are now viewed as organic, learning systems, pulsing with life, ready for regeneration and new knowledge. *People,* we now know, are the life force that propels companies ahead. Organizational mission, once buried beneath the surface of a world dominated by numbers, is pushing its head above the waters begging for the attention it deserves. And all of the organizations' processes are being examined to make them work more effectively.

Business leaders are recognizing that companies have cultural identities that permeate every part of a business, influencing how people think, what they say, and how they act. Shaped by the people and formed by the corporate purpose, culture drives the organization's approach to business.

Each organization has its own distinct culture, and every aspect of an organization is influenced by the way in which its culture operates. Therefore, it is of ultimate importance for organizations to understand what culture is and how it works. It is strategically important to know if the organization's culture is helping it to meet the demands of the environment, or if the culture is hindering it from moving ahead, from reaching its fullest potential in productivity, profitability, and performance.

This chapter unearths the basic components of organizational culture, enabling managers to get a better understanding of the interconnectedness of the system and how each component influences the way the organization works.

KEY CONCEPT — CULTURE INFLUENCES PERFORMANCE AND PROFIT

"This is the way we do things around here." Organizational cultures contain systems of shared meaning which unite people, providing a context for them within which to live and work. Cultural shared meanings are expressed in a variety of forms, both informal and formal, explicit and implicit. They influence how the organization operates, how members accomplish their work, and how people interact with each other.

Culture is the accumulated shared values, beliefs, attitudes, assumptions, interpretations, habits, customs, practices, knowledge, and behaviors of a group of people which bind them together. (See Table 2.1.) Culture in an organization operates like an iceberg: Values, beliefs, assumptions, and interpretations lie invisible below the surface of the water, while customs, practices, and behaviors are the visible attributes above the water line.

TABLE 2.1 COMPONENTS OF ORGANIZATIONAL CULTURE

Assumptions

Subjective interpretations and assessments, not based on objective data, which become collectively accepted as fact.

Norms, Customs, and Routines

Day-to-day ways in which members behave, interact, and work. Linked to core assumptions, norms determine acceptable behaviors and are usually implicit, numerous, and powerful. New members are rewarded or sanctioned, depending on their acceptance of these behavior patterns. Norms and customs provide benefit, but they also protect core assumptions and can be extremely difficult to change.

Power

The ability to get things done. Power comes from the dependency of others, from relationships with key figures, or from access to or control over key resources. Power bases exist throughout the organization and can be derived from formal structures or informally through interpersonal skills.

Rites and Rituals

Ceremonies, events, training programs, etc., which highlight accomplishments, mark turning points, and signify what is important to the organization. They can include negative events, like the firing of senior managers, as well as positive ones. Rites and rituals reinforce norms, contain history, and can exist long after their functional basis has disappeared.

Roles and Responsibilities

The positions held by individuals and groups within the organization including what is expected of them and what tasks they are responsible for completing.

TABLE 2.1 (Continued)

Stories and Myths

Tales and stories told by organizational members to people inside and outside the organization. They impart the organization's history and highlight significant events, people, and turning points.

Structure

Framework, formal and informal, which portrays how the organization works. Structures reflect and preserve power bases and reveal important relationships.

Symbols

Logos, language, terminology, titles, and status symbols, like offices and cars, which portray the organization's values and beliefs.

Systems and Rules

The formal methods used to control behavior and to measure and reward performance. Systems and rules reflect organizational values and attitudes. They explicitly determine how the organization will motivate, monitor, and reinforce behaviors.

Values

The essential, deep beliefs of the organization—what it cares about the most, regardless of the external environment.

Researchers are beginning to believe that the *software* of culture in a highly competitive environment may have even greater influence on performance and the bottom line than the *hardware* of organizational structures, systems, and strategies. In fact, some studies indicate that "corporate culture can have a significant impact on a firm's long-term economic performance."[1]

 THE PRIORITY OF PURPOSE

In *Built to Last: Successful Habits of Visionary Companies,* James C. Collins and Jerry I. Porras compared the core ideologies of 18 pairs of companies. Their work provides evidence that what lies at the heart of a company plays a role in determining how well it performs. The companies they called "visionary" have "woven themselves into the very fabric of society." They have made a significant impact on the world— between 1926 and 1990, their stocks have performed 15 times better than the general stock market.[2]

Although these visionary companies experienced reversals and made mistakes, they demonstrated "resiliency" and have performed exceedingly well through multiple life cycles and multiple leaders. The "timeless" management principles of these organizations operate contrary to business school doctrine. According to Collins and Porras, these companies, rather than being driven by profit and numbers, are guided by an internal *core ideology*, made up of *core values* (essential, guiding principles) and *purpose* (fundamental reasons why the company exists) that extend beyond making money.[3]

At Johnson & Johnson, for example, the health of customers is its top priority, more important even than the bottom line; hence, its total recall of Tylenol after the product was tampered with in the '80s. The exemplary way Johnson & Johnson handled the crisis not only reflected the strong leadership of then-CEO James Burke, but also reflected shared ethical values that were a deep part of the company's culture.[4]

For visionary companies, business transcends economic considerations. Profit is necessary, but it's not the sole focal point of business life. Success requires living up to principles and fulfilling purpose. 3M's strong attachment to innovation and individual initiative and its tolerance for mistakes have raised it from its origin of being a failed mine, to a huge manufacturer of 60,000 products. GE's commitment to improve the quality of life through technology and innovations— "GE . . . We bring good things to life"—and its responsibility to customers, employees, shareholders, and society have turned it into a company with a market value of almost $90 billion.

 REVOLUTIONARY CONSERVATIVES

Concrete organizational systems and policies enable workers to act in support of abstract values. Visionary companies are *both* conservative in their unrelenting adherence to their ideology *and* revolutionary in boldly tackling the unknown. Because ideology without the means to implement it won't provide performance, these visionary companies create "tangible mechanisms aligned to preserve the core and stimulate progress." GE didn't just pronounce it valued technological improvement, it created "one of the world's first industrial R&D laboratories." 3M doesn't merely value individual initiative, it allows researchers the freedom to devote 15 percent of their time to work on ideas they believe will benefit the company.[5]

CORE VALUES MUST BE ARTICULATED

Formal belief and mission statements communicate core values. They help inspire and encourage members to commit to the organization's purpose. Leaders who start out by clearly communicating their ideology and values have greater impact on establishing, or on changing, the culture of their organizations. If they put those values down on paper in the form of mission or vision statements, they seem to have even more impact. When used as "living documents," they can be powerful control levers that guide behaviors.[6] Hence, the growing popularity of these corporate statements.

Written documents are visible instruments which clarify the abstract, and written words tend to have a sacredness about them. They can be referred to when questions arise, providing a solid foundation for guiding actions. They can also be widely distributed through a variety of channels, providing a constant and consistent way for people to put their hands on intangible ideals and beliefs.

Many highly successful companies have organizational documents, which are cherished, tangible records of values and beliefs. Paul Galvin, founder of Motorola, linked purpose to profit in the organizational booklet "For Which We Stand: A Statement of Purpose, Principle and Ethics." Later, Robert, his son wrote 31 essays for employees explaining who the company was and why it existed. These essays focused on the organization's attitude toward creativity, quality, ethics, and innovation.[7] When Masaru Ibuka founded Sony, he created a prospectus describing the company's ideology, even though he could not clearly define the company's products.[8] When David Kearns led Xerox through its cultural change in the '80s, he had his team write a 92-page document detailing the changes needed; it served as a cornerstone from which the senior management team leading the effort could work.[9]

 THE ENERGY OF VISION

When vision is articulated as part of the organization's purpose, it provides focus and clarity. When it is articulated enthusiastically by the leader's words and actions, it becomes a powerful force of energy that mobilizes and unites people behind the cause of the organization.

Vision calls for creativity. To have a vision for the organization means to have a tremendously positive image of what the organization can be or can do in the future. Vision needs passion. The leader who creates a vision must be emotionally attached to it and believe in it with his or her heart and soul. Vision holds possibilities. It's motivational. As the visionary process unfolds and evolves, the vision will take shape, become sharper, and offer unmistakable guidance. When CEO Jack Welch was leading GE's change effort in the '80s, the company defined its vision in "broad, but clear terms"—"To become #1 or #2 in every market we serve and revolutionize this company to have the speed and agility of a small enterprise."[10]

Vision and values are interconnected: They link the organization's goals with action, with the everyday decisions and activities that will get the organization closer to those goals. When strong leadership links vision and values, an organization can achieve the impossible.

THE RATIONALE OF MISSION

The mission statement explains why the organization exists and why the vision is meaningful. Mission is rational, leading to action, while vision carries passion. Leaders create vision, pulling people together and instilling them with motivation to achieve the organization's purpose. They turn vision into reality with their interpersonal skills, sending powerful messages that galvanize and energize employees. The mission carries the vision a step further, guiding everyone to act in ways that fulfill the organization's objectives. Together vision and mission provide the "clarity, consensus, and commitment" necessary for successfully steering the organization forward."[11]

Tom Chappell, cofounder and president of Tom's of Maine, understood the importance of putting the company's vision and beliefs down on paper. He realized these statements helped define the future for the company and provided guidelines for employees. The company's core beliefs focus on human dignity, respect for nature, and responsibility. All decisions are based on these values. Once the employees had vision and mission statements, they no longer had to second-guess what was expected from them. His management team developed belief and mission statements, and, in the process of formulating the statements, answered questions about core values the company had been struggling with.[12]

Companies should have only a few core values. Tom's of Maine has eight core beliefs and eleven ways in which the company fulfills its mission. (See Tables 2.2 and 2.3.)

NOTHING IS WRITTEN IN STONE

Just because the mission is written down doesn't mean it's written in stone. Flexibility is significant. After Tom's of Maine had written and implemented its original mission statement, the management team realized it lacked any reference to expectations of competence in employees. This was an omission that caused some confusion, and both the belief and mission statements were amended to include competence and a commitment to skill and effectiveness at work as a responsibility of employees.[13]

VISION IS INCLUSIVE

To help create vision in the organization, leaders should bring teams or groups of managers together to

TABLE 2.2 TOM'S OF MAINE STATEMENT OF BELIEFS

WE BELIEVE that both human beings and nature have inherent worth and deserve our respect.

WE BELIEVE in products that are safe, effective, and made of natural ingredients.

WE BELIEVE that our company and our products are unique and worthwhile, and that we can sustain these genuine qualities with an ongoing commitment to innovation and creativity.

WE BELIEVE that we have a responsibility to cultivate the best relationships possible with our co-workers, customers, owners, agents, suppliers and our community.

WE BELIEVE that different people bring different gifts and perspectives to the team and that a strong team is founded on a variety of gifts.

WE BELIEVE in providing employees with a safe and fulfilling work environment, and an opportunity to grow and learn.

WE BELIEVE that competence is an essential means of sustaining our values in a competitive marketplace.

WE BELIEVE our company can be financially successful while behaving in a socially responsible and environmentally sensitive manner.

participate in conceiving the vision. When people are involved in the process of creating something, they are more invested in the outcome and are more likely to endorse and support it.

The visioning process should be held off-site to stimulate creativity and free expression, away from the distractions of everyday routines and removed from the conscious reminders of roles and reporting relationships. The process should stimulate thinking and create productive interaction, increase camaraderie, and unify organizational perspective as well as uncover any conflicts and negative feelings. It should also provide direction for the next steps to be taken.[14]

VISION HAS PSYCHOLOGICAL IMPACT

DANGER!
As organizations become increasingly complex and employees more diverse, it will be more difficult to create a unified vision. Additionally, vision has a "psychological significance"—it binds people together. If vision is lost, it can traumatize people and they will need time to grieve. It is particularly important to give people time to transition from one type of culture to another. Leaders must operate with high levels of integrity and take responsibility for the vision they create. Vision involves trust and humility, characteristics identified with good leadership.[15]

TABLE 2.3 TOM'S OF MAINE MISSION

TO SERVE our customers by providing safe, effective, innovative, natural products of high quality.

TO BUILD a relationship with our customers that extends beyond product usage to include full and honest dialogue, responsiveness to feedback, and the exchange of information about products and issues.

TO RESPECT, value, and serve not only our customers, but also our co-workers, owners, agents, suppliers, and our community, to be concerned about and contribute to their well-being, and to operate with integrity so as to be deserving of their trust.

TO PROVIDE meaningful work, fair compensation, and a safe, healthy work environment that encourages openness, creativity, self-discipline, and growth.

TO CONTRIBUTE to and affirm a high level of commitment, skill, and effectiveness in the work community.

TO RECOGNIZE, encourage, and seek a diversity of gifts and perspectives in our worklife.

TO ACKNOWLEDGE the value of each person's contribution to our goals, and to foster teamwork in our tasks.

TO BE DISTINCTIVE in products and policies which honor and sustain our natural world.

TO ADDRESS community concerns, in Maine and around the globe, by devoting a portion of our time, talents, and resources to the environment, human needs, the arts, and education.

TO WORK TOGETHER to contribute to the long-term value and sustainability of our company.

TO BE A PROFITABLE and successful company, while acting in a socially and environmentally responsible manner.

TiP CORPORATE CULTURES ARE NOT TOTALLY HOMOGENEOUS

Companies, especially large, complex organizations, have more than one culture operating. Although the core values of the organization should be the same across the entire organization, functional departments, divisions, and business units tend to develop distinct subcultures of their own. Historically, skills, practices, and policies valued in one area are not necessarily valued in another.

Talents admired and respected by scientists in R&D, for example, are likely to be completely different from those admired and respected by staff members in public relations or by plant workers in manufacturing. Perceptions, assumptions, and beliefs can vary, depending on the context of each environment. What's important for the organization, however, is to create a unified vision that everyone can see and embrace and a mission that everyone understands and can work toward.

CULTURES CAN GET SICK

Companies, like people, can get sick. Corporate cultures start to show signs of dysfunction when leadership is missing or no longer valued, when the organization forgets about its important constituents, when success leads to a loss of humility, and when change is resisted.[16] (See Figure 2.1.)

CONCEPT

A STRONG CULTURE ISN'T ALWAYS A HEALTHY CULTURE

Organizations, both small and large, have cultures that vary in strength and weakness. Strength is determined by the degree to which the members uniformly share all the values, beliefs, assumptions, interpretations, meanings, practices, and behaviors. A strong culture

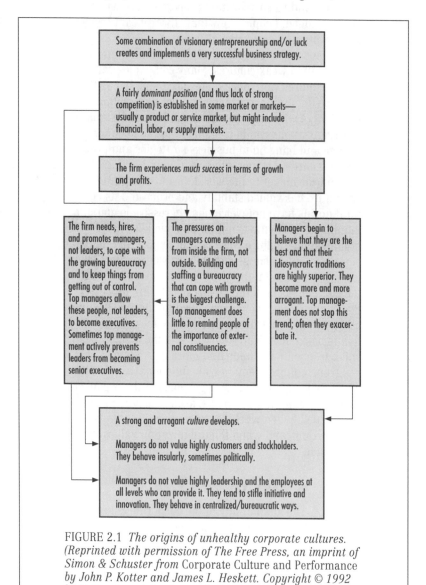

FIGURE 2.1 *The origins of unhealthy corporate cultures. (Reprinted with permission of The Free Press, an imprint of Simon & Schuster from* Corporate Culture and Performance *by John P. Kotter and James L. Heskett. Copyright © 1992 by Kotter Associates Inc. and James L. Heskett.)*

can be an enormous advantage: Its image is easily recognizable by those outside the culture.

The U.S. Army, for instance, has a strong culture. When you hear its name, you know what it stands for. You can envision the soldiers. You know what to expect from them, from the organization, and from its leadership. And with strong cultures, there is tremendous clarity about roles, values, expectations, and behaviors. In strong cultures, ambiguity and uncertainty, which can confound decision making, are absent. In the army, each soldier is readily identified by rank and is clear about his or her roles and responsibilities.

In the corporate world, IBM provides a good example of a strong culture. For years, the symbols of the IBM culture—the tailored business suit, worn as a uniform, along with the company's strict code for personal behavior and its socialization process—were widely acknowledged. People knew that "IBM" meant loyalty and devotion to work above all else.

However, strong cultures can be even more prone to sickness than weak cultures. Many companies with strong cultures were once quite successful, but as they grew, so did their arrogance and their dysfunction: They lost sight of why they were successful in the first place.

Organizations can become blind to the need for change and hang on to business strategies and practices that are no longer effective. General Motors, number one car maker in the world, has a strong tradition. Its culture has valued stability and order and its cultural norms have not welcomed aggressive leadership in managers. Even when it became evident that the organization's culture was starting to hurt, not help, the company found change a gruelingly slow process. Now, led by CEO Jack Smith, who came on board in 1992, the company is undergoing a restructuring process. Plants are finally being overhauled to improve flexibility and quality standards, but, in the meantime, production is being negatively affected. And the company is still burdened with union and morale problems.[17]

Strong cultures remain truly functional and healthy when they support the strategic goals of the organization. They link with strong performance when goals are aligned, when workers are motivated by work that is rewarding, and when the organization values the individual.

KEY CONCEPT: IT PAYS TO STAY FIT

The adaptability of the corporate culture, or its ability to fit itself into a changed environment, is a key variable for success. According to studies conducted by John P. Kotter and James L. Heskett, successful organizations adjust their cultures to fit with business strategies, which fit with the competitive situation in significant markets—financial, products or services, and labor. Companies that value "all three key constituencies—stockholders, customers, and employees" seem to adapt better. And companies with strong managers who remain aware of the shifting context of their important markets and adapt their strategies and cultures to their environments tend to perform well in the long run.[18]

In the 1980s, Anheuser-Busch's more flexible culture enabled it to adapt much more easily to market demands than Coors, whose slow-changing values and beliefs that "a good product sells itself" impeded the company when it ventured into new territory beyond its Colorado domain.[19] In new markets, it wasn't quite prepared for the lack of brand recognition and the tougher competition it faced. Back home, the beer drinkers bellied up to the bar and ordered Coors; in the East, the beer drinkers and the bars were different. Meanwhile, Anheuser-Busch developed a segmented marketing strategy targeting a wider variety of drinkers. The company tripled the types of beer it sold and used marketing techniques, such as background music and voice-overs in Spanish, to appeal to consumers in parts of California, Florida, and New York. By 1990, Anheuser-Busch had 43.4 percent of the market.[20]

Corporate cultures stuck in unhealthy patterns, however, can be changed to enhance performance if the organization has strong and competent leadership.[21] Like people, even the strongest cultures can begin to show signs of stress. Hewlett-Packard, a visionary company by almost everyone's standards, has had enduring success, but it has not been without stressful times. The company's tremendous performance can be attributed in part to the strong leadership of Bill Hewlett and Dave Packard, whose consistent, sound principles gave the organization a solid foundation from which to grow and prosper. When HP's bureaucracy began bulging in the mid-1980s, causing the company to become bloated and slow, it was their leadership that shepherded the organization back on a leaner, and once again highly profitable track.

UNHEALTHY CULTURES ARE COSTLY

DANGER! Nonadaptive, unhealthy cultures have an internal focus. They are so concentrated on themselves, they fail to foresee changes in the marketplace. With their slow response to market demands and their constituents, they simply don't perform as well.[22]

HEALTHY CULTURES PROSPER

In an ideal culture, managers throughout the organization are leaders who initiate responsive strategic and tactical changes. When leadership can mesh values with market flexibility and intelligent strategies, compa-

Stellar Performer:
Hewlett-Packard
Deep Core Values, Strong Leadership, Cosmic Performance

Bill Hewlett and Dave Packard founded their company in 1939 with $538. Determined to create a company together, they set up shop in a garage. Hewlett-Packard (HP) first produced innovative electronic instruments aimed at scientific and engineering markets. Higher performance at a lower price was a core value from the beginning. By 1942, the company had grown to 60 employees. By 1943, sales were nearly $1 million. By 1950, the company was introducing 20 new products a year. Sales climbed to $60 million by 1960. Today, HP is a major player in the calculator, printer, and computer businesses, with computers making up 66 percent of sales. Annual revenues are $25 billion, and the company employs 98,600 people.

Hewlett and Packard shared the same basic values and deep beliefs about how to run a company. They hired and promoted people with similar mind-sets and explicitly communicated key values of serving everyone with integrity, fairness, trust, and respect. Individuals are recognized for achievements and offered opportunities. Products and services are unique or technically superior. Self-finance, growth, and absence of long-term debt are strong beliefs. The core values include technical innovation to benefit customers, creativity, initiative, effective problem solving, and teamwork. HP is known for management-by-objectives, management-by-walking-around, and its open-door policy.

HP, however, has not been without its problems. In the '80s, its bureaucracy had grown with its size. There were 38 committees overseeing all major decisions, and the company was losing speed getting products to market. By 1988, it was also losing ground to competitors. CEO John Young and Chairman David Packard began a program of renewal. The committees were dissolved. The company was decentralized and reorganized around core computer operations. The management structure was made leaner: 5,400 employees were laid off. The strategic focus shifted from instruments to computers to adapt to the changing, highly competitive market. Products were stripped of costly features, creating less expensive models. HP adopted a highly competitive philosophy of "killing off its own products with new technology," which proved to be extremely successful: HP's revenues, profits, and market value soared.

(Continued)

(Continued)

Although HP experienced a period of setbacks, and even though some of its strategies and practices changed, HP's *timeless philosophy and basic values never changed.* In the long run, HP has proven to be a stellar performer.

Sources: John P. Kotter and James L. Heskett, Corporate Culture and Performance (New York: The Free Press, 1992); James C. Collins and Jerry I. Porras, Built to Last (New York: HarperBusiness, 1994); Elizabeth Lesly, et al., "The Nimble Giants," Business Week, 28 March 1994 (America Online: McGraw-Hill, 1994); "Executive Update: Fifty Years of Insight from David Packard," Investor's Business Daily, 24 May 1995 (American Online: Investors Business Daily, 1995).

nies can prosper. Adaptive, healthy cultures act proactively. They have an outward focus and are concerned about the market and their constituents.[23]

At Xerox, periods of undisciplined practices and lack of strong, identifiable values brought it close to a corporate abyss. However, through the leadership of David Kearns, the company began a cultural transformation that pushed profits and performance back on a path of ascension.

 **SHIFTING CULTURAL CONTEXT IS NOT EASY**

Managing culture is not easy, and changing culture is even more difficult—not impossible, but extremely difficult. Culture runs deep. What lies below the water line continually influences attitudes and actions above the water.

Tangible rules and regulations and intangible stories and myths work together. They not only express the underlying beliefs and assumptions of the culture, but they also serve to keep the culture alive. If management wants to shift its strategies and alter its course, it must consider the underlying values and beliefs that have been keeping the ship afloat. Because it embraces these deep human concepts, attempts to change culture produce emotional reactions. Managers need to be able to create a new context, within which people will choose to act in the desired ways of the organization. In this altered context, new expectations about roles and performance can be created that will help shape employees' behaviors and actions.

Behaviors can be modified to some degree by altering formal systems and structures. Financial incentives, bonuses, and benefits can motivate workers to behave differently, but alone they will not produce the commitment that is needed in a real change effort. Managers can change culture by treating employees as

Xerox: Still in Orbit

Founded in 1906 as the Haloid Corporation, the company grew slowly and profitably manufacturing photographic paper, but it had no identifiably distinctive culture.

In 1945, when revenues were less than $7 million, Joe Wilson became president. Looking for growth, he brought ownership of a number of significant patents. In 1955, he built the first factory, expanded the product line, enlarged the sales force, and sold internationally. Sales were $26 million by 1957. In 1960, the "show-stopping" 914 office copier was introduced and Wilson predicted it would double sales by 1965. He was wrong: Sales soared to $392.6 million. "The 914 would go on to be the most profitable product in the history of US business." The firm grew. Executives were recruited from the best firms. Revenues in 1968 were slightly over $1 billion and net income was $138 million. Xerox should have continued skyrocketing, but it almost crash-landed.

In the culture of the 1950s, Wilson valued customers and employees, but in the late '60s, the culture changed for the worse. Managers grew arrogant. Concern for customers decreased. Money was spent on buildings and perks, not new, low-cost products. The company became insular with intensive internal competition. There was little initiative from the ranks. Decision making was centralized. Experimentation was discouraged and errors weren't allowed. Numbers ruled. Communication was poor. Response to the marketplace and competitors was slow. Copier revenue share "fell from 82 percent in 1976 to 41 percent in 1982."

In 1983, on the brink of disaster, chairman David Kearns began to turn the culture around, emphasizing commitment to quality products, customer needs, and key constituencies. As the culture changed, so did the profit picture. Return on assets rose from 5 percent to 12.4 percent between 1983 and 1989; revenue more than doubled. And Xerox won the Malcolm Baldrige National Quality Award.

In 1990, Paul Allaire became CEO and started restructuring, focusing on core business processes and on cutting costs. In a 1994 interview, he said the company was "three-quarters of the way" through restructuring, but still had "three-quarters of the way to go." Xerox's earnings are up and it's still orbiting, still searching for its place in the highest heavens.

Sources: John P. Kotter and James L. Heskett, Corporate Culture and Performance (New York: The Free Press, 1992); Interview, Community TV of South Florida, Inc. (America Online, 1994); Gary Hamel and C. K. Prahalad, "Competing for the Future," Harvard Business Review, July/August 1994; "Executive Update," Investors Business Daily, 1 February 1995 (America Online: Investors Business Daily, 1995).

valuable assets, by providing opportunities for growth and development, and by clarifying roles and responsibilities. These issues are examined in more depth in later chapters, but it is important to note here briefly that lasting change comes when intangible incentives provide satisfaction, helping employees to identify with organizational goals, accept and internalize core values, and commit to shared meanings on a deep level.

Change, however, can be a difficult and sometimes painful process. When a large industrial products company was slow to respond to declining markets, the CEO decided the company had to restructure. Yet, many upper-level managers just didn't seem to understand how deeply affected the employees would be by the changes that were beginning to take place. In order to make the managers realize how drastic the cuts and the changes were going to be, the CEO closed the executive dining room. Having to sit next to the workers, many of whom they would have to fire, the managers were forced to reassess their roles and responsibilities. Any assumptions the managers had that changes would not disturb them were eliminated along with the executive silver and linen. Forced to change their behavior patterns, they became more deeply aware of the impact that restructuring would have on all facets of the organization's culture.[24]

END POINT

The evidence points to a strong link between culture and success—and to the price, both economical and social, that everyone pays for unhealthy cultures. The studies mentioned in this chapter have shown that firms with healthy cultures increased revenues, stock prices, and net income, far beyond the companies with culture problems. They also employed greater numbers of people. When companies are profitable, there is more cash available for growth. When companies thrive, people have jobs. When organizational cultures are healthy, the workforce is well. If workers feel good about themselves at work, they will become more productive and their sense of well-being will be enhanced. As their well-being expands, it not only has a positive influence on productivity, but it has an impact that reverberates beyond the walls of their organizations, to customers and suppliers, influencing a wider sphere of people.

As organizations learn how to manage their cultures better, they will make greater progress toward enhancing performance and improving productivity. The next chapter continues to focus on the "softer" side of business—the organization's most important asset: its people. It examines the changing role of the human resource department and its responsibilities in competitively positioning the organization for the future.

MORE READING

Collins, James C., and Jerry I. Porras. *Built to Last: Successful Habits of Visionary Companies.* New York: HarperBusiness, 1994.

Conrad, Charles. *Strategic Organizational Communication: An Integrated Perspective.* Fort Worth: Harcourt Brace Jovanovich, 1990.

Davis, Keith, and John W. Newstrom. *Human Behavior at Work: Organizational Behavior.* New York: McGraw-Hill, 1985.

Deal, Terry E., and Allan A. Kennedy. *Corporate Culture: The Rites and Rituals of Corporate Life.* Reading, Mass.: Addison-Wesley, 1982.

Donaldson, Gordon, and Jay Lorsch. *Decision Making at the Top.* New York: Basic Books, 1983.

Drucker, Peter. *Managing for the Future: The 1990s and Beyond.* New York: Truman Talley Books/Plume, 1993.

Kilmann, R. H., et al., eds. *Gaining Control of the Corporate Culture.* San Francisco: Jossey-Bass, 1985.

Kotter, John P., and James L. Heskett. *Corporate Culture and Performance.* New York: The Free Press, 1992.

Likert, Rensis. *The Human Organization.* New York: McGraw-Hill, 1967.

Peters, Tom, and R. W. Waterman. *In Search of Excellence.* New York: Harper & Row, 1982.

Sathe, Vijay. *Culture and Related Corporate Realities.* Homework, Ill.: Richard D. Irwin, 1985.

Schein, Edgar H. *Organizational Culture and Leadership.* San Francisco: Jossey-Bass, 1985.

———. *Organizational Psychology.* Englewood Cliffs, N.J.: Prentice-Hall, 1988.

Weick, K. W. *The Social Psychology of Organizing.* Reading, Mass.: Addison-Wesley, 1979.

People:
The Management
of Human Resources

People are an organization's most important resource. As organizations attempt to become more entrepreneurial in spirit, more focused on learning, and more competitive in the marketplace, the function of the human resource (HR) department has grown. No longer is its role simply to recruit new employees and to fulfill regulatory requirements. Its responsibilities include making sure employees have capabilities that will help the company compete in the present and the future, matching workers' skills and abilities with the changing needs of the organization. As an important organizational link, HR ensures that organizational practices and policies are in sync with the external demands of the market and assists workers in developing to their full potential, enhancing both the individual's strengths and the organization's competitiveness.

THE ROLE AND FUNCTION OF HR

HR enforces the organization's values and beliefs, shapes and supports cultural norms and roles, and implements cultural change in support of organizational goals. It also plays a significant strategic role by helping the corporate culture adapt to shifting environments so that the organization is well positioned to meet the challenges it faces.

The traditional organization is undergoing a transformation that requires a new way of managing and leveraging the company's most valuable assets: its employees. Technological advances and global operations are demanding that organizations become more flexible, more efficient, and more entrepreneurial. HR helps the organization to manage its human assets more strategically so that it can attain higher levels of performance and greater profitability. The HR manager assists employees in finding ways to increase produc-

tivity and to reinforce the organization's core competencies by teaching skills that contribute to organizational growth. Additionally, HR works to develop an
environment that encourages affiliation, responsibility,
and commitment. (See Table 3.1.)

SHIFTING STRUCTURES

Traditional, hierarchical structures don't
respond well to the individual initiative, innovation, and
change that is needed to compete in a modern, technological world. Modern corporations are under pressure
from customers demanding special attention and from
incredible technological advances which speed the flow
of information, opening up global marketplaces.

In 1776, writing in his famous treatise, *The Wealth
of Nations,* Adam Smith theorized that specialization
and the division of labor increased productivity. At the
turn of the twentieth century, Frederick Taylor introduced the principles of scientific management and
tested his theories about making workers more efficient with his time and motion studies. Henry Ford
linked specialized tasks together on the first assembly
line, creating an efficient factory system. And Alfred
Sloan of General Motors created a divisional model of
management in which managers watched over their
divisional operations from corporate headquarters.
Sloan's formal, divisional structure incorporated tight
planning and disciplined control systems and paved
the way for the command and control structures, with
the separated functions and systematized tasks, that
we know today.

The traditional organizational structure helped
organizations in the '30s, '40s, and '50s to grow,
expand their product lines, and operate a variety of

TABLE 3.1 HUMAN RESOURCE MANAGEMENT FUNCTIONS

- Analyzes jobs and skills needed in the organization
- Assesses, develops, and implements policies, procedures, and systems
- Recruits and selects workers
- Appraises performance
- Rewards workers through the implementation of compensation systems
- Designs and delivers training, development, and educational programs for employees to provide the organization with the skilled resources it needs
- Capitalizes on the human resource potential available to gain strategic advantage

businesses. But by the 1980s, corporate growth in U.S. companies was stagnating and market share and profit margins were falling.

Companies have now recognized the deficiencies of this vertical, hierarchical structure. It worked well when organizational life was stable and predictable, but in a fast-paced, high-tech world, it has outgrown its usefulness. It no longer works efficiently and effectively. Created to meet the demands of mass production, it thrived on stability. But today's business environment is much more competitive and chaotic. Tables 3.2 and 3.3 show the difference between the values, structures, systems, and policies of traditional and entrepreneurial organizations.

KEY CONCEPT — CHANGING ROLES AND RESPONSIBILITIES

Enlightened companies are realizing that frontline managers working closer to the customer have better information with which to make decisions.

In traditional organizations, power and influence are not in the hands of the workers. In a top-down hierarchy, responsibility resides at the top of the pyramid: The top manager is the chief decision maker and strategist whose orders flow down through the troops to those at the front lines. Information from the front lines slowly filters back up the pyramidal structure, but it tends to become distorted on the way. This structure is based, therefore, on the presumption that senior managers can successfully lead alone. However, as organizations are becoming flatter, rather than being ruled by a narrow group at the top, organizational tasks and responsibilities are being relegated across the organization.

As the structure of the organization shifts, the roles of those working inside the organization are also shifting, as are the talents and skills needed. The rigid structures and systems of the past are giving way to more versatile configurations that provide environments which support creativity, innovation, and an entrepreneurial spirit. As structures flatten, entrepreneurialism, usually associated with smaller firms, is being adopted by larger companies. Big corporations, like 3M, Canon, ABB, and Intel have successfully maintained entrepreneurial environments, often by decentralizing and keeping units and divisions small and autonomous. At 3M, for instance, there are approximately 42 product divisions that average $200 million in sales. And plants located in 40 states average 115 people per plant.[1]

A sense of partnership is being fostered throughout the modern corporation. Companies are getting closer to their employees and relying on them in new ways. A

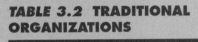
TABLE 3.2 TRADITIONAL ORGANIZATIONS

Structure

- Bureaucratic, hierarchical
- Vertical, isolated functions and departments
- Internally focused
- Rigid and formal with strong control systems

Values

- Conformity, predictability, and stability
- Command and control
- Mass-produced products in volume

Jobs: Policies, Roles, Responsibilities

- Screens new hires for past performance, using references and individual interview
- Hires the best and trains to climb up corporate ladder
- Assimilates new employees into culture with careful procedures
- Clarifies roles and responsibilities with explicit job descriptions
- Utilizes assembly line and specialized jobs
- Focuses on individual
- Supports lifetime employment
- Values longevity and loyalty

Performance and Reward Systems

- Appraises individual performance
- Specifies outcome of activities and assesses individual on those outcomes
- Appraises performance in comparison to past performance or to others
- Promotes from within along well-defined paths in functional silos
- Provides security and steady pay with perks and benefits to motivate and bond, but with little incentive to change

Training and Development Programs

- Training for specific job
- Development programs for managers and senior executives

new partnership is developing between the organization and its employees, who are experiencing broader freedom as well as greater responsibility. Rules and regulations exist in entrepreneurial companies, but rather than creating a restrictive environment, they are designed to guide employees and provide means for them to develop and grow.

At Nordstrom, a high-end retailer, employees set their own sales goals. Rules for employees' behavior are printed on a single card, which contains only one rule:

TABLE 3.3 ENTREPRENEURIAL ORGANIZATIONS

Structure

- Informal, nonhierarchical
- Flatter, egalitarian
- Externally focused
- More flexible structure and systems

Values

- Innovation, creativity, individuality, risk taking
- Cooperation, communication, relationships, and alliances
- Quality, customization, and speed in making products

Jobs: Policies, Roles, Responsibilities

- Takes time recruiting right individual, and screens for abilities and cultural fit
- Recruits internally and externally
- Defines jobs as needs or opportunities arise
- Moves employees in response to environment
- Stresses egalitarian teamwork and cross-functional teams
- Offers a variety of career paths, multiple ladders, and more complex, less-structured jobs needing cross-functional cooperation
- Tolerates mistakes in learning process

Performance and Reward Systems

- Participative performance evaluation with more than one appraiser
- Appraisal is based on potential value and future contributions
- Performance measures have individual and group criteria, with some compensation tied to team outcomes
- More flexible pay and greater incentives, both monetary and symbolic, encourage better performance, although tendency is toward lower pay scales
- Stress placed on efficiency and results

Training and Development Programs

- Emphasizes training in teamwork and participative skills
- Develops new skills and knowledge through training and development programs
- Long-term development for future challenges

"Use your judgment in all situations." Employees are also given an organizational chart—an inverted pyramid with customers at the top followed by sales and support people. The board of directors sits at the very bottom point of the pyramid. Nordstrom salespeople, who are known for their excellent customer service, are given training in entrepreneurial behavior and are expected to act independently in making decisions about the service they provide to meet customers' needs.[2]

TiP OUTSOURCING WORK SUPPORTS FLEXIBLE STRUCTURE

Larger, entrepreneurial companies are outsourcing work as well as decentralizing. Companies are learning that outsourcing projects, parts of projects, or non-strategic functions can provide cost benefits as well as better products and services. Maintaining a flexible approach to handling who does what gives the organization a competitive advantage.

FLEXIBILITY ALSO MEANS JOB INSECURITY

DANGER! There is, however, a downside to all this flexibility and change—workers no longer feel the security they once took for granted. The framework of traditional organizations provided employees with an understanding of their job parameters and their roles. Employees knew what was expected of them and what to expect from their employers in the present and in the future. In today's rapidly changing corporate environment, employees live with ambiguity and uncertainty. Employees now know that jobs might disappear and roles might alter dramatically as the organization adjusts itself to the demands of the marketplace. Managing effectively during times of chaotic change puts greater demands on human resource departments and on individual managers.

 CAREFUL HIRING PRACTICES

Entrepreneurial companies are careful about who they employ. They want to make sure that new hires will have the ability to contribute to the corporate objectives, will perform well, and will easily fit into the corporate culture. When companies make sure they hire the right person for the job, not only do they provide the company with a highly suitable pool of people, they also send a message to other employees that they are a very special group of people.

Southwest Airlines is a good example of an entrepreneurial company that has clear hiring objectives. Its culture fosters a "chip-in-and-help" attitude. In order to get planes turned around on time, flight attendants and crew members sometimes perform a variety of tasks on the ground. Employees are carefully screened before they are hired to make sure they have personality traits that mesh with these attitudes. Hiring can be "a time consuming process," but putting time in up front pays off: Southwest's employee turnover is about "half the industry average."[3]

USE A VARIETY OF INTERVIEW TECHNIQUES

Use interview techniques and tests that will reveal whether or not the applicant has the characteristics that match the organization's and the job's requirements. Rather than the solitary interview process used by traditional companies, entrepreneurial firms use a variety of assessment techniques such as psychological tests, group interviews, simulations, and stress tests to derive clues about personality and creativity.

At Southwest, the company assesses some job applicants in group setting interviews, where candidates sit together and converse while a Southwest manager observes behaviors; at Honda, personal essays are used as an assessment tool. Job applicants are asked to write essays linking their personal goals with Honda's—only 10 percent of applicants make it through this phase of the interview process.[4]

YOU'VE GOTTA LIKE THE PLACE

DANGER! One caveat: Strong cultures, even entrepreneurial ones, put enormous pressure on employees to conform to organizational norms. Although workers at Nordstrom are given freedom to develop customer service as they see fit, there are powerful customs operating that guide the behavior of salespeople. The same holds true for Southwest Airlines, which is why the company takes so long to select new hires—it wants to make sure new employees are attuned to the culture even before they come on board. Individuals with personality traits that are aligned with the cultures of these organizations will be more quickly assimilated and will more readily accept the company's strong values and beliefs.

KEY CONCEPT — PERFORMANCE AND PRODUCTIVITY

Performance and productivity are influenced by employees' behavior—by their capabilities, skill levels, motivation, and effort. Ability and skills can be developed through training and education, but workers must be motivated to improve their performance. Therefore, HR managers must understand the nature of human behavior and motivational theory—what motivates workers to perform better, to take on new roles and responsibilities, and what stimulates them to gain new skills and competencies in support of the organization.

Effective HR managers consider all motivational factors and support the future growth of the company by creating systems and policies that enable workers to embrace the attitudes, beliefs, and values that will produce required behaviors and competencies. With help from HR, these characteristics can be implanted in the collective corporate consciousness and reflected in turn in the performance of individuals.

It can, however, be more difficult to motivate people, or to understand their behavior than it first seems. Organizational life is systemic, made up of a complex web of interactions, and behaviors can be more complex than they appear on the surface. HR managers must have a total understanding of the way the corporate culture operates and the dynamics of interpersonal communication.

As organizations make changes that create more flexible, less hierarchical structures and demand greater versatility in roles and responsibilities, it will be up to HR to devise systems and methods that not only help workers learn new skills, but also ensure they get fair performance appraisals and receive proper compensation and rewards.

KEY CONCEPT — MOTIVATION, PERFORMANCE SYSTEMS, AND REWARDS

Research shows that different kinds of tasks require different kinds of leadership. When tasks are simple and clearly defined, supervision should be tighter and more controlled. With the complexity and changing nature of tasks in the flatter organizations of the present, supervision gives way to a more participative exchange and employees must assume greater responsibility for their actions and decisions. HR, therefore, must create systems that not only allow employees to discuss their roles, but that also permit them to provide suggestions for improving their own performance. Additionally, employees should have the freedom to critique the evaluation process itself.

Employee motivation and effort are partially determined by compensation and rewards. In fact, the reward system itself impacts behavior. The fulfillment of employees' expectations can affect levels of performance. If employees believe they are being treated fairly and recognize they are being valued through equitable compensation, openly tied to their performance, they will be more motivated to continue performing well. Inequity and unfair treatment breed discontent, which lowers motivation and leads to poor performance.

Studies show that, with effective performance management programs, the company's financial performance improves: Profits are greater, cash flow is better, and stock increases in value.[5] HR managers need to create ways for employees' performance to be tied to profitability. Many companies are implementing pay-for-performance, gain sharing, and stock option plans. Although base pay structures in entrepreneurial organizations tend to be lower, workers increase their salaries through these incentive systems.

Whirlpool established a pay-for-performance system, gain-sharing programs, and a 401K program that pays on the basis of return-on-equity (ROE) and return-on-asset (ROA) goals. More important, employees have a very clear understanding of the link between these incentive programs and shareholder value.[6] At Nucor Corp., steelworkers receive productivity and quality bonuses, which average "130 percent to 150 percent of base pay," putting them on a par with unionized workers and giving them a tremendous reason to work productively.[7]

DESIGN EFFECTIVE PERFORMANCE MEASURES

Incentive programs work when performance measures are clearly defined. Effective programs promote employee involvement, emphasize coaching and feedback skills, and use common performance measures.[8]

EMPLOYEES NEED FEEDBACK

Full-circle or 360-degree feedback is an easy-to-implement, diagnostic assessment tool that works to increase employee participation. It helps align an individual employee's focus with the preferred behaviors of the organization. (See Table 3.4.) The process includes gathering observations about the employee's performance from all levels of the organization—from peers, team members, managers, and direct reports—and links their feedback to the employee's own self-evaluation. The data offer the individual insight into the ways he or she can improve, and help to remove individual bias that might come when only one person is providing feedback. Additionally, the information helps the organization to gather information about the effectiveness of its own processes and systems.

More companies are beginning to use this technique, including GE, AT&T, Nabisco, and Digital Equipment Corp. Using the tool requires planning. Issues to be decided include whether to use the tool alone or in conjunction with other appraisal programs, what training is necessary to use the tool effectively, and whether to use off-the-shelf or customized versions.[9]

COMMUNICATE GOALS AND REVIEW PERFORMANCE

HR managers must communicate organizational goals and help workers understand how job responsibilities relate to those goals. By continually reviewing performance, adjustments can be made to ensure tasks and responsibilities are aligned with goals and objectives. As companies take on more entrepreneurial postures, managers need to provide clarity about how the com-

TABLE 3.4 FULL-CIRCLE REVIEW GIVES FULL 360

- Reveals competencies, showing relationship between strategic plan and performance ability of those implementing it
- Increases the focus on customer service
- Reinforces TQM and continuous improvement programs
- Supports and promotes team initiatives
- Creates a high-involvement workforce
- Decreases hierarchies and promotes streamlining
- Reveals barriers to success
- Assists in planning and assessing development and training needs
- Avoids discrimination and bias, reducing potential for legal action
- Identifies employee's strengths and weaknesses

Source: Robert Hoffman, "Ten Reasons You Should Be Using 360-Degree Feedback," HRMagazine (April 1995), pp. 82–85. Reprinted with permission of HRMagazine published by the Society for Human Resource Management, Alexandria, Va.

pensation system really works and to explain the full range of rewards that are available. Traditional systems generally provided employees with raises, which were supposed to be based on merit, but in reality were often based on the length of service to the company. These merit pay systems were not strategically used to leverage performance. By clearly stipulating what types of rewards are offered and tying them to specific behaviors, companies can truly affect performance.[10]

REWARD WITH MORE THAN MONEY

In addition to formalized systems that offer monetary rewards for improved performance, systems that provide intrinsic rewards should be created as well. HR managers need to be aware of how the culture operates and what types of behaviors are rewarded by peer groups among employees. What ways of acting provide employees with a feeling of belonging, with a feeling of being part of something bigger than themselves? What will elicit feelings of loyalty? Rites, routines, and rituals impact behavior. What ones are necessary to reinforce cultural norms, or what ones will change cultural norms?

Since 1987, the Malcolm Baldrige National Quality Award has been presented to companies that have been the most successful in utilizing their human resources to improve quality and to enhance strategic practices. This prestigious award is highly revered and difficult to win. Employees involved in helping their companies earn it are proud of their performance and are widely recognized and applauded for their hard work. Companies that have received this honor include Federal Express, Xerox, Motorola, IBM, GM, and Westinghouse.

Nonmonetary rewards also include career opportunities, challenging assignments, mentoring programs, and the right to help in the design of one's work.

PAY-FOR-PERFORMANCE MUST BE EQUITABLY MEASURED

DANGER!

Performance is never clear-cut and simple, and should never be appraised in isolation. Many factors, such as the quality of supervision, procedures, materials, and the work environment, enter into an employee's ability to perform well, and they should all be considered. Additionally, pay-for-performance systems must be set up to assure that they accurately measure what they are supposed to measure. With teamwork becoming the norm, performance measures need to be designed to assess the team's success and the individual's contribution. If large pay disparities exist within a group, the reason should be uncovered. If performance of an employee is truly lacking, the employee should receive further training or should be transferred to an area where his or her skills better match the responsibilities and tasks.[11]

KEY CONCEPT EMPOWERMENT: THE ULTIMATE REWARD

Managers empower employees by helping to bring out the best in them. Empowerment strengthens employees' beliefs in their own effectiveness. In entrepreneurial firms, authority and decision making are pushed to lower and lower levels, creating an atmosphere of sharing in which all employees have the opportunity to contribute ideas. When employees realize they can determine outcomes, they feel more powerful. A main ingredient of the entrepreneurial environment is respect for the individual; another is an atmosphere which builds competence. Entrepreneurialism builds corporate power by harnessing the power of the individual through competence building. When competence exists, it can be linked and leveraged, providing the organization with the valuable skills and resources it needs.

Employees are truly empowered when they feel free to take initiative and make mistakes without fear of retribution. In entrepreneurial firms, managers are similar to coaches. They spend time getting to know those who report to them, helping them develop individual skills and a personal sense of mastery—all this ends up benefiting the corporation. Companies must provide the opportunity and support for personal and professional growth. HR helps managers to acquire these coaching skills through training programs.

OPEN-BOOK MANAGEMENT

One of the latest tools for motivating and empowering employees and for helping them to improve performance and productivity is open-book management. With this tool, employees are taught how to observe progress so that they will have greater understanding of the company's position, why it might need to change, or why following particular pathways will lead to competitive advantage. With open-book management, everyone gets to understand more clearly that numbers are important.

Using this system, employees are empowered because they "learn to think and act like owners, like business people, and not like hired hands."[12] Open-book management also helps employees learn how to make good decisions. When workers become involved in budgeting processes, they become more aware of the factors that must be weighed into a decision and they learn how to take responsibility for making determinations about spending and costs.

Open-book management "communicates *all* relevant information" to people throughout the organization on a monthly, weekly, or even daily basis.[13] Its objective is to help people understand the financial condition of the company, with the belief that enhanced understanding will motivate and empower employees to perform better and to work together to meet the organization's goals and objectives. The principles are fairly simple: Employees receive information that they are taught to understand. Thus, everyone shares more directly in the company's success or failure.

DOCUMENTS FOR OPEN-BOOK MANAGEMENT

- Balance sheet
- Income statement
- Cash-flow statement
- Sales and marketing plan
- Capital plan
- Inventory plan
- Organizational chart
- Compensation plan

Everyone means both blue-collar and white-collar workers. At Springfield Remanufacturing Corp. (SRC), everyone, including the union mechanics, can provide details about the costs for components used in his or her department and how those figures relate to the overall costs of running the company. In 1983, when the company was purchased by Jack Stack (who wrote *The Great Game of Business* in 1992), it was in bad shape. Stack and 12 other investors purchased SRC from International Harvester. The group started out with a debt-to-equity ratio of 89 to 1. Mistakes were made as the group learned how to run the company, and, in the process, Stack pioneered the "open" concept, realizing that all the employees had to be involved and motivated to turn the company around. A stock ownership plan was instituted, and SRC employees were taught open-book management principles. In fact, the company invested heavily in education, providing financial training to its entire workforce. These actions resulted in tremendous growth: The company has expanded from 119 employees to 750, and revenues have increased annually from $16 million to $105 million.[14]

When employees understand the finances, they can become involved in planning. When they are granted stock ownership, they realize they have a stake in the outcome. Open-book management principles are also used at Manco, an Ohio consumer distributor, where the sales compensation system is tied to profitability and the profit each salesperson generates is individually calculated. A year after being introduced to this open system, one Manco salesman figured out how to increase his compensation by cutting his freight bill 14 percent.[15]

When Sandstrom Products, a paints and coatings manufacturing company located in northern Illinois, started to use open-book principles in 1991, two significant changes occurred: Red ink turned black, and employees had an opportunity to flourish. Blue-collar worker Leo Henkelman, a man with ideas about how to improve processes, had little chance to test his theories under the old system. But with principles of openness and teamwork in play, Henkelman was given access to formulas, technology, responsibility, and a better life. He seized the opportunities that were given him, and now, as the director of the laboratory, the color he wears to work each day has changed from blue to white.[16] The bottom line is: Companies that encourage employees to understand the numbers profit from opening their books.

APPLICATION DEPENDS ON CULTURE

The application of open-book management depends on the company and its culture. Moreover, it does not take the place of strategy—it just helps get people aligned toward the strategy. And it can assist in change processes by helping employees to see why change is needed.[17]

IT'S A GOOD TECHNIQUE FOR SMALLER COMPANIES

The pioneers that have forged ahead on this path tend to be small- and medium-sized companies; however, it is interesting to note that entrepreneurial companies like Intel, Sprint, and The Body Shop also have experienced success by exposing their numbers.[18]

IT'S A GOOD WAY TO BUILD TRUST

Open-book management provides an ultimate method for communicating honestly with employees and for building high levels of trust. As John Case writes in *Open-Book Management: The Coming Business Revolution:*

> *When the books are open, everyone can see what is going on. It's harder for managers to fall back on excuses or to point the finger at someone else. Open-book management gets people involved and helps them take responsibility rather than shirk it. It's a way by which everyone in the business can hold each other accountable.[19]*

TRAINING AND DEVELOPMENT

The best way for companies to build bridges strong enough to support their organizations as they move into the next century is by educating their workforces. In the fast forward speed created by information technology, some skills quickly become obsolete, while new ones are required. As advanced technologies are installed and new ways of operating are instituted, workers will be called on more and more to adapt their capabilities to changed working environments. Employees, therefore, must have access to methods for improving their skills to keep pace with the rapid changes taking place.

Training prepares employees to meet immediate job requirements, improves skills, and provides learning relevant to the organization, while development is broader and prepares employees for future challenges. Both enable people to advance themselves and to learn new and better ways of working.

The mix of training and development that each firm offers depends on its organizational goals and financial resources. AlliedSignal put each of its 80,000 workers through total quality training in two years,[20] while some companies, like Motorola (see Stellar Performer) have spent millions investing in educational facilities as well as training and development programs.

International Service Systems (ISS), a Danish office-cleaning contractor, has grown into a $2 billion multi-national company, employing 114,000 in 16 countries, due in part to the training and development offered to employees. Founder and president Poul Andreassen has great respect for workers and sees development as a way for them to advance themselves. He encourages supervisors of cleaning teams to act as independent businesses and provides training for them in finance, problem solving, customer relations, and interpersonal skills. They are taught how to read financial reports, which contain cost figures on direct labor, materials, and overhead, and to interpret these data in order to learn how to control costs for their units. These supervisors now generate business and help with team building. As well as making the company more productive, the training has created a happier workforce: Turnover at ISS is below the industry average.[21]

REMEMBER TO CHANGE BELIEFS BEFORE BEHAVIOR

Before behaviors change, the underlying belief system has to change. When employees receive mixed messages, they cling to old patterns. Caterpillar trained thousands of workers in the 1980s in preparation for the adoption of more flexible processes. But management and the union ended up disagreeing, and because of the conflict in their beliefs and values, behaviors were slow to change, causing the company's quality program to suffer.[22]

MANAGING DIVERSITY

When tension exists around issues of diversity, it impedes the organization from being as productive as it could be because the tension depletes energy and distracts employees from focusing on their performance. For the organization to operate at peak performance, the environment must be supportive of all workers. Issues around diversity have increased in recent years due to changes in family structures, more women in the workforce, and global developments that bring people of different races and countries together more often. Diversity reaches beyond gender and race to include a host of characteristics that make people feel different: age, sexual orientation, physical abilities, educational levels, and personal backgrounds.

Managing diversity means the organization is operating in an ongoing manner to enable and empower its entire workforce—all its employees, not just a specific, targeted group. Diversity includes both similarities and differences and, unless managers focus on both, the organization will not be managing diversity effectively. When diversity is managed properly, the organization, the manager, and the individual all work together to adapt to the differences and to build "a productive relationship between the individual and the organization." This approach focuses on making sure the organization utilizes all the resources it has available and produces the best results as naturally as possible.[23] (See Table 3.5.)

Stellar Performer: Motorola
Educational Power

Education empowers everyone. Motorola, a giant electronics manufacturer, has a history of creating, supporting, and implementing educational programs. Spending "about 4 percent of its payroll cost on training and development, compared with an average of 1.2 percent for all U.S. companies," Motorola deserves the title "stellar performer."

In 1979, when Motorola began its highly successful commitment to total quality, it focused enormous energy on education, investing millions in a training and education center, now known as Motorola University. From the beginning, training had a total quality orientation; however, the more deeply Motorola became involved in educating its workforce, the more it found out how much education was needed. Along with teaching employees how to use standard quality tools, how to problem solve, and how to communicate more effectively, it also discovered it needed to teach a significant number of employees how to read.

Because the company realizes it must have an educated workforce to maintain the high level of quality it demands from itself and because it is concerned about the quality of education being provided to Americans, Motorola president Gary Tooker has made education a top priority. The company has instituted a broad educational initiative, lobbying at the federal and state levels as well as working with colleges and school districts to reshape education in the United States.

Motorola has a deep respect for the value of training and development and a sense of responsibility about helping employees reach their full potential, but Motorola also expects its employees to be responsible. Employees must now pass entrance tests and have at least a high school diploma. And if employees turn down training that is offered, they are dismissed from the organization.

Managers at Motorola are taught to apply the knowledge they receive from their extensive training to make operations run more efficiently and to bring higher levels of satisfaction to the customer. The company's educational efforts have paid off: Motorola "is first or second in most of the markets it serves around the world."

Sources: D. MacCormack, L. J. Newman III, D. B. Rosenfield, "The New Dynamics of Global Manufacturing Site Locations," Sloan Management Review, vol. 35, no. 4 (Summer 1994), p. 73; Robert H. Waterman, Jr., What America Does Right (New York: Penguin Books, 1994), pp. 256–262.

LEVI STRAUSS: LEADER IN DIVERSITY

 Levi Strauss values diversity. Since Robert D. Haas became chairman and CEO in 1984, "Levi's has doubled the percentage of minority managers to 36% . . . women have climbed . . . to 54%"— way above the average U.S. company.[24]

A year after Haas came on board, women employees pressured the company to practice more fully what it preached. The company exceeded equal opportunity employment standards—50 percent of Levi's professionals were women or minorities—but none of them were senior managers. When meetings were held off site to discuss the diversity issue, tension that was simmering below the surface erupted. Haas and his HR department resolutely set out to change things. The HR

TABLE 3.5 MANAGING DIVERSITY IS A BOTTOM-LINE ISSUE

- When corporate environments are supportive of diversity, organizations can confidently recruit the best people from a diverse pool.
- With growing numbers of minorities and women in the workforce and with work being increasingly accomplished by teams in participative work settings, managers will not achieve quality or productivity goals without effectively managing diversity.
- As the organization continues to turn outward, it will face a more diverse group of customers.
- As companies become involved in global strategies, they will interact with more diverse populations.

Definitions

Affirmative Action: Goes against organization's natural order to include and utilize selected targeted groups.

Understanding Differences: Facilitates understanding of differences to enhance interpersonal relationships.

Managing Diversity: Focuses on changing the organization's natural order to include and utilize different people.

Guidelines

- Conduct an audit, using formal and informal systems to find the root assumptions operating in the culture, and determine whether those root assumptions will support diversity goals.
- Develop a plan to modify or change culture or systems as needed, using a strategic business approach.
- Adopt a long-term time frame to institutionalize diversity.
- Use techniques from traditional HR, Affirmative Action, Understanding Differences, and Managing Diversity.

Source: R. Roosevelt Thomas, Jr., "Managing Diversity: Utilizing the Talents of the New Work Force" in The Portable MBA in Management, ed. Allan R. Cohen (New York: John Wiley & Sons, Inc.), pp. 315–339.

department created three core educational programs covering leadership, diversity, and ethics, which employees around the world attend to learn skills in managing diversity, problem solving, and teamwork.[25]

Haas claims that regardless of race or gender, it's the contribution the employee makes and his or her desire for self-improvement that counts. Workers now consider themselves an integral part of the operations and feel like they are valuable contributors to the company. Harassment is simply not tolerated. The company has a "Diversity Council, which is a direct link to senior management for groups representing Blacks, Asians, Hispanics, gays, and women," and benefits, like health coverage, are extended to nontraditional partners. Haas claims the company's approach to diversity makes for a more responsive company and better marketing decisions. He was quoted in a *Business Week* article as saying, "We are not doing this because it makes us feel good—although it does. We are not doing this because it is politically correct. We are doing this because we believe in the interconnection between liberating the talents of our people and business success."[26]

KEY CONCEPT — WITHOUT QUESTION: A NEED FOR ETHICS

Experts are advocating the development of strategies that deal specifically with ethical issues. When ethics is institutionalized, it provides the organization with guiding values that support "ethically sound behavior" and "shared accountability among employees." An ethics policy holds the organization to higher standards. When strong ethical values become part of the context of the organization, they shape systems and decision-making processes. With ethics as an underlying, unifying force, the organization is steered toward right behavior, which in the end does far more than just keep the organization out of trouble.[27]

In response to charges of illegal behavior in 1994, Martin Marietta Corporation implemented an integrity-based ethics program, which has grown in scope and size. Although it was first viewed quite skeptically, it's now recognized as being "an early warning system for poor management, quality and safety defects, racial and gender discrimination, environmental concerns, inaccurate and false records and personnel grievances." The program has helped to change perceptions and has raised awareness about the "long-term consequences of short-term thinking." As a result, it has enhanced its reputation and developed a better relationship with the U.S. government, its major customer.[28]

Sometimes organizations need to get in big trouble before they begin to take action. But once they're in motion, they not only learn from their mistakes but also seem to reach for lofty goals. Ford Motor Co. provides an example. Its ethical debacle with the dangers of the Pinto demonstrated how the whole company had gotten out of touch with its customers. Ford realized it had to change its ethics and its relationship with its employees, who had become more concerned with looking good internally than with being responsible for the quality of their products and the safety of customers. Ford increased training and development programs, stressing employee involvement, and targeting team building, entrepreneurship, and efficiency. It also initiated profit-sharing plans for all employees. By the latter part of the '80s, not only had Ford's profitability increased, but Ford cars started winning awards for quality and excellence.[29] By 1994, the company had record earnings of $5.3 billion and the Taurus was the best-selling car in the United States.[30]

END POINT

HR is the doctor, the therapist, the lawyer, and the advisor, looking out for the health of the organization, while making sure the employee is also in good shape. The changing nature of the environment is altering structures, roles, and responsibilities. HR is now finding itself in a position to influence behavior and advance the competitive position of the organization. HR is even becoming a profit center in some companies. Corporations like Walt Disney, Xerox, and IBM, which have experienced success in particular HR practices, are selling their services to outside customers. Walt Disney offers leadership and management courses, Xerox offers benchmarking seminars, and IBM sells HR reengineering and benefits consulting.[31] The next chapter continues to explore the people side of the business: It examines the nature of teamwork as employees seek better ways of working together in a changed and highly competitive environment. And it looks at the company's new focus on developing lasting relationships with customers in today's market-driven economy.

MORE READING

Beer, Michael, et al. *Managing Human Assets: The Groundbreaking Harvard Business School Program.* New York: The Free Press, 1985.

Devanna, Mary Anne. "Human Resource Management: Competitive Advantage" in *The New Portable MBA,* eds. Eliza G. C. Collins and Mary Anne Devanna. New York: John Wiley & Sons, 1994.

Fombrun, Charles, M. A. Devanna, and Noel Tichy. *Strategic Human Resource Management.* New York: John Wiley & Sons, 1984.

Johnston, William B., and Arnold H. Parker. *Workforce 2000: Work and Workers for the 21st Century.* Indianapolis: Hudson Institute, 1987.

Kanter, Rosabeth Moss. *The Change Masters.* New York: Simon and Schuster, 1983.

Mervis, Phillip. *Building the Competitive Workforce: Investing in Human Capital for Corporate Success.* New York: John Wiley & Sons, 1993.

Pasmore, William A. *Creating Strategic Change: Designing the Flexible High-Performing Organization.* New York: John Wiley & Sons, 1994.

Pfeffer, Jeffrey. *Competitive Advantage Through People: Unleashing the Power of the Workforce.* Boston: Harvard Business School Press, 1994.

Roosevelt, Thomas Jr. *Beyond Race and Gender: Unleashing the Power of Your Total Work Force by Managing Diversity.* New York: AMACOM, 1991.

Schein, E. H. *Organizational Psychology.* Englewood Cliffs, N.J.: Prentice-Hall, 1964.

Schuler, Randall, and Drew L. Harris. *Managing Quality: A Primer for Middle Managers.* Reading, Mass.: Addison-Wesley, 1992.

Tichy, Noel, and Mary Anne Devanna. *The Transformational Leader.* New York: John Wiley & Sons, 1986.

Waring, S. P. *Taylorism Transformed: Scientific Management Theory Since 1945.* Chapel Hill, N.C.: The University of North Carolina Press, 1991.

Weick, K. W. *The Social Psychology of Organizing.* Reading, Mass.: Addison-Wesley, 1979.

New Relationships: Teamwork and the Customer Connection

As companies recreate themselves to gain competitive advantage, they are changing the nature of their relationships with key constituents. Closer cooperation and communication is being stressed. Partnership is important—inside and outside the company.

Within the organization, employees are teaming up, partnering in new ways as they learn how to work together to solve complex problems in a turbulent, competitive environment. As employees learn to collaborate more effectively, they are not only improving efficiency and quality, but they are also creating greater value for their customers.

Outside the organization, the relationship to the customer has changed dramatically—in a competitive world, the customer reigns supreme. The company that can give the customer the most value wins the profitability prize. The company that can forge a bond with the customer, create a partnership, and build loyalty, gains competitive advantage and secures a stronger position in the marketplace.

KEY CONCEPT

TEAMWORK: AN INTEGRAL PIECE OF THE NEW BUSINESS STRUCTURE

In the turbulent environment of the 1990s, multifunctional teams enable companies to respond with greater flexibility. Teams are becoming the organization's building blocks, "replacing the boss-employee pair."[1] Team members who work in closer proximity to the changing external environment and who are more familiar with customer requirements, are more capable of successfully adjusting to competitive demands. With the complex and multifaceted problems of today's business, no one person has all the answers to problems, nor does one person have the level of expertise needed to tackle all the changes occurring in the workplace. Well-functioning teams are much more likely to produce better solutions than one person working alone.

Although the concept of self-managed teams was introduced in the '70s, when decentralized matrix organizations were first introduced, teams never quite achieved the success that most had hoped for. Teams back then "were formed to create more democratic and more humanitarian workplaces"; teams today are being created for competitive advantage. The self-managed team of the '90s is viewed from a pragmatic perspective rather than an idealistic one.[2] Today, the purpose of the cross-functional team "is to create a structure . . . that is responsible for a complete value-delivery process."[3] Teams are proving to be important internal links in the organization, changing its basic structure by giving it more interconnected nodes.

Percy Barnevik's approach to teamwork at ABB provides a good illustration of how a huge multinational organization relies on self-managed teams to save time and respond more quickly to customers. With ABB's T-50 program, which was created to cut cycle time in half, frontline local managers and teams work together to handle problems. Because they are provided with the information, resources, skills, knowledge, and authority needed to make quick decisions, the program is progressing toward accomplishing its goals. Teams operate throughout ABB's global network of companies. At the ABB Switchgear plant in Ludvika, the defect rate in the production of transformers was 30 percent, so a team was formed to find out why. After mapping out the process, the team was able to pinpoint the machines causing difficulties. The team worked so well and had such great success with the project that team members decided to continue meeting once a week for an hour to solve other problems, with the result that production defects in the plant have been almost entirely eliminated, and production volume has increased by 10 percent.[4]

KEY CONCEPT **TEAMS COME IN DIFFERENT SIZES AND SHAPES**

Cross-functional teams are often organized around the flow of production. They become responsible for seeing a product through production from beginning to end. Many manufacturing plants are taking this whole-process approach. Any size team can be formed, with the size being determined by the scope of the process involved. For example, in creating a new product, both engineers and production people might work together in creating the design of the product. Salespeople might also be included because they have much closer contact with customers and know what customers want. In developing its "next-generation switching system," Northern Telecom created a large cross-functional team that "included representatives from its Bell Canada customer organization, marketing people, design and development engineers, and members of the manufacturing organization that would ultimately build the switch."[5]

Depending on the goal, these cross-functional teams can be made up of both blue-collar and white-collar workers. Whirlpool instituted One-Company Challenges, a program in which managers gather employees from across the organization to work on teams that tackle specific problems. One cross-cultural team created a TQM program that combined the best of the European ISO-9000 and American Baldrige Award approaches, resulting in the company's successful quality program: the Whirlpool Excellence System.[6]

Table 4.1 provides guidelines for designing successful teams.

 MAKING TEAMS WORK

Making teams function well can be challenging. They must be designed and developed in context with the organizational environment. When they are, and the strength of a team is harnessed, its power can be truly dramatic.

Well-functioning teams not only have the ability to provide top-notch solutions, but they have the force to make sure that solutions are implemented. Teams provide employees with an arena where creative ideas can be born. Additionally, they provide a source of learning for the organization.[7]

However, people require training in order to make teams work well, and training entails both cost and time. Good team performance is not achieved overnight. For success as a team, members need to work together to develop a common direction. When the group's energies are aligned, there is harmony and coherence. A synergy develops as individual visions merge together to form a shared vision. In fact, "the shared vision becomes an extension of the personal vision." Unless the team is aligned, it will not become empowered. Instead, empowered individuals will create chaos in the team.[8]

In order for the team to learn, it must use the collective intelligence of its members. This can be more difficult than it seems. Although well-functioning teams can create better solutions than a single individual, there is rampant evidence that bringing intelligent people together in a team does not ensure that the collective intelligence will be greater than the sum of the parts. Often, it ends up being dramatically lower.

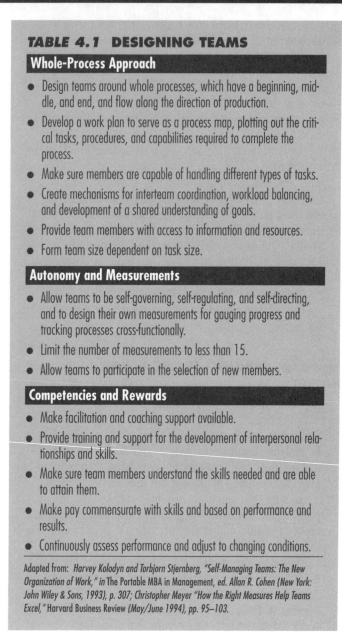

TABLE 4.1 DESIGNING TEAMS

Whole-Process Approach

- Design teams around whole processes, which have a beginning, middle, and end, and flow along the direction of production.
- Develop a work plan to serve as a process map, plotting out the critical tasks, procedures, and capabilities required to complete the process.
- Make sure members are capable of handling different types of tasks.
- Create mechanisms for interteam coordination, workload balancing, and development of a shared understanding of goals.
- Provide team members with access to information and resources.
- Form team size dependent on task size.

Autonomy and Measurements

- Allow teams to be self-governing, self-regulating, and self-directing, and to design their own measurements for gauging progress and tracking processes cross-functionally.
- Limit the number of measurements to less than 15.
- Allow teams to participate in the selection of new members.

Competencies and Rewards

- Make facilitation and coaching support available.
- Provide training and support for the development of interpersonal relationships and skills.
- Make sure team members understand the skills needed and are able to attain them.
- Make pay commensurate with skills and based on performance and results.
- Continuously assess performance and adjust to changing conditions.

Adapted from: *Harvey Kolodyn and Torbjorn Stjernberg, "Self-Managing Teams: The New Organization of Work," in* The Portable MBA in Management, *ed. Allan R. Cohen (New York: John Wiley & Sons, 1993), p. 307; Christopher Meyer "How the Right Measures Help Teams Excel,"* Harvard Business Review *(May/June 1994), pp. 95–103.*

Team members must be able to investigate complex issues. This requires active listening skills and a dialogue process, in which complex issues are examined from many points of view, and judgment and assumptions are suspended. MIT's learning guru Peter Senge points out the importance of understanding the difference between discussion and dialogue. He recognizes them as complementary, but he warns that discussion alone can lead to defended stances that impede learning.[9] There must also be enough trust operating to support innovative and coordinated action. And if a team is truly learning, it will be interacting on some level with other teams, fostering learning throughout the organization. (See Table 4.2.)

TABLE 4.2 FIVE STEPS TO TEAM PROBLEM SOLVING

1. Identify and diagnose problems

- Assume nothing; look for the cause of problems.
- Focus on core problems, not symptoms.

2. Generate alternatives

- Understand the problem before evaluating suggestions.
- Look at a range of options; don't grab at the first possible solution.

3. Evaluate options

- Make evaluations using objective data, not subjective assessments.
- Don't count on numbers alone; add judgment to numbers.
- Search for integrative solutions.

4. Make decisions

- Don't close too quickly at the first attractive option.
- Allow for disagreements.
- Make sure all members are committed.

5. Implement decisions

- Make sure all members are supportive of the plan.
- Agree on who will do what by when.

Adapted from: *David L. Bradford, "Building High-Performance Teams," in* The Portable MBA in Management, *ed. Allan R. Cohen (New York: John Wiley & Sons, 1993), p. 50.*

LOSS OF COHESION UNGLUES THE PROCESS

Teams fail when they lose cohesiveness, when team members remain more concerned with their individual agendas than with the common goal of the group. When this happens, there is an enormous amount of wasted energy. Teams also can fail when they jump ahead and begin to implement solutions without clearly defining problems and without thoroughly assessing the entire situation. And they fail when they ignore the manner in which they are operating as a group.

These problems are endemic to small groups. And when these conditions are present, rather than working together synergistically, the group's ability to align is lowered and the commitment is reduced. Teams need cohesion to be effective.

Teams fail when management claims there is a participative environment, but, in fact, a consultative decision-making process, not a consensual one, is operating. In a consultative process, the final decision is always the leader's, not the group's, and the leader really holds onto his or her control. "When members know that the leader is the crucial person to influence, they tend to advocate their personal interests and pass up to the boss the responsibility for developing an integrated solution." Consensual solutions force all members to take responsibility for decisions.[10]

PROVIDE CLARITY AND GUIDANCE

Team members may not have received sufficient guidance about their new roles and what they entail, because companies themselves have not been clear about what those roles are or how this new structure should really function.

Some teams fail because of poor change management processes. As well as having to learn new team-based behaviors, many managers, schooled in traditional work methods, are understandably having difficulty "unlearning" practices they have used for years. It is difficult to change long-established patterns of behavior, especially if expectations for new roles are not clear.[11]

EMPOWER TEAMS WITH DECISION-MAKING AUTHORITY

Teams that make decisions have much greater ability to attract committed members than teams that simply share information. And teams that make decisions by consensus have far more appeal than teams that provide advice for leaders. In entrepreneurial organizations, consensus is one of the major keys in determining the success of teams. Consensus is a potent method of decision making for a team because it involves give and take: Members truly influence each other.[12]

 RESPONSIBILITY IS A KEY ISSUE

Teams cannot be effective unless they accept responsibility. Empowerment and responsibility go hand in hand.

Teamwork changes the dynamics within the organization. It shifts accountability and responsibility. In order to foster good teamwork, the manager has to let go of control, both over the outcome and over the group dynamics. When a leader relinquishes control, control is not lost; it is changed. The base of control moves from the leader to the group. Coordination and control reside in the group's ability to create its own purpose, to discipline itself in the decision-making process, and to establish mutual influence among members. Responsibility is a key word here. When decision making is pushed up the pyramid, it disempowers those below, relieving them of responsibility for decisions that are made.[13]

Organizations today need to push decision making back down the pyramid. Nucor Corp., a $2 billion steelmaker, operates with a highly decentralized structure: There are only 23 people at the home offices in Charlotte, North Carolina. Decision making is the responsibility of frontline managers, who have greater access to customers and who know what's happening in the market. "Each of Nucor's 21 plant managers is responsible for sales, purchasing, and personnel."[14]

SILENCE IS DEADLY

DANGER! When silence overtakes a team, and members don't communicate openly and honestly, it can doom a project. When questions aren't raised and opinions aren't challenged, a collusion of silence develops and the team can become dysfunctional. Rather than operating with responsibility and consensual agreement, members become protective. Harvard researcher Chris Argyris, well known for his work on defensive routines, says that keeping quiet not only protects others by not putting them on the spot or not opening up a can of worms, but it protects the "self" as well: By keeping quiet, the individual doesn't appear negative, isn't viewed as a troublemaker, and doesn't have to admit to what he or she doesn't know.[15]

Andy Grove, Intel CEO, knows silence is deadly. At Intel, constructive confrontation is a company norm. Employees have permission to challenge; in fact, at meetings, managers are expected to give their honest opinions. However, they are also expected to commit once a decision has been reached. This process empowers everyone and reinforces dedication to the goal because everyone knows that all stakeholders have had a chance to agree or disagree, and to make suggestions for improvements. Grove wants managers to be dedicated to their work, "putting aside self-interest and territoriality for cooperation and mutual support," while allowing space for respectful, honest differences to be aired.[16]

TEAMS NEED SOME CONFLICT

Good teams need some amount of conflict. Disagreement is necessary. Two indications of trouble in a team are a total absence of conflict or extreme polarization. When disagreement is valued and when members are encouraged to articulate their doubts, solutions are apt to be more innovative and creative.

Dissenting views can be highly valuable. In a collaborative, consensual problem-solving mode, members are free to admit what they don't know and to examine differing points of view. However, because of pressure to conform and issues of defensiveness, individuality should be established as a group norm. Teams need to

Stellar Performer: 3M
Innovation and Teamwork

Founded in 1902, 3M started as a failed mine, and its first president wasn't paid a salary for 11 years. Yet with the company's ability to innovate and its entrepreneurial engine, 3M's 19 divisions presently manufacture approximately 60,000 products, from protective face masks to surgical tape to cleaning pads. In 1990, 3M made Fortune's 10 Most Admired Companies list for the sixth time; the company is now worth $14 billion.

In 1914, William L. McKnight was made general manager and began propelling the organization forward. From 1926 to 1966, he led 3M, instilling the belief that managers need to trust employees who have the best direct knowledge of the market, operations, or technology. At 3M, frontline engineers and sales representatives are nurtured and employees are encouraged to be creative. The famous "Post-it Notes" are the result of an environment where people are given time to play with ideas. There is less emphasis on top-down planning and control. Innovation and individualism are core values: Individual entrepreneurs can present their ideas directly to management at face-to-face meetings. Mistakes are accepted and seen as part of the learning process.

3M operates by a "grow-and-divide" principle. Project teams are the organization's building blocks, forming the foundation of the company's 3,900 profit centers. Departments grow from small units which grow from successful teams started by entrepreneurs with innovative ideas. As the departments grow, some spin off as separate divisions, which thus seed new projects. Cross-unit collaboration has been in effect for decades at 3M, building interdependence and mutual respect across the organization. "Products belong to divisions, but technology belongs to the company" reflects the way 3M values collaboration. The company has a portfolio of more than 100 technologies, which it applies in multiple markets through a strong broad-based distribution system.

The role of 3M managers is to support initiatives and ideas and to help in their development rather than to direct and control. Managers act as coaches, who both challenge and encourage their teams. 3M has deep historical technologies and knowledge bases in abrasives, adhesives, and coating-bonding that far exceed its major competitors, but

(Continued)

(Continued)

some experts claim that 3M's "real core competence is its well-oiled competence-building process."

With 100 laboratories around the globe, 3M has a wide collegial network of scientists and technologists who work openly with one another and who participate in forums and councils that facilitate the communication of cross-unit technology and scientific knowledge. And everyone in the organization has the opportunity to learn: Each year scientists showcase their research and findings at the annual technology fair.

3M balances discipline and support. As well as being innovative, the company also has extremely clear guidelines and management practices, which are shared across the organization. One of the reasons the company has had so many entrepreneurial initiatives is because of the company mandate that "30 percent of a unit's sales must come from products introduced within the past four years." All parts of the organization are expected to contribute to the company's goals for 10 percent growth in sales and earnings, 20 percent pretax profit margins, and 25 percent return on shareholder equity.

Like other organizations in recent years, 3M has had its problems. Although sales increased 60 percent in the late '80s, between 1991 and 1993, sales growth was a meager 2 percent. CEO L. D. DeSimone aggressively began to drive innovation. He pushed R&D to become more competitive, to apply the company's proprietary technology wherever possible, and to propel products out faster. His strategy seems to be working: By the end of 1994, 3M's profits and revenues were again climbing at a steady rate.

Sources: Christopher A. Bartlett and Sumantra Ghoshal, "Changing the Role of Top Management: Beyond Systems to People," Harvard Business Review (May/June 1995); Christopher A. Bartlett and Sumantra Ghoshal, "Changing the Role of Top Management: Beyond Structure to Process," Harvard Business Review (January/February 1995); James C. Collins and Jerry I. Porras, Built to Last: Successful Habits of Visionary Companies (New York: HarperBusiness, 1994); James Brian Quinn, "Building the Intelligent Enterprise," in The Portable MBA in Strategy, ed. Liam Fahey and Robert M. Randall (New York: John Wiley & Sons, 1994).

set aside time periodically to assess their own dynamics and performance and ask themselves how they are doing. Just as a manager needs self-awareness, a team needs to be aware of itself. Its environment should permit appraisal and feedback and should foster development of individuals.

A team is a dynamic subsystem operating within the larger system of the organization. Like the organizational culture, it is not static, but evolves and changes as it matures. Regardless of the environment, groups tend "to go through relatively predictable stages of development." And each stage provides a crucial function. (See Table 4.3.) This is important for leaders to understand as they implement group processes into their organizations: Teams take time to bond and will go through several stages before they reach their point of highest functioning.[17]

TEAMS NEED PROCESS MEASUREMENTS

Teams need good methods for measuring success. Because the structure and use of cross-functional teams is somewhat recent, new performance measurements must be devised and used along with traditional measures. Teams should be heavily involved in creating their own measurements. Working together and blending skills from different functions, they end up creating a "common language," which enables them to define problems and goals more clearly.

Functional measurements—whose real intent is to inform management about progress and activities—tell organizations where they are in the process of attaining goals, but they don't tell the organization how it got there or "what it should do differently."[18] Results measurements, such as cost, schedule, market share, and profit, "keep score" on the organization's performance. But they do not "monitor the activities or capabilities that enable it to perform a given process. Nor do such measures tell team members what they must do to improve their performance." Process measures, on the other hand, "examine the actions and capabilities that contributed to the situation." Process measures might, for example, include tracking the number of new parts used in a product—the more parts, the greater the probability of difficulty. This measurement can provide insight into parts causing the problems and might lead to ways to reduce or consolidate parts.[19]

Measures, once created by the team, are not set in stone. Flexibility is the rule as team members assess the value of the measures they create. Some measurements will be worthwhile for a period of time and some will become obsolete. Members must maintain flexibility and the freedom to throw out any measure that is wasting time and not producing the information that is

TABLE 4.3 STAGES OF GROUP DEVELOPMENT

Stage One: Membership

Commitment is being decided. Interaction is polite and guarded. Managers need to increase members' attraction to the group by tying members' goals to the group's purpose, and identifying and linking core issues with the specific expertise of members.

Stage Two: Subgrouping

Individuals seek allies and tend to speak from subgroups. Conflict is indirect and positions are not yet clear. It is important at this stage to make sure the group takes time to discuss how it is operating and what issues might be inhibiting its effectiveness.

Stage Three: Conflict

Conflict emerges across subgroups. This stage tests whether relationships and the group can survive battles. This is a crucial turning point. Managers should not rush in to put out fires; they must show members the value of differences and encourage the expression of disagreement. Members must learn how to raise questions and difficult issues, to disagree, and to resolve their conflicts. Conflict cannot be suppressed; it will surface in other, more indirect, harder-to-handle ways. By learning how to negotiate their way through this stage, members grow in competence. At this stage, members can improve their interpersonal communication skills and learn how to give feedback on behaviors without personally criticizing others. Groups should again take time for self-evaluation.

Stage Four: Individual Differentiation

If conflicts from Stage Three have been successfully resolved, members feel comfortable in being themselves. Low group conformity exists as members accept each other's individuality. It is difficult to get to this stage, but if a group gets this far, it is likely to be a high-performance team. Greater autonomy is achieved at this level. Greater trust exists because problems have been resolved, and individual skills can be more fully utilized.

Stage Five: Collaboration

The team works collectively to solve problems and to support each other in implementation. A synergistic outcome results in which the whole is greater than the sum of the parts. At this stage there is true integration. The team gets to Stage Five by stressing its centrality. It benefits from the individuality that was achieved in Stage Four. Members know they can influence each other and give feedback without loss of status. Once this stage is reached, it takes constant work to remain at this integrated, holistic level.

Source: *David L. Bradford, "Building High-Performance Teams" in* The Portable MBA in Management, *ed. Allan R. Cohen (New York: John Wiley & Sons, 1993), pp. 61–68.*

needed. Additionally, the process of establishing measurements can be systematized to a degree, but each team will need to establish measurements particular to its own process and the environment.[20]

DON'T GET CAUGHT UP IN OLD PATTERNS

Traditional measures can distract a team from its goals. When Ford first used multifunctional teams in the early 1990s, one product development team used a collection of functional measurements. In the process stage between design and engineering, a controversy arose over the design of a door handle for the new car. "Each function made different assumptions about the relative importance of the factors contributing to the product's costs and competitiveness." Team members were locked into their own traditional measurements and lost sight of the bigger picture. Throughout the controversy, a critical issue was never raised: "Would the new handle increase the car's ability to compete in the marketplace?"[21]

K E Y CONCEPT (CUSTOMERS ARE NUMBER ONE)

Sam Walton's customers were his number one concern. At Wal-Mart the customer comes ahead of everything else. "Every time a customer comes within ten feet of me, I will smile, look him in the eye, and greet him. So help me Sam." This is more than an employee pledge; it's a deeply valued practice.[22]

The ability not only to discover what customers want, but to empathize with them and gain knowledge from them is a key to success in a market-driven, competitive environment. When companies can supply customers with exactly what they want, it is much more difficult for competitors to lure them away.

When companies meet customers' needs, customers develop feelings of loyalty, and every company wants loyal customers—they help ensure profitability, are repeat buyers, pay premium prices, and bring in new business.[23] Customers who are loyal save the company money by reducing the promotional cost of attracting new customers and cutting the production cost incurred from meeting new customer requirements.

In the new world of business, the customer is becoming a business partner who can be counted on to provide "a stream of revenues and profits over a long period of time." In the new relationship with customers, companies develop a "buyer-seller partnership" that goes beyond the simple purchase of a product. This approach is more inclusive and broader than strategies used in the past. It takes a knowledge-based service approach, which demands a shift in values and beliefs, and establishes the customer as the focal point for the activities of all employees in the company, not just the marketing people.[24]

At Wal-Mart, employees are motivated to excel in customer service. The chain operates with "a store-within-a-store" concept. Department managers have the freedom and authority to run the department as if it were their own business. They are encouraged to think creatively and to experiment in their efforts to please customers and to run efficient operations.[25]

KEY CONCEPT — LISTEN TO THE CUSTOMER

Listening can result in feedback that leads to breakthrough products and services, while failure to listen to customers can result in missed opportunities. Understanding and loyalty can be increased through the development of interactive communication with customers. Greater clarity about expectations and desires can be attained, rectifying misunderstandings and enhancing relationships.

AlliedSignal CEO Lawrence Bossidy believes in direct customer contact. In his first three months on the job, he made sure he spoke directly with employees and customers, and claims he "really got an earful." He also discovered some disturbing facts: The company was under the assumption that it was "delivering an order-fill rate of 98%," while customers thought the fill rate was 60 percent. The company, which usually operated with the belief that it was right, had to start believing the customer. But before it could do that, it had to get honest feedback from the people in the field. When the sales force told headquarters what the customers really felt, the company finally realized it had to do something. So, Allied went directly to the customers and asked them to team up and help identify problems. Almost every customer agreed. Multifunctional teams now work together, providing customers with higher quality service and products.[26]

Customers want products that offer them particular benefits and value. Companies that have an understanding of what features, designs, and services will bring customers the most value and the highest levels of satisfaction will succeed in building business and profitability. Beyond just fulfilling customers' immediate needs, companies that know their customers well can anticipate what innovations in products and services will create even deeper levels of satisfaction. In a *Harvard Business Review* interview, Whirlpool CEO David Whitman advises making projections about what customers will want in the future by thinking innovatively and creatively. He points out the microwave was developed because someone thought about easier and quicker food preparation, not about making better stoves and ovens. Whitman provides examples of ways to change thinking patterns to stimulate innovation. It's better, he counsels, to think about being in the "fabric-care" business than in the washing machine business, to be in the "food-preservation" business than in the refrigerator business.[27]

TIP DO WHAT IT TAKES TO GET CLOSE

Work with customers to find ways to help them with their communication needs. Speak at customers' events, hold seminars for them, join together in making presentations. Support them in ways that provide the opportunity to get to know them better.

Face-to-face communication works wonders. It provides better insight and offers the opportunity to elicit more detailed information. One-to-one visits enable managers to gain competitive advantage by developing partnerships with customers in which both parties benefit and learn. But while visiting, managers need to dig below the surface and invest more time really understanding their clients. By becoming more aware of their own assumptions, managers can set aside any preconceived ideas. Approaching a visit with an open mind affords an opportunity to be more curious and to ask a greater number of questions, which can elicit more valuable, detailed information.

Managers' personal involvement with customers drives organizational change, because managers end up "feeling" what their customers feel. The recommendation "to spend a day in the life of your customer" should not go unheeded. It is time well spent. Besides generating insights into new possibilities, it can become a catalyst, spurring managers to put ideas into action.[28]

KEY CONCEPT NEW ONE-TO-ONE RELATIONSHIPS

By dealing with customers on a one-to-one basis, managers can get detailed feedback that enables them to discover the products or services their individual customers value most.

One-to-one marketing and *mass customization* (more thoroughly discussed in Chapter 9) are new marketing concepts being emphasized in today's competitive market. By focusing on individual customer requirements and developing customized products, companies build a base of loyal customers. One-to-one marketing entails interaction with customers to determine what they want and need. With mass customization, the company adapts mass-produced products to fit the individual customer's requirements after collaborating with the customer about design features.

For example, sales representatives of Andersen Corporation, a window manufacturer, help customers at retail centers design and order customized windows by using a multimedia system that offers 50,000 different components. Together the sales representative and the customer determine the manufacturing specifications that meet the customer's individual preferences. The system fulfills customers' needs efficiently by linking sales and production together.[29]

TiP LEARN ABOUT CUSTOMERS BY BEING CREATIVE

Devise ways to initiate interaction with customers in order to learn their preferences. The Ritz-Carlton, for example, teaches its employees how to communicate with hotel customers and glean their preferences. Employees enter customers' desires and requests into a global database to enable future tracking. Not only can the hotel learn how to provide repeat customers the service they want, but the hotel learns how to stay on top of trends. It provides better overall service by finding ways to solve problems that show up on a repeat basis.[30]

TiP CREATE A NEW ROLE

Create the role of *customer manager* to serve as a vital communication link between the company and the customer. These managers should be responsible for working with customers to define their needs, to oversee production and delivery, and to make sure the capacity exists to produce and deliver goods.[31] Ross Controls, a uniquely successful manufacturer of both mass-produced and mass-customized pneumatic valves (highlighted in Chapter 9) has *integrators*—employees who don't just provide customer service, but who manage the entire process, ensuring the best in design, production, and delivery.

TiP LEARN FROM OTHERS: BENCHMARK

Smart companies have learned the importance of developing effective systems for gathering and analyzing customer and competitor information. By benchmarking themselves against others who are best in the field, companies can learn more efficient ways of operating.

Again and again, evidence supports the concept that knowledge derived from the proper compilation and assessment of information is a key success factor in the marketplace. Companies can learn from Honeywell's experience. (See Stellar Performer.) When Honeywell realized it was having customer satisfaction problems, it benchmarked companies in other industries that were leaders in customer service and in the utilization of information. It used the knowledge it gained to reengineer its fragmented customer-service process,

Stellar Performer: Honeywell
Customer Service

Since Honeywell's Home and Building Control division revamped its customer service operations, the special attention it pays to customers has reaped enormous rewards for the company and customers:

- Order-delivery defects have been reduced by more than 80 percent.
- Breakthrough products like the Perfect Climate Comfort Center System, developed in partnership with customers, reached 100 percent of its 1995 sales plan within five short weeks of its introduction.
- Customer satisfaction ratings have increased dramatically—customers rating themselves "very satisfied" have grown 23 percent.
- The company won the International Customer Service Award for Excellence in manufacturing in 1991.

These achievements are the culmination of Honeywell's efforts to become a service leader and to raise the bar in communication and information exchange with customers.

In 1986, Honeywell, an industry leader in products for controlling the environment of homes and commercial buildings, discovered its customer service function had to change. Customer surveys reflected customers' frustrations—Honeywell was "hard to do business with." Lack of coordination and communication were common problems and there was an enormous amount of inefficiency and redundancy: Fifteen fundamental areas, reporting to various parts of the organization, were doing the same things. Customer service was slow and customers were bounced around due to multiple contact points and the reporting structure. Additionally, no one was responsible for the overall process of customer service. The company simply wasn't utilizing information or information technology properly.

Honeywell started redesigning its customer services process by benchmarking itself against leaders in other industries. It upgraded its information technology and developed new systems and software. In 1989, it realigned its numerous and scattered customer service functions under the umbrella of the Customer Satisfaction Department, and headed it with a director of customer satisfaction, who became directly responsible for the process of meeting customers' needs.

Realizing that it was no longer sufficient just to fulfill customers' expectations, the company began educating customers, many of whom were mom-and-pop shops, on the significance of incorporating technology into everyday operations. Honeywell trained interested customers in the use of its newly developed system and offered them free software.

(Continued)

(Continued)

With access to Honeywell's database, customers can now track their products in one or two minutes and find out what has been shipped, what mode of transportation is being used, and where goods are enroute to their destination. The database is continuously updated, and 80 percent of Honeywell's volume utilizes the system. It greatly reduces time on the phone, saves customers money, and frees up customer service reps to work with customers on more complex issues, providing them with far more valuable service.

Customers receive highly individualized treatment, made possible through segmentation and precise differentiation of needs. Dedicated teams and customer representatives are trained to meet the particular requirements of each customer within these segmented groupings. Each team member is educated to answer all types of questions, so that the customer does not get bounced between different departments looking for answers.

In the process of upgrading its customer satisfaction service, Honeywell has gone beyond being simply a manufacturer or supplier to being a partner in the development of products. Honeywell's Home and Building Control division employs more than 10,000 people in the United States and 15,000 people worldwide. In 1994, it had $2.6 billion in sales. It has a huge customer base and its commitment to partnering with customers is just as huge. Its customer satisfaction goals go beyond meeting customers' needs to ensuring that products exceed customer expectations. Its latest breakthrough, the Perfect Climate Comfort Center System, is the first integrated all-in-one temperature and indoor air quality control system, and was designed with input from over 400 distributors and contractors who provided information about the benefits and features they wanted. Over 7,000 hours of simulated testing were conducted even before the product entered the pilot mode. The end result was a product that exceeded everyone's expectations. Customers have nothing but praise, claiming it's "everything we've been asking for. We now have a product that is the be-all and do-all of home control."

Through technical training and marketing support offered by Honeywell, customers develop additional expertise that enables them to provide better service to their own customers, demonstrating that Honeywell's sense of partnership is ongoing. Honeywell works with customers throughout the entire production cycle—before, during, and after—to create innovative products that make life more comfortable.

Source: Interviews with Barbara Hensley, Honeywell's first director of customer satisfaction; Honeywell corporate material.

and it ended up with a customer satisfaction department that other companies can use as a model.

END POINT

Relationships require communication. Listening and good interpersonal skills are especially important for customer relations and teamwork. These "soft" aspects of the organization—its culture and its people—are core elements which must be properly managed for success. But "hard" issues must be managed, too. Focusing too much on soft issues won't guarantee success any more than focusing too much on hard issues. A balanced approach ensures a greater chance of supporting an environment that leads to productivity and profitability. People need knowledge of all the underpinnings of the organization. And that knowledge can't be built without information—information that is communicated in ways that make it understandable. The next section provides a means for understanding those hard numbers, for placing them in perspective, and for seeing their interrelatedness and their value.

MORE READING

Argyris, Chris. *Overcoming Organizational Defenses: Facilitating Organizational Learning.* Needham, Mass.: Allyn and Bacon, 1990.

Beer, Michael, et al. *Managing Human Assets.* New York: The Free Press, 1981.

Birch, David. *How Our Smallest Companies Put the Most People to Work.* New York: The Free Press, 1987.

Bradford, D. L., and A. R. Cohen. *Managing for Excellence.* New York: John Wiley & Sons, 1984.

Drucker, Peter. *Post-Capitalist Society.* New York: HarperBusiness, 1993.

Hackman, J. Richard (ed.), *Groups that Work (and Those that Don't): Creating Conditions for Effective Teamwork.* San Francisco, Calif.: Jossey-Bass, 1990.

Janis, I. L. *Victims of Groupthink.* Boston: Houghton Mifflin, 1982.

Pine, Joseph B. II, *Mass Customization: The New Frontier in Business Competition.* Boston: Harvard Business School Press, 1993.

Quinn, James Brian. *Intelligent Enterprise.* New York: The Free Press, 1992.

Schafer, Robert H. *The Breakthrough Strategy: Using Short Term Successes to Build the High Performance Organization.* Cambridge, Mass.: Ballinger, 1988.

Sexton, Donald L., and John D. Kasards. *The State of the Art of Entrepreneurship.* P.W.S. Kent, 1992.

Vroom, V. H., and P. Yetton. *Leadership and Decision-Making.* Pittsburgh: University of Pittsburgh Press, 1973.

Webster, Frederick E., Jr. *Market-Driven Management: Using the New Marketing Concept to Create a Customer Driven Company.* New York: John Wiley & Sons, 1994.

Zeithaml, Valarie A., A. Parasuraman, and Leonard A. Berry. *Delivering Quality Service: Balancing Customer Perceptions and Expectations.* New York: The Free Press, 1990.

The Hard Numbers

When you can measure what you are speaking about, and express it in numbers, you know something about it; but when you cannot measure it, when you cannot express it in numbers, your knowledge is of a meager and unsatisfactory kind: It may be the beginning of knowledge, but you have scarcely, in your thought, advanced to the stage of science.

William Thomson, Lord Kelvin

Accounting and Finance: Showing How the Numbers Count

Delivering value to customers is important. Motivating employees to work together effectively is important. And providing shareholders with profit is important.

In the past, the primary corporate focus was directed toward satisfying shareholders' needs. As new management practices take hold, the focal point has widened to include customers and employees. All three groups of constituents count. And all three groups need executives who know how to manage the company's finances, using capital wisely to protect the solvency of the organization and give it a secure financial base from which to grow and prosper.

In every company, there is competition for financial resources as investment strategies are evaluated and timed. These next two chapters offer insight into the fundamentals of accounting and financial management. Having a basic understanding of essential financial concepts helps managers in every area of business make intelligent, informed decisions which contribute to profitability and lead to better performance.

KEY CONCEPT   HOW A COMPANY WORKS

Companies operate on cash flow. They raise money to purchase assets so they can perform operations that produce and provide products and services for customers, which in turn provide profit for the company.

In the process of operating, the company needs cash to purchase materials and pay its employees for their labor. Cash is turned into products, which become the company's inventory. When inventory is sold, it gets turned back into cash, either at the point of sale or when the amount due is collected as an account receivable. This movement of cash is known as the "operating or working capital cycle."[1]

ACCOUNTING

In its simplest form, accounting gives the organization a means of measuring the competence of those in charge. As a control function, it provides a scorecard that reflects the company's performance. Accounting enables decision making through the analysis of data for both day-to-day cash management and long-term planning, and it acts as an internal control, documenting records, account books, and taxes.

Auditing, another control device, assures that the accounting is accurate. Audited financial statements are considered reliable documents. Every country has its own particular requirements for filing financial accounts, and the kinds of documents required are determined by the company's classification. Private companies and partnerships have different requirements than corporations that trade stock publicly. A discussion of requirements and types of companies is beyond the scope of this chapter; however, the basics offered here contain general principles that can be applied to most businesses.

There are two methods of accounting: accrual and cash. With *accrual accounting,* revenues and expenses are recorded in the tax period in which transactions take place. Accountants record a sale or revenue figure as the amount that will be generated when the transaction is totally complete. However, as soon as the sales effort is completed and it is believed that payments will be received, accountants add the sales figure to the income ledger. For instance, if sales receipts on a credit basis are normally received within 60 days of purchase, the cash from sales made in December 1995 won't actually be received until 1996, but the figures will be entered as sales on the 1995 books. The accrual system is most commonly used by corporations in their financial reports.

With *cash accounting,* revenues are recorded at the time in which the payment is actually received—sales made in December 1995, but paid for in January or February of 1996 appear on the 1996 books.

The basic financial documents used by most companies, public or private, big or small, include:

- A balance sheet
- An income statement
- A cash flow statement

THE BALANCE IN THE BALANCE SHEET

The balance sheet provides a picture of the company at a point in time and shows the company's assets (what it owns), its liabilities (what it owes), and shareholder equity (its net worth, which is also known as owners' equity, stockholders' equity, or just plain equity).

The balance sheet equation is simple:

$$\boxed{\text{Assets} = \text{liabilities} + \text{shareholder equity (net worth)}}$$

This equation can be restated to show the company's net worth:

$$\boxed{\text{Shareholder equity (net worth)} = \text{assets} - \text{liabilities}}$$

Assets, financed through liabilities and equity, include the inventory and equipment that enable the company to run its business. Assets and liabilities are current if they can be converted into cash within one year—otherwise they are long-term. Inventory is considered current because it generally sells within a year.

) current assets

Note the balance sheet for Company ABC shown in Table 5.1: Its total assets and total liabilities and shareholder equity in 1995 were each $3,480,000. Note also

TABLE 5.1 COMPANY ABC: BALANCE SHEET
(December 31, 1995)
($000)

Assets	1995	1994
Current assets		
Cash	$ 280.	$ 50.
Accounts receivable	660.	700.
Inventory	780.	830.
Total current assets	**$1,720.**	**$1,580.**
Fixed assets		
Land	$ 220.	$ 220.
Plant and equipment	2,100.	2,040.
Less: Depreciation	(560)	(440)
Total fixed assets	**$1,760.**	**$1,820.**
Total assets	**$3,480.**	**$3,400.**
Liabilities and Shareholder Equity (Net Worth)		
Current liabilities		
Accounts payable	$ 780.	$ 860.
Notes payable	190.	220.
Total current liabilities	**$ 970.**	**$1,080.**
Long-term debt	$ 1,100.	$ 1,130.
Total liabilities	**$2,070.**	**$2,210.**
Shareholder equity		
Common stock	1,000.	1,000.
Retained earnings	410.	190.
Total shareholder equity (net worth)	**$1,410.**	**$1,190.**
Total liabilities and shareholder equity	**$3,480.**	**$3,400.**

that the shareholder's equity or the net worth of the company is $1,410,000, calculated by subtracting the total liabilities of $2,070,000 from the total assets of $3,480,000 ($3,480,000 − 2,070,000 = $1,410,000).

INCOME STATEMENT: A PICTURE OF PROFITABILITY

Income Statement = Profit + Loss Statement

The income statement, also known as the profit and loss statement, provides a picture of the company's profitability, the net profit it makes over a period of time. This statement shows how the company made a profit by displaying how much money it took in through sales and how much money it costs to run the business. The equation used to determine net profit or loss, which is commonly called *the bottom line,* is:

> Net profit (loss) = gross sales − total expenses

OPERATING INCOME

EARNINGS after Expenses, But Before Interest + Taxes "EBIT"

A key distinction managers need to make is that operating income is not the same as net profit. Operating income is the amount determined by subtracting costs from sales; it does not take into account taxes owed or interest charges. Operating income is the amount the company earns after expenses, but before interest and taxes. Note that operating income is sometimes referred to as EBIT (earnings before interest and taxes) and profits are often referred to as *income* or *earnings.* And sales are often referred to as *revenues.*

> Gross sales − sales costs − operating expense − depreciation = operating income

NUMBERS ALONE MEAN NOTHING

Numbers by themselves mean nothing. Numbers in relation to other numbers tell the story. Some things are obvious: If sales go up and costs go down, the picture has a rosy glow; if sales go down and costs go up, the picture starts to look dark and gloomy. But what about the shades of gray created by sales that go down slightly and costs that remain the same, or sales that go up slightly with costs that go up severely? These numbers give managers questions to ponder. Should prices be raised or costs cut? If costs should be cut, how? What is the most cost-efficient way to make, sell, and distribute the product?

When looking at income statements, check out the cost and expense pattern. When expenses decrease substantially, it is generally an indication that management is on top of issues. On the other hand, if expenses have continued to creep up, it could be an indication that management does not have the organization under control. Whether costs have gone up or down, it's good to find out what has caused the changes. Compare expenses with standards in the industry to get a better idea of how a company spends in relation to others. Use financial ratios (which will be explained shortly) to calculate percentages and compare figures on the statement.

Company ABC's income statements for 1994 and 1995 (see Table 5.2) show a modest increase in sales and a significant decrease in total expenses. In 1995, management moved to improve every area of performance, and the result was a markedly improved profit over 1994.

PROFITABILITY DOES NOT EQUAL CASH FLOW

DANGER!

The numbers on paper might look good at first glance, but if large amounts of money are owed to the company or cash is tied up in inventory and equipment and not available to use for growth, then the company can be short on working capital. Profitability does not assure solvency. Cash flow statements provide insight needed to understand more clearly how the company is protecting its operating flexibility and how much working capital is available. Astute managers analyze both earnings and cash flow. In 1995, Company ABC's earnings were $220,000.

TABLE 5.2 COMPANY ABC
(for period ending December 31, 1995)
($000)

Income Statement	1995	1994
Gross income (sales)	$4,000.	$3,700.
Less cost of goods sold	(2,667.)	(2,553.)
Gross profit	$1,333.	$1,147.
Gross margin	33.3%	31.0%
Expenses		
Selling	$ 620.	$ 700.
General and administrative	140.	160.
Less depreciation	120.	115.
Total costs and expenses	$ 880.	$ 975.
Operating income (EBIT)	$ 453.	$ 172.
Interest charges	115.	123.
Income before taxes	$ 338.	$ 49.
Taxes @ 35%	118.	17.
Net income	$ 220.	$ 32.

Due to improved management practices, the company not only enhanced profitability, but cash flow increased as well.

DIFFERENTIATE BETWEEN FIXED AND VARIABLE COSTS

Differentiate between fixed and variable costs. Firms with greater fixed costs have more vulnerability: When sales decline, so do their profits because they have more limited means of adjusting their costs. Generally speaking, operating costs are considered fixed and cost of goods sold is considered variable. Determining gross margin provides a way to distinguish between variable and fixed costs.

$$\text{Gross margin} = \frac{\text{gross profit}}{\text{sales}}$$

For example, if a company had a gross profit of $240 million and had $600 million in sales, its gross margin would be 40 percent, which means that 40 cents of every sales dollar is available to pay for fixed costs. Note that in 1995 Company ABC's gross margin increased to 33.3 percent.

KEY CONCEPT — CASH FLOWS THROUGH THE COMPANY

The cash flow statement shows where cash comes from and how it is used for a given period of time. It enables managers to see the amount of working capital or *liquidity* the company has available to pay bills and stay in business. Information for the cash flow sheet comes from both the income statement and balance sheet; however, the cash flow statement provides more precise information about a company's state of liquidity. Additionally, by analyzing the cash flow statement, it is possible to discern a company's operating strategy and judge its viability.

The company derives its cash from sources both inside and outside the organization. Cash flows from three main areas: operating activity, investment activity, and financing activity. (See Table 5.3.)

COMPARE SOURCE OF NUMBERS

For a better understanding, take a closer look at what the numbers in Table 5.3 indicate. One of the first things to determine is whether the numbers are showing in the positive or the negative. Numbers in parentheses are subtracted: They represent cash disbursed. Look at the relationship between cash made available through operations and cash from finance and investment.

TABLE 5.3 COMPANY ABC: CASH FLOW STATEMENT 1995
($000)

Operating activities

Net income	$ 220.
Depreciation	120.
Accounts receivable	40.
Notes payable	(30)
Inventories	50.
Accounts payable	(80)
Net cash flow from operations	**$320.**

Investing activities

Property, plant, and equipment	(60)

Financing activities

Long-term debt	(30)

Cash flow	**$230.**

Cash balance at beginning of year	**50.**
Cash balance at end of year	**$280.**

BOOK VALUE VERSUS MARKET VALUE

Accounting figures usually reflect the historical cost of assets (the book value), not present market value, and generally state the original transaction. For example, if a company purchased land 20 years ago for $500,000, but for one reason or another never developed the land, its real estate value has most likely increased in the market. It might be worth as much as $5 million today. Yet accountants will report the land at its original cost as a $500,000 asset on the balance sheet.

ANNUAL REPORT: READ THE WHOLE THING

The company's annual report contains the financial reports previously outlined and provides an overview of the financial health of a corporation. It also contains an analysis and discussion section, which provides management's view of the company strengths, weaknesses, and future direction. The notes or footnotes to the financial statement found in annual reports offer additional significant information for those assessing the worth of a company. They provide information on any changes or structural reorganization, new systems of compensation, and details of legal matters that may affect the well-being of the company. Table 5.4 lists a dozen ways in which financial statements can be used. And Table 5.5 defines significant terms.

TABLE 5.4 FINANCIAL STATEMENTS AND BUSINESS DECISION MAKING: A DOZEN REASONS WHY FINANCIAL STATEMENTS ARE USEFUL

User	Use
1. Management	Assess operational effectiveness
2. Suppliers and customers	Evaluate financial strength
3. Equity and debt investors	Monitor performance of management
4. Prospective investors	Find companies in which to invest
5. Banks and lenders	Determine credibility for loans
6. Investment analysts, money managers, and stockbrokers	Make investment recommendations to clients
7. Rating agencies	Assign credit ratings
8. Competitors	Benchmark
9. Potential competitors	Assess profitability of industry and strength of potential competitor
10. Corporate raiders	Seek hidden value
11. Labor unions	Assess financial status
12. Government agencies	Assess taxes and compliance

Source: John Leslie Livingstone, "Accounting and Management Decision Making," in The Portable MBA (New York: John Wiley & Sons, 1994), pp. 245–246.

 INVENTORY AND DEPRECIATION

Inventory is a balance-sheet asset, and changes in inventory affect the bottom line on the income statement. The value of inventory can be determined using a *first-in/first-out* (FIFO) method or a last-in/first-out (LIFO) method. Because inventory is never one single item, because prices can fluctuate over time, and because of the effect of inflation, there can be a difference between the cost of inventory at the beginning of the year and the cost of inventory later on in the year. The key is to know how to make the numbers pro-

1995 Production Cost			FIFO	LIFO
Mar.	$46.00	Sales price	$70.00	$70.00
June	47.00	Cost of goods sold	46.00	50.00
Sept.	48.00	Sales income	24.00	20.00
Dec.	50.00	Other expenses	12.00	12.00
		Taxable income	12.00	8.00
		Tax @ 35%	(4.20)	(2.80)
		Earnings after tax	$7.80	$5.20

TABLE 5.5 COME TO TERMS WITH TERMS

Understanding financial definitions and their relationship to the overall financial health of the company helps.

Accounts receivable are moneys owed to the organization due to sales. They need to be managed so that they are received in a timely fashion, providing adequate cash flow.

Accounts payable are moneys owed by the organization to others. They need to be managed so they don't grow to the point where they become too large, creating an imbalance that threatens the health of the company. Compare payables and receivables.

Net income represents the profitability of the company and differs from operating income. It is the bottom line on the income statement. Determine whether net income shows growth from one period to another.

Retained earnings are surplus earnings not distributed as dividends, but kept and reinvested in the business.

Common stocks are securities that represent ownership in a company. Common stockholders receive a return on their investment through growth, which increases the value of the stock, and through dividends. When companies are profitable, stockholders benefit; when firms fail, stockholders suffer.

Preferred Stocks are securities with fixed dividend rates. Preferred dividends are not tax deductible for the company. Although dividends are fixed, the board of directors decides when they are issued; unless the company is sufficiently profitable, stockholders might not receive dividends. However, preferred stock dividends are cumulative, which means that when dividends are paid, arrears for accumulated payments must be distributed before common stock dividends are distributed.

duce the desired effect for the organization. Overstating the value of inventory using FIFO, management can enhance apparent net worth. Understating inventory using LIFO can reduce taxable income.

Depreciation allows companies to spread the cost of an asset over the life of the asset. Rather than deducting the full amount of costs for fixed assets like plants and equipment in one year, depreciation enables the company to determine an asset's useful life and to spread the costs out over that time period. Companies normally use one of two depreciation methods: straight line or accelerated.

In *straight line depreciating,* the original cost is equally divided over the appropriate time period with one exception: It is assumed that assets (other than properties) are acquired in midyear. Therefore, in the first and last years, 50 percent of the annual depreciation is deducted. For example, Swayback, a two-year-old racehorse, was purchased in March 1995 for $24,000. His owner is depreciating him as an asset over three years.

Year	Depreciation	Book Value
		$24,000
1995	$4,000	20,000
1996	8,000	12,000
1997	8,000	4,000
1998	4,000	0

In *accelerated depreciation,* more depreciation is charged in the first years of deduction, with deductions declining as time passes. With this approach, earnings are understated early in the life of the asset and over-stated later. The percent of the depreciation doubles the straight line method and is applied to the declining balance, not to the original cost.

Using this method, Swayback's depreciation schedule would be:

Year	Depreciation	Book Value
		$24,000
1995	$8,000	16,000
1996	10,667	5,333
1997	3,555	1,778
1998	1,778	0

IRS STIPULATES USEFUL LIFE

The IRS has established the useful life, or cost recovery period, for different types of assets, ranging from 3 to 31.5 years.

ACCELERATE TO ZERO

The Modified Accelerated Cost Recovery System (MACRS) uses double the straight line percentage. When the straight line depreciation exceeds accelerated depreciation, the schedule converts to straight line. Therefore, the asset's book value automatically becomes zero at the end of the cost recovery period.

SMALL COMPANIES CAN DEPRECIATE FULLY IN ONE YEAR

Small businesses may depreciate a purchase 100 percent in the first year if the asset cost is less than $10,000.

CHECK FINANCIAL HEALTH WITH FINANCIAL RATIOS

Financial statements help managers check the health of companies—their own and others. Using numbers from financial statements, financial ratios can be developed which provide tests that measure a company's short-term solvency, long-term solvency, and profitability. But financial ratios aren't precise measures: They're only rough guides. And they're only as good as the numbers on which they're based: If the numbers are wrong, the ratios will be misleading. But they do provide a systematic way of examining the company to gain insight into how well it operates.

Standards for industries vary and managers should be aware of the best standards in their industries. Additionally, as already mentioned, accountants use different accounting methods depending on what they are trying to accomplish; therefore, caution is advised. If ratios do not provide an answer, it's an indication that further investigation is required. Furthermore, numbers and ratios get their meaning in relationship to other factors that influence them. For example, some industries, such as retail, are affected by the seasons.

A good practice is to compare a company's ratios against another company's in the same industry, against the industry as a whole, and against the company's own ratios in other years. Trends over time can provide critical and useful information.

FIRMS NEED WORKING CAPITAL TO WORK

CONCEPT

Poor liquidity ratios are danger signals for companies. The current ratio is a measure of working capital or liquidity.

$$\text{Current ratio} = \frac{\text{current assets}}{\text{current liabilities}}$$

current ratio

For a margin of safety, a current ratio greater than 1 is desired.[2] If a company has a low current ratio, it means it probably doesn't have enough working capital to meet debts that are maturing and must rely instead on operating income or additional financing. For example, Company ABC has a 1995 current ratio of 1.8 (1,720/970 = 1.8), an improvement over its 1994 current ratio, which was 1.5 (1,580/1,080 = 1.5).

Current ratio is looked at by lending institutions when they are determining creditworthiness: They usually require minimum levels of net working capital.

THE ACID TEST IS A QUICK RATIO

QUICK RATIO

CONCEPT   Current ratios can also be calculated on cash that is quickly available. Quick ratios exclude inventories not easily liquidated and include only cash and highly liquid current assets such as accounts receivable and marketable securities. This is known as the *acid test*. Quick ratios above 1 are desirable.

Liquidity in assets is important because assets that can be converted easily to cash enable companies to conduct business without having to raise cash in the short term.

$$\text{Quick ratio} = \frac{\text{current liquid assets} - \text{inventory}}{\text{current liabilities}}$$

 CONTROLS THAT TEST
CONCEPT **FOR LIQUIDITY**

Turnover controls help operating managers determine how efficiently the company uses specific assets, such as inventories or accounts receivable. The following measure of liquidity deals with the relationship between sales and accounts receivable. How quickly a company converts sales into dollars determines how much liquidity the company has—how much working capital it has at its disposal. For instance, if Company DEF sells $1,600,000 worth of services in a year, but its customers owe it $400,000 in outstanding accounts receivable, the firm can calculate its average turnover by dividing its sales by its outstanding receivables.

$$\text{Accounts receivable rate of turnover} = \frac{\text{sales}}{\text{accounts receivable}}$$

In this case, Company DEF's rate of turnover is 4 (1,600,000/400,000 = 4). Or to put it more bluntly: It takes three months (12/4 = 3) to collect payment on bills. If company policy gives customers 90 days to pay their bills, then this turnover is acceptable. If, however, payment is expected every month, or every 60 days, then this three-month cycle is slow and endangers the company's liquidity.

Another liquidity ratio tests the rate of turnover for inventory. In this ratio, the cost of goods sold (which represents how much it cost to make the product, not how much the product sold for) is divided by the cost of inventory. For example, suppose the BestValve company started 1995 with 2,500 valves in inventory. During the year, it made 10,000 more, with each valve costing $25 to make. In the course of the year, 10,500 valves were sold, leaving 2,000 valves in inventory at the end of the year.

The cost of goods sold equals the number sold during the year times the cost per unit. Thus, BestValve's cost of goods sold for 1995 was $262,500 (10,500 × $25 = $262,500). The rate at which inventory was turned over—the average length of time the valves stayed on the shelves—is calculated by dividing the cost of goods sold by the cost of inventory. The length of time that inventory sits on shelves depends on the industry. But, generally, the higher or faster the turnover rate, the better; slow turnover can cause cash flow problems.

Beginning inventory	$2,500 \times \$25 =$	$\$\ 62,500$
Ending inventory	$2,000 \times \$25 =$	$\$\ 50,000$
		$\$112,500$
Average inventory	$\$112,500/2 =$	$\$\ 56,250$

$$\text{Inventory rate of turnover} = \frac{\text{cost of goods sold}}{\text{average inventory}}$$

On average, BestValue's inventory is sold and converted into cash 4.67 times a year ($262,500/56,250 = 4.67$), which means that each valve has an average shelf life of 78 days ($365/4.67 = 78$).

DEBT-TO-EQUITY RATIO

CONCEPT One of the most common measures for testing a company's long-term solvency is debt-to-equity ratio. It compares the amount of financing provided by creditors as opposed to financing provided by shareholders.

$$\text{Debt-to-equity ratio} = \frac{\text{total liabilities}}{\text{total shareholders' equity}}$$

By calculating the relationship between the company's total liabilities and shareholders' equity, managers can determine long-term solvency. For example, Company ABC has total liabilities of $2,070,000 and shareholders total equity of $1,410,000. The debt-to-equity ratio is 1.47 ($2,070,000/1,410,000 = 1.47$). Safety margins for debt-to-equity ratios vary among industries and depend on the volatility of the industry. But, generally, companies want low debt-to-equity ratios—the lower the better.

Another ratio that measures a company's ability to meet long-term debt is the interest earned ratio. It tests the company's ability to pay interest on long-term debt. It examines the earnings before interest and taxes (EBIT) in relationship to the interest owed on long-term debt. This ratio helps to determine whether the company has the ability to meet its interest expenses on loans. Interest earned ratio is calculated by dividing the company's profits by the interest on its loans.

$$\text{Interest earned ratio} = \frac{\text{EBIT}}{\text{annual interest}}$$

Company ABC, for instance, has an EBIT of $453,000 and an annual interest charge of $115,000. This ratio is calculated by dividing EBIT by the annual interest; thus, it has a better margin of safety ($453,000/115,000 = 3.9$) for repaying interest, as compared to 1.4 the previous year.

KEY CONCEPT — PROFITABILITY RATIO: RETURN ON EQUITY (ROE)

Return on equity (ROE) measures profitability and is one of the most popular indicators of financial performance. ROE measures how efficiently management uses the shareholders' capital. ROE is net income divided by shareholder equity.

$$\text{Return on equity} = \frac{\text{net income}}{\text{shareholder equity}}$$

Management has three levers of control over ROE:

- *Profit margin*—the earnings from each dollar of sales. The profit margin summarizes performance from the income statement. Profit margin reflects pricing strategy and management's ability to control operating costs. Profit margins vary enormously depending on the industry, the products, and the competitive strategy.

- *Asset turnover*—sales generated by each dollar of assets used. The asset turnover focuses on the left side of the balance sheet, indicating how well management has utilized assets in generating revenues.

- *Financial leverage*—equity used to finance assets. Financial leverage looks at how effectively management has financed assets.[3]

With a few exceptions, whatever management does to improve these levers improves ROE. These three levers capture the main elements of financial performance. Another way of looking at ROE is to incorporate all levers into the equation to see how they link together to form profitability:

$$\text{ROE} = \%\text{ profit margin} \times \%\text{ asset turnover} \times \%\text{ financial leverage}$$

determined by

$$\text{ROE} = \frac{\text{net income}}{\text{sales}} \times \frac{\text{sales}}{\text{total assets}} \times \frac{\text{total assets}}{\text{shareholder equity}}$$

Hewlett-Packard provides an example. Its 1989 ROE was 15.3 percent. That same year, Kmart Corp. had a similar ROE of 15.9 percent, but its combination of profit margin, asset turnover, and financial leverage was quite different. How a company manages its significant leverage points and interrelates them factors into its success.[4]

	PM $\times$ AT $\times$ FL =	ROE
Hewlett-Packard:	$(.070 \times 1.18 \times 1.85 = .153$ or 15.3%$)$	
Kmart:	$(.029 \times 2.27 \times 2.42 = .159$ or 15.9%$)$	

Another point worth noting is the inverse relationship between profit margin and asset turnover. Companies with high profit margins, like Hewlett-Packard, tend to have low asset turnover. The ability to manufacture unique and value-added products usually requires a large investment in assets. Conversely, companies with high asset turnover, like retailer Kmart, tend to have low profit margins.[5]

$$\text{ROE} \quad = \quad \text{ROA} \quad \times \% \text{ financial leverage}$$

$$\frac{\text{Net income}}{\text{shareholders equity}} = \frac{\text{net income}}{\text{total assets}} \times \frac{\text{total assets}}{\text{shareholder equity}}$$

By illustrating relationships, managers can form "what-if" questions, such as: What if sales grow by 25 percent instead of by 18 percent? If price is cut and volume increases, how is ROA affected? If inventory turnover slows down, how will ROE be affected? "What-if" analysis, also known as "sensitivity analysis," can provide the key to improving ROE by helping to point the way to effective strategies.[6]

ROE CONTAINS QUESTION OF RELIABILITY

ROE is a significant indicator, but it does have some drawbacks. It is not a totally reliable measure of financial performance for the following reasons:

- It examines returns without examining risk factors.
- Its annual time frame keeps it from providing a full assessment of long-term decisions—results of actions might not show up immediately.
- It uses book value, not market value, of shareholders' equity.

Like everything else, ROE must be judged in relation to its environment: "No analyst should mechanistically infer that a higher ROE is always better than a lower one."[7]

ROE AND FINANCIAL LEVERAGE

KEY CONCEPT

When companies increase the proportion of debt to equity in order to finance their business activities, they are using financial leverage. Although over-indebtedness threatens long-term solvency, that does not mean firms should not carry some debt. The home-owner provides a good analogy. Buying a house by taking out a mortgage is generally more advantageous than paying with cash for two reasons: Mortgage interest payments are tax deductible, and the original cash outlay is reduced, freeing capital for other uses and investments. The astute manager leverages corporate debt in response to the market, using a variety of strategies.

However, managers need to use caution when increasing debt, even if it increases ROE. More is not always better. The right balance must be found. Financing with current liabilities involves lower cost than financing with long-term debt, but it has higher liquidity risk. The greater the debt maturity, the longer the loan; the longer the loan, the more uncertain the outcome. The higher the risk and the longer the time, the greater the final cost. Some companies have greater ability to leverage finances than others. Generally, the more stable and predictable the operating cash flow, the greater the ability to leverage. Increased financial leverage usually increases ROE, but it also has a tendency to increase risk. The trick for managers is to find the way to balance increased performance and increased risk.[8]

Two common measures of financial leverage are the debt-to-asset ratio and the debt-to-equity ratio. The debt-to-equity ratio, described earlier, demonstrates how the company is financed by creditors in comparison to shareholders. Debt-to-asset ratio shows what percentage of assets comes from creditors.

$$\text{Debt-to-asset ratio} = \frac{\text{total liabilities}}{\text{total assets}}$$

For example, Company ABC, with liabilities of $2,070,000 and assets totaling $3,480,000, has a debt-to-asset ratio of 0.59. This means its creditors fund 59 percent of those assets ($2,070,000/$3,480,000 = 0.59). As demonstrated earlier, Company ABC has a debt-to-equity ratio of 1.47. With a debt-to-asset ratio of 0.59, Company ABC relies fairly heavily on its creditors. It better be able to continue to increase EBIT annually or it could find itself on the fault line of an earthquake.

Determining how to leverage financing can be tricky—each company is different—but there is a generalization that can be made: Companies with stable and predictable operating cash flows can use financial leverage with greater comfort levels than companies operating in unstable environments.

A key function for managers is to have a deep understanding of the company's business, the way it competes, and the interdependencies of these leverages so that strategies can be created that contain the proper mix and utilization of assets and liabilities.

KEY CONCEPT — PROFITABILITY RATIOS: ROA AND ROI

Return on assets (ROA) measures how well management is utilizing all the firm's assets in relation to net income.

$$\text{Return on assets} = \frac{\text{net income}}{\text{total assets}}$$

or

$$\text{ROA} = \% \text{ profit margin} \times \% \text{ asset turnover}$$

$$\frac{\text{net income}}{\text{total assets}} = \frac{\text{net income}}{\text{sales}} \times \frac{\text{sales}}{\text{total assets}}$$

Using Hewlett-Packard's figures, its ROA in 1989 was 8.26 percent ($7.0 \times 1.18 = 8.26$). This means it earned an average of 8.3 cents on each asset dollar, while Kmart earned 6.6 cents ($2.9 \times 2.27 = 6.58$). Capital-intensive companies have low asset turnover. High profit margins and high asset turnover are considered ideal, while low margins and low turnover point the way to insolvency. Management's ability to control assets is often the determining factor of success or failure in competitive environments where companies have access to similar product technology.[9]

Return on investment (ROI) measures profitability relative to asset investment and is used to determine whether a company or division is operating as efficiently as possible.

$$\text{Return on investment} = \frac{\text{operating income}}{\text{assets}}$$

RATIOS ARE CLUES

Before leaving the topic of ratios, it's important to drive the point home that ratios by themselves mean nothing. They are only crude measures and can be misleading. Ratios provide insight only when the information they hold is combined with other knowledge. The questions to ask are not whether the ratios are high or low by themselves, but when viewed in relation to other numbers and other pieces of information, what do they indicate about the nature of management at the firm, about the competitive strategy that is being used, or about the health of the organization. For example, ROE provides information on the performance of the company as a whole. Look at ROE for a pattern or trend over a period of time. Then find out what changes in profit margin, asset turnover, and financial leverage helped to make that pattern. Look to see how those segments of the business added to or detracted from ROE. And then take a closer look at the accounts, the income statements, and balance sheets to find explanations for the changes.[10]

END POINT

In addition to understanding accounting principles and the methods for analyzing profitability, cash flow, and the company's worth, managers across all levels of the organization need to understand the basics of financial management. The next chapter discusses some of the fundamental concepts.

MORE READING

Altman, E. I. (ed.). *Handbook of Corporate Finance.* 6th ed. New York: John Wiley & Sons, 1986.

Anthony, Robert N. *Essentials of Accounting.* 4th ed. Reading, Mass.: Addison-Wesley, 1988.

Bernstein, Leopold A. *Financial Statement Analysis: Theory, Application and Interpretation.* 4th ed. Homewood, Ill.: Richard D. Irwin, Inc., 1988.

Boutell, Wayne S. *Accounting for Anyone.* Englewood Cliffs, N.J.: Prentice-Hall, 1982.

Brealey, R. A., and S. C. Myers. *Principles of Corporate Finance.* New York: McGraw-Hill, 1988.

Cooper, W. W., and Yuri Ijiri (eds.). *Kohler's Dictionary for Accountants.* Englewood Cliffs, N.J.: Prentice-Hall, 1983.

Davidson, Sidney, Clyde P. Stickney, and Roma L. Weil. *Financial Accounting: An Introduction to Concepts, Methods, and Uses.* 5th ed. Chicago: The Dryden Press, 1988.

Davidson, Sidney, and Roman L. Weil (eds.). *Handbook of Modern Accounting.* 3d ed. New York: McGraw-Hill, 1983.

Donnahoe, Alan. *What Every Manager Should Know About Financial Analysis.* New York: Fireside/Simon & Schuster, 1989.

Downes, John, and Jordan Elliot Goodman. *Dictionary of Finance and Investment Terms.* 2d ed. New York: Barron's Education Services, Inc., 1987.

Dun & Bradstreet. *Industry Norms and Key Business Ratios.* New York: Dun & Bradstreet, 1992.

Finkler, Steven A. *Finance & Accounting for Nonfinancial Managers.* Englewood Cliffs, N.J.: Prentice-Hall, 1992.

Gallinger, George W. *Liquidity Analysis and Management.* 2d ed. Reading, Mass.: Addison-Wesley, 1991.

Higgins, Robert C. *Analysis for Financial Management.* 3d ed. Burr Ridge, Ill.: Richard D. Irwin, Inc., 1992.

Horngren, Charles, and Gary L. Sundem. *Introduction to Management Accounting.* 7th ed. Englewood Cliffs, N.J.: Prentice-Hall, 1987.

Livingstone, John Leslie. "Accounting Management Decision Making" in *The New Portable MBA,* eds. Eliza G. C. Collins and Mary Anne Devanna. New York: John Wiley & Sons, 1994.

Needles, Belverd E., Henry R. Anderson, and James C. Caldwell. *Financial & Managerial Accounting.* Reading, Mass.: Houghton Mifflin, 1988.

Ross, S. A., and R. W. Westerfield. *Corporate Finance.* St. Louis, Mo.: Times Mirror/Mosby College Publishing, 1988.

Seidler, Lee. J., and Douglas R. Carmichael (eds.). *Accountants' Handbook.* 6th ed. New York: John Wiley & Sons, 1981.

Tyran, Michael R. *The Vest-Pocket Guide to Business Ratios.* Englewood Cliffs, N.J.: Prentice-Hall, 1992.

Financial Function:
Hard Values

The financial function has several key goals: to ensure assets are well-managed, to invest wisely, supporting operations and providing means of future growth, and to make decisions about how best to finance the company.

Along with meeting the needs of customers and employees, a key organizational goal is to compensate shareholders for the risks they encounter in offering the organization their capital. Shareholders invest in a company with the expectation of future returns; thus, "the ultimate financial objective of most firms is to maximize common share value," increasing the rate of return investors receive on the stock they purchase.[1] The shareholder suffers if the company incurs losses. Conversely, the shareholder also stands to gain a great deal when the company operates profitably. This chapter examines financial management principles that can help guide managers in making investment decisions.

 CONCEPT

CAPITAL PLANNING

Capital planning evaluates long-term investments, helping managers to decide where to commit the company's money. It provides a disciplined process that includes estimating the cost of capital investments and forecasting future cash flows.

The capital planning process starts by determining the strategic business activities in which the company will be involved. Corporate goals are set by analyzing the competitive nature of the market and the company's strengths and weaknesses. Then specific capital investments based on that strategic direction are proposed, and operational and capital budgets are established. Capital budgets generally focus on long-term investments, while operational budgets concentrate on day-to-day expenditures.

Some investments are better than others in terms of risk and rates of return; therefore, capital investment projects are ranked, enabling managers to select the ones that will provide the greatest value for the company. In the capital planning process, managers generally make projections several years into the future, determining the availability of funds for capital investment. Capital planning includes making decisions in the following areas:

- New products or support services
- Equipment—purchase or replacement
- Facilities—buying, leasing and renting decisions, and possible expansion
- Debt refinancing
- Mergers and acquisitions

Table 6.1 describes the variables that are considered in the investment planning process.

KEY CONCEPT — KNOWING THE COST OF CAPITAL

The "cost of capital," also referred to as the "opportunity cost of capital" or the "weighted-average cost of capital," is "the return on a new, average-risk investment that a company must expect in order to maintain share price."[2] It is the "weighted sum of the

TABLE 6.1 CAPITAL INVESTMENT PLANNING VARIABLES

Core Businesses

Core businesses influence profitability. Managers can reduce the impact on cash flow and the sensitivity to risk by diversifying. However, caution should be taken to make sure companies don't scatter themselves too widely and stray too far from the core businesses at which they excel.

Liquidity and Degree of Leverage

The financial manager is always performing balancing acts to ensure the best state of liquidity, return on equity (ROE), and growth.

Internal vs. External Growth

If internal growth is not forthcoming, the company must decide how to obtain growth externally, for example, through mergers and acquisitions.

Dividends and Stock Repurchase

Dividends and stock repurchases compete with capital investment for available cash flow.

Market Conditions, Interest Rates, Tax Regulations

The rise and fall of stock prices and interest rates affect managers' investment decisions. Managers also consider tax regulations when structuring and timing investments in order to obtain the least possible tax liability.

after-tax costs of the diverse components that make up the capital structure."[3] Knowing the cost of capital is an essential guide for making investment decisions.

The cost of capital is weighted by the ratio of the market value of each investment project to the total market value of the capital structure. The cost of capital continually varies as capital investment projects get added to or subtracted from the total.

ANALYZING RISK IN CAPITAL INVESTMENTS

Managers must know how to assess rates of return accurately. The financial manager creates value for the shareholder in the present by buying future cash flow through capital investments.

Every capital investment opportunity cannot be acted on due to the limits of funding resources. Knowledgeable managers evaluate capital investments in relation to the organization's goals and resources, and to the uncertainty and risk involved with making the investment.

There are a number of assessment methods to help managers decide what capital investment proposals have the greatest value, the best potential, and most closely match the resources of the organization. The most commonly used methods are: net present value (NPV), internal rate of return (IRR), payback period, and profitability index (PI).

Net present value (NPV) is the difference between the present value of future cash inflows and the present value of cash outflows. NPV acts as a guide for assessing particular investment opportunities. It simply calculates the present value of the expected stream of cash as a result of the investment against the present value of the cost of the investment. When estimating NPV it is necessary to use a "discounted rate" of money that reflects the rate of return that could be earned from an investment with similar risk. For example, assume a manager is presented with an investment opportunity of $6,000 that will generate variable income totaling $6,750 over three years. The discount rate is 9 percent. Using readily available discount tables or a financial calculator, the manager can make the following calculation:

	Income stream		Discount factor @ 9%		Discounted income stream
year 1	$2,000	×	.917	=	$1,834
year 2	3,500	×	.842	=	2,947
year 3	1,250	×	.772	=	965
	$6,750				$5,746

Discounted income	–	initial investment	=	NPV
present value of future cash inflow	–	present cash outflow	=	NPV
$5,746	–	$6,000	=	($254)

If the initial investment is greater than the discounted income stream, as in the preceding example, the NPV is negative and the investment is ill advised. Even with a positive NPV, it is important to compare the investment opportunity with alternatives.

Internal rate of return (IRR) is the "discount rate at which the project's net present value equals zero."[4] When a manager seeks IRR, she is simply trying to find the rate of return at which the present value of the cost of the investment and the present value of the future income stream equate.

	Income stream	Discount factor @ 6.5%		Discounted income stream
year 1	$2,000	× .939	=	$1,878
year 2	3,500	× .882	=	3,087
year 3	1,250	× .828	=	1,035
	$6,750			$6,000
Discounted income		– initial investment	=	NPV
$6,000		– $6,000	=	-0-

In the preceding example, the IRR is 6.5 percent. It is unlikely that this investment is attractive; generally, companies target a higher rate of return or hurdle rate.

The *payback period* is the time it takes the cash flows generated by the investment to recover the invested capital. In other words, it provides the point in time at which the initial investment is recouped. Knowing how long it will take to make the investment show profit helps managers determine whether or not to pursue the investment. The payback period can be determined by dividing the investment by the annual cash inflow.

$$\text{Payback period} = \frac{\text{investment}}{\text{annual cash inflow}}$$

Profitability index (PI) is based on NPV calculations and is also known as the *benefit-cost ratio*. It is determined by dividing the present value of future cash inflows with the present value of cash outflows. A PI over 1 indicates a good investment possibility; a PI less than 1 does not. PIs are helpful in determining the best investments when using capital rationing and, in that process, carry greater weight than individual NPVs and IRRs.

$$PI = \frac{\text{present value of future cash inflows}}{\text{present value of cash outflow}}$$

COMPANIES TEND TO SET HIGH HURDLE RATES

A hurdle rate is the minimum rate of return on an investment that a company will accept. A 1987 study found that hurdle rates ranged "from 8 percent to 30 percent, with a median of 15 percent and a mean of 17 percent," and more recent studies have shown that hurdle rates "are often three or four times their weighted average cost of capital."[5] Capital asset pricing establishes a financial model that rigorously determines appropriate hurdle rates.

CAPITAL ASSET PRICING MODEL

The *capital asset pricing model* (CAPM) enables managers to assess the minimum rate of return, or hurdle rate, on investments in order to satisfy stockholders' expectations. It is "an accepted and sensible way of rationalizing the manner in which assets in general and common stock in particular are priced." As an assumption-based model (see Table 6.2), CAPM stipulates that the required rate of return (the cost of equity) should be equal to the riskfree rate (the U.S. Treasury Bill rate), plus the relevant *beta* times the market risk premium (the market rate minus the riskfree rate).[6] For instance, if an investment has a riskfree rate of 6 percent, a beta of 1.7, and a market

---

TABLE 6.2 CAPITAL ASSET PRICING MODEL (CAPM) ASSUMPTIONS

- Investors are rational and willing to accept expected rates of return and standard deviations of rates of return as measures of reward and risk.
- Investors are risk averse, meaning they expect to be rewarded for risk and they expect management to lower risk as much as possible.
- Markets are highly competitive.
- Buyers and sellers are numerous, operate independently, and do not affect prices individually.
- Investment horizons are usually one year.

Adapted from: *John Leslie Livingstone and James E. Walter, "Financial Management: Optimizing the Value of the Firm," in* The New Portable MBA, *eds. Eliza G. C. Collins and Mary Anne Devanna (New York: John Wiley & Sons, 1994), p. 270.*

risk premium of 7 percent, its required rate of return is a 17.9 percent.

$$\text{Riskfree rate} + \text{beta} \times (\text{market risk rate} - \text{riskfree rate})$$
$$= \text{required rate of return}$$
$$.06 + 1.7 \times (.13 - .06) = 17.9\%$$

 UNDERSTANDING BETA

Beta assesses sensitivity to risk. It "is the regression coefficient that relates the return on the individual security or portfolio to the return on the market portfolio. In effect, it measures—in a relative sense—that part of asset risk that cannot be diversified away."[7]

If managers do not want to calculate beta themselves, betas can be obtained from investment services. A beta of 1 indicates average volatility. The lower the beta, the lower the risk, the lower the cost of equity; the higher the beta, the higher the risk, the higher the cost of equity. A company's beta coefficient is likely to fluctuate over time.[8]

 **TIME HAS VALUE**

Unless today's dollar is wisely invested, it will be worth less in the future, because its value will be discounted. Wisely invested, it will increase in value due to compounding. Discounting reveals the present value of a future sum. With compounding, the future value of a present sum is determined.

 MISSED OPPORTUNITIES COST MONEY

When investment opportunities are not pursued, the investment income not received is called an *opportunity cost*. The opportunity cost equals what would have been the return on an investment that wasn't made.

KEY CONCEPT **CAPITAL RATIONING**

When a company has a fixed investment budget and has several investment alternatives, the investments should be ranked in order of their value to enable the company to make the best investment choice. Considering the budget available, the company should look for the best bang for its buck and select the investments that are going to generate the highest NPV per dollar invested. For example, suppose a company has $240,000 to invest at a discount rate of 11 percent. Proposals received from its division managers determine that the following investment opportunities exist:

Investment	Initial Cost	NPV @ 11%	PI @ 11%	IRR
#1	$240,000	$27,900	1.12	13.6%
#2	140,000	19,400	1.14	14.1%
#3	90,000	16,800	1.18	15.2%
#4	$ 40,000	$ 9,700	1.24	16.5%

In order to achieve the highest total NPV, the company should invest in #3 and #4 and, if possible, allocate $110,000 to Investment #2.

Investment	Initial Cost	NPV @ 11%
#3	$ 90,000	$16,800
#4	40,000	9,700
#2	110,000	15,240
	$240,000	$41,740

If no investments can be split, then the company should invest in #2 and #3, borrowing less than the full credit line. But either combination is better than investing in #1 because, in capital rationing, the best return per dollar invested is what counts the most.[9]

Investment	Initial Cost	NPV @ 11%
#2	$140,000	$19,400
#3	90,000	16,800
	$230,000	$36,200

DON'T SINK WITH SUNK COSTS

When costs in investments are irreversible, when they can't be recovered, they are considered sunk costs. Once capital has been expended, it's gone. Most investments in areas like advertising are considered sunk costs because once the money is spent on a campaign it can't be recovered; therefore, these investments need to be approached carefully, and all options should be weighed about how and when to invest capital. If a campaign doesn't work, there is no way to recapture the loss.

However, sometimes companies get caught up in trying to salvage sunk costs. For example, suppose a marketing department spends $2 million on a year-long national campaign investing in videos, advertising, and costly promotional material, but the campaign doesn't get the anticipated response. Extending the campaign will require additional expense. The department is split about what to do: One group wants to give it more time since $2 million was already spent; the other wants to start over with a different approach. Which is the best investment strategy? The first thing to do in making this investment decision is to let go of the lost money. It's gone. The real question is whether the original approach had merit. If there is value in the campaign, how much will it cost to extend, and will the benefits merit the cost of that extension? Or is there a different, more beneficial campaign that will provide greater return on a new investment?

USE PRO FORMA STATEMENTS FOR FORECASTING

Pro forma statements are used for predicting what the financial statements will look like at the end of a specific period. They are a good means of financial forecasting, providing information in a consistent and logical manner. They help in forecasting the company's need for external financing as well as offering a way to evaluate alternative operating and financing strategies. Using pro forma statements, managers can systematically change one assumption and see how the change alters the forecast. For example, what happens if the cost of goods as a percentage of sales increases? What happens if it decreases? Knowing the degree to which one variable impacts another enables managers to focus on critical paths.

One method for projecting financial performance is to connect the income and balance statement with future sales in a percent of sales forecast. Most current liabilities and current assets fluctuate with sales, and this forecast offers a simple approach that may yield a fairly good prediction:

- Examine historical data to pinpoint connections.
- Estimate sales.
- Create pro forma statements.
- Extrapolate historical patterns and compare to estimated sales forecasts.[10]

USE STATISTICAL TOOLS

Statistical analysis is often used for financial forecasts, marketing forecasts, quality control, and inventory controls. Statistical methods are meaningful when applied to large population groups. Tables 6.3 and 6.4 describe commonly used statistical and forecasting tools.

THE VALUE OF STOCK

Management's responsibility is to maximize profitability and to satisfy stockholder requirements. Essentially, stockholders are customers who expect value, and providing value to them through performance is of major concern to the organization. Managers must, therefore, understand how the value of the corporation's stocks and bonds relate to the financial marketplace.

TABLE 6.3 STATISTICAL TOOLS HELP WITH DECISION MAKING

Frequency distribution is the range along which data from findings are distributed. The range is the spread between the lowest and the highest number. In a frequency distribution, findings are usually displayed graphically, forming one of three types of frequency distributions: symmetrical, skewed, or bimodal.

Symmetrical distribution, known as the bell curve, is a normal distribution in which most of the data are clustered in the center, with extremes falling equally on both sides of the midrange. The center cluster is considered representative of the average population. In a **skewed distribution,** most of the data are clustered off center. And in a **bimodal distribution,** the data fall within two clusters.

Measures of central tendency work hand in hand with distribution and standard deviations to reveal more precise information about the data. Three measures of central tendency are the mean, median, and mode. The **mean** is commonly known as the average, and is the sum of the samples divided by the number of samples. The **median** is the number in the middle of the range of numbers, and the **mode** is the number that appears most often. The mean, as well as providing an average figure, helps to pinpoint variations. The median, by casting off extremes, provides a truer view of the central tendency, which is a more accurate representation of the average. And the mode can help to prioritize efforts.

Standard deviation is the extent to which a particular finding deviates from the mean; it is the extent to which the data points spread out along a distribution. Standard deviation is used in calculating the rate of return on investment and is the square root of the weighted sum of individual investment variances and covariances. The standard deviation is a significant measure used in assessing investments and helps managers view data more clearly. In a normal distribution, 68 percent of all data points fall within plus or minus one standard deviation, and 94 percent fall within two standard deviations.

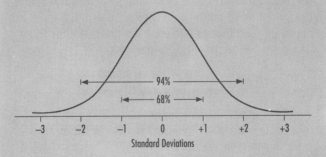

94%

68%

−3   −2   −1   0   +1   +2   +3
Standard Deviations

Probability value (P value) quantifies the margin of error in a test. For example, a $P \leq 0.05$ indicates the margin of error is not likely to be greater than 5 percent, or that the findings are likely to occur 95 percent of the time.

TABLE 6.4 FORECASTING TOOLS

Exponential smoothing is a forecasting tool, good for the short term, that is used for measuring production, inventory, sales, and financial data. This tool assumes the future is dependent on the most recent past; therefore, it gives heavier weight to the most recent data, with the weight declining the older the data get. This method has drawbacks because it doesn't include any environmental factors, such as economic or market conditions, or seasonal fluctuations.

Regression analysis examines the relationship between dependent and independent variables and is commonly used in forecasting. It is generally used to forecast sales, income, and financial data, and is especially good for short-term forecasting. It is also helpful in determining when change occurred. For example, regression analysis can correlate a positive relationship between sales and advertising efforts. Likewise, regression analysis can be used to demonstrate the negative relationship between sales and interest rates. In regression analysis, the *correlation coefficient*, or relationship between two variables, is shown as *r*. The closer *r* is to +1, the stronger the positive relationship; the closer *r* is to −1, the stronger the negative relationship.

Trend analysis (times series) plots a variable over time, providing information about general trends, periodic variations, cyclical variations, and random variations. It is also commonly used in forecasting. A trend line is plotted on a graph through a time series of data, showing the relationship of the variables over a period of time. Trend analysis is helpful in both short- and long-term forecasting.

Price-to-earnings ratio is a commonly used ratio which measures the relationship between the market price per share of common stock and the earnings per share. The P/E ratio is a good indicator of what investors believe the future profitability of the company will be. The P/E ratio helps in making across-the-board comparisons about the value of stocks with different earnings. Two factors influence the P/E ratio: the prospects for future earnings and risk.

$$\text{P/E ratio} = \frac{\text{price per share of common stock}}{\text{earnings per share (EPS) of common stock}}$$

All corporations offer common stock, but only certain companies offer preferred stock. P/E ratios always refer to common stock. Preferred stock has a fixed dividend rate, a fixed amount it earns; common stock doesn't—its dividends fluctuate with the earnings and the number of shares. Over time, the amount of outstanding shares usually grows in publicly traded companies due to dividend reinvestment programs and exercise of stock options by management.

Earnings per share (EPS) is the amount each share of stock earns. EPS is the net income, less the preferred stock dividends, divided by the number of common shares outstanding. If, for example, a company has a net income of $4.5 million and it has 2 million shares of common stock and no preferred stock outstanding, it has an EPS of $2.25 (4.5/2 = 2.25). If the stock is selling for $26, then the P/E is 11.5 (26/2.25 = 11.5). When more stock is issued, the EPS is diluted and goes down until earnings increase.

Another important ratio to understand regarding stocks is the market-to-book ratio. It measures the market price per share to the book value per share of common stock. The book value of stock is the total common equity divided by the number of shares outstanding. This ratio measures the value of the company—what it is worth in relation to the cost it paid for its assets. If the ratio is greater than 1, the market value exceeds the book value. This means that management has provided value to the stockholder above the costs incurred in acquiring assets.

THE VALUE OF BONDS

Bonds are fixed-income securities that are forms of long-term indebtedness. Bondholders receive a specified annual interest and a specified amount at maturity. Par value, coupon rate, and maturity date are three bond characteristics. Companies that issue bonds may be required to periodically make a payment to creditors, and this process is known as a *sinking fund payment.* Companies may help to meet sinking fund obligations by repurchasing bonds in the securities market or by retiring bonds and paying bondholders par value.

Bond values and interest rates work in opposition: Bond prices fall when interest rates rise and vice versa. When interest rates drop, bonds may have call options, which allow companies to pay off the existing bonds and issue new bonds with lower interest. This provides the company with flexibility in arranging its capital structure.

Bonds are given credit ratings, which reflect their rate of risk and, in turn, reflect the rate of interest that can be charged to the issuing company. AAA is the highest rating and means the company's ability to pay interest and repay principal is extremely good. D is the lowest rating and means that the company is expected to default on payment.

END POINT

The warning not to judge figures in a vacuum has been repeatedly presented. Therefore, in addition to being able to understand the meaning and relationship of numbers to each other, it is also necessary to understand what finances and investments mean in relationship to the business climate. The next chapter looks at the impact of micro and macro economics, providing advice for managers on how to manage their companies' finances and operations in relation to the external environment.

MORE READING

Altman, E. I. (ed.). *Handbook of Corporate Finance.* 6th ed. New York: John Wiley & Sons, 1986.

Averill, E. W. *Elements of Statistics.* New York: John Wiley & Sons, 1972.

Berenson, Mark L. *Basic Business Statistics.* Englewood Cliffs, N.J.: Prentice-Hall, 1983.

Bierman, Harold, Jr., and Seymour Smidt. *The Capital Budgeting Decision: Economic Analysis of Investment Projects.* 7th ed. New York: MacMillan, 1988.

Brealey, R. A., and S. C. Meyers. *Principles of Corporate Finance.* New York: McGraw-Hill, 1988.

Donaldson, Gordon. *Managing Corporate Wealth.* New York: Praeger Publishers, 1984.

Grant, Eugene L., et al. *Principles of Engineering Economy.* 8th ed. New York: John Wiley & Sons, 1990.

Higgins, Robert C. *Analysis for Financial Management.* 3d ed. Burr Ridge, Ill.: Irwin, 1992.

Livingstone, J. L. *The Portable MBA in Finance and Accounting.* New York: John Wiley & Sons, 1992.

Logue, D. E. (ed.). *Handbook of Modern Finance.* Boston: Warren, Gorham, Lamont, 1994.

Parket, I. Robert. *Statistics for Business Decision Making.* New York: Random House, 1973.

Ross, S. A., and R. W. Westerfield. *Corporate Finance.* St. Louis, Mo.: Times Mirror/Mosby College Publishing, 1988.

Stigum, Marcia. *The Money Market.* 3d ed. Homewood, Ill.: Dow Jones-Irwin, 1989.

Van Horne, James C. *Financial Market Rates and Flows.* 3d ed. Englewood Cliffs, N.J.: Prentice-Hall, 1990.

The Macro and Micro of Economics

Economics studies the behavior of individuals, society, businesses, and industries as they utilize resources in the process of producing and consuming goods. Economics has two interdependent branches: microeconomics, which measures the individual behavior of households, companies, and industries, as well as the quantity and price of specific commodities; and macroeconomics, which measures the overall behavior of the economy.

Economic indicators are measures of activity, which include figures on production, the price of goods, and employment. These indicators are significant to managers because they can provide information vital to effective decision making. By knowing whether unemployment is up or down, astute managers can make better decisions with regard to increasing or reducing production (output), structuring wage levels, or making hiring decisions.

Both micro and macroeconomics have as objectives the ability to predict the future and to facilitate decision making by evaluating the impact of alternative strategies and decisions.[1] Managers should be familiar with all indicators, what they measure, and what the measures mean.

MACROECONOMICS

Economic activity is reflected in four basic macroeconomic indicators derived from different sources: gross domestic product (GDP), industrial production, employment, and personal income.[2] Short-term changes in these measures provide managers with indications of their companies' outlooks in the context of the macroenvironment. (See Table 7.1.)

GDP is the broadest indicator of total economic progress, combining figures on consumption, invest-

> **TABLE 7.1 PUTTING ECONOMIC DATA TO WORK**
>
> - Personal income and consumption data provide managers with knowledge about the real and potential strength of consumer demand.
>
> - Industrial production reflects output, measuring economic activity. Increases in production strengthen the economy, push interest rates, and reflect the supply side of the economy. Managers can determine the state of the overall market by watching production figures and, by observing how those changes affect interest rates, they can structure their financing accordingly.
>
> - GDP gives a country's broadest measure of economic activity. Because GDP figures can be separated into real dollars and inflation prices, GDP is a valuable tool for assessing what's actually happening in an economy. Increasing real GDP indicates the economy is expanding, while decreasing real GDP means recession.

ment, exports, and government purchase activity. In the United States, GDP is compiled by the Commerce Department's Bureau of Economic Analysis. Variations in GDP occur from year to year because of changes in the level of economic activity and shifts in prices. *Real GDP* means the effects of inflation on prices have been removed, with figures representing a *real* constant dollar. Prices are reflected in the *consumer price index* (CPI) for retail prices, and the *producer price index* (PPI) for wholesale prices. The PPI and the CPI are measures of inflation in the United States and are published monthly. The PPI measures price changes for goods produced in the United States, and the CPI measures price changes in a representative sampling of goods and services consumed during the month. Producer prices provide price trends for raw materials and goods used in manufacturing other products. Consumer prices show price changes in product categories, enabling managers to follow the competitive cost of their products.

Industrial production is a measure of all goods, but not services, produced. The Federal Reserve Board reports figures in aggregate as well as by industry. This indicator is also useful to the service sector because services generally support production activities.

Employment figures are derived from the number of workers in the workforce as reported by the Bureau of Labor Statistics. Jobs, not wages, are rapidly compiled in aggregate and by industry; as a result, employment is the earliest indicator of change in the economy.

The *personal income* indicator is the total of wages and salaries paid, plus income from other sources. The Bureau of Economic Analysis compiles these data, from which both disposable income (a measure of purchasing power) and personal savings (a measure of invest-ment capacity) can be derived.

THREE TYPES OF UNEMPLOYMENT

Employment is reflected in the unemploy-ment level. It is not influenced by inflation: It is mea-sured by the number of jobs, not by the money paid out in wages. There are significant differences among the kinds of unemployment people experience and their impact on the economy.

- *Frictional unemployment* indicates workers who are temporarily out of work for short periods of time. This unemployment is not due to market conditions, but rather to personal situations—for example, career changes or pregnancies. Workers intend to be employed again within a short amount of time.

- *Cyclical unemployment* refers to workers who are without jobs due to downturns in the business cycle.

- *Structural unemployment* refers to those people who are out of jobs for long periods of time due to lack of skills or education. Structural unemployment has deep-rooted social and economic causes.

Two different measures offer insight into how many jobs and how many hours are involved in employment. Employee-hours worked (number of payroll jobs times the number of workweek hours) measures labor input—how intensely labor is utilized—while employ-ment (number of payroll jobs) measures how exten-sively labor is utilized.[3]

USE GDP AS A GUIDE TO INFLATION AND INTEREST RATES

Generally, rapidly growing economies utilize existing capacities. This signals that demand is being strength-ened relative to supply. It also can be an indicator that inflation is increasing and interest rates may rise. On the other hand, a decrease in GDP or slower growth implies a lessening of demand, less tendency to infla-tion, and lower interest rates.

BE AWARE OF CYCLES

A cycle contains the three phases of economic activ-ity: recession, recovery, and expansion. Managers need to be aware of future economic conditions, especially short-term fluctuations, in order to make accurate business decisions. For example, clothing retailers, who need to order in advance of the season, must know what demand for merchandise will be like in the future. If summer's bathing suits are ordered the previous fall based on the buyer's assessment that the future economy will be stronger, and her assessment is wrong, she might be stuck with a pile of bathing suits when fall rolls around again.

SEASONS SHIFT DATA

Seasons affect economic data on a regular basis. Time series used in forecasting need to be seasonally adjusted. For example, in looking at unemployment, summertime is a factor. Students work in summer and, depending on geographical location, some types of employment, such as landscaping and outdoor painting, are available only in warm weather. Employment tends to peak in summer and bottom out in the middle of winter. Prices and sales also peak due to seasonal factors. For instance, retail sales are generally higher in December because of Christmas.

MONEY IS ALWAYS AN ISSUE

Every country has a total amount of money to spend that influences its economic condition. Interest rates and the country's monetary policy affect economic activity. The supply and demand of money result from a complex interaction of a number of forces. One of these forces is a demand for credit by institutions, organizations, and individuals, and another is the response by the commercial banking system to that demand. Banks provide money through loans and charge interest on the money. However, the rate of interest that they charge is dependent on the supply and demand for credit and the country's monetary policy.

When money supplies are constant and people are spending, prices rise. When people are reluctant to spend, prices fall. When the economy is *inflationary,* there is a general rise in price levels and the buying power of currency is diminished. Inflation means there has been a difference between real growth and nominal growth due to changes in the index (average level) of prices. In a *recession,* the economy is in a downturn. In a *depression,* it is in a severe downturn, during which time unemployment dramatically increases, production severely decreases, and businesses tend to fail.

A LITTLE HISTORY HELPS

Until the late eighteenth century, economists did not believe a decentralized, free-market economy would work without a detailed system of government regulations. In 1776, Adam Smith contradicted that philosophy in his famous *Wealth of Nations.* He claimed government regulation was not required because prices in the marketplace provide the regulation needed. In effect, according to Smith, the system would regulate itself, guided by its own "invisible hand." On the other hand, John Maynard Keynes, perhaps the most famous advocate of fiscal policy, believed government has a role to play. In *General Theory of Employment, Interest and Money,* he wrote that governments should intervene in economic downturns by stimulating growth through reducing taxes and increasing government spending.

INTERNATIONAL ECONOMICS

KEY CONCEPT

International macroeconomics encompasses international trade flows, foreign exchange, and international finance. Businesses and individuals in one country purchase goods and services in another country. Balance-of-payment accounts represent these international transactions. They are divided into *current accounts* (short-term), which compare exports (goods, income, and services) with imports, and *capital accounts* (long-term), which compare the outflow of capital (direct investment and long-term lending *to* foreigners) with the inflow of capital (direct investment and long-term lending *by* foreigners). Current accounts generally show the nation's balance-of-payment position. If they show a deficit, there is an adverse imbalance in international payments; if it shows a surplus, the nation has a healthy international payment position.

FOREIGN EXCHANGE RATE

KEY CONCEPT

All these transactions are based on the currencies of the countries involved. In order to buy and sell across national borders, countries must exchange currency. The supply and demand for each country's products are dependent on the country's currency. When goods or services are exchanged or investments made, a conversion of currencies takes place between the two countries involved. The *foreign exchange rate* is the rate at which currencies are exchanged. The value of the currency depends on supply and demand for the currency in the international currency market.

Exchange rates are set in three ways: fixed rates, floating rates, and managed floating rates. With fixed rates, countries agree to a set rate. When rates float, the exchange rate is determined by the demand for the currency in the international money market, and when floating rates are managed, as they are in the United States, the rate fluctuates. But in the United States, for instance, if the dollar is valued too high or too low, the Treasury Department and the Federal Reserve adjust the dollar supply by selling or buying dollars.[4]

The fact that money floats on the international market is extremely significant. The higher the demand for a currency, the higher its value. Money traders and speculators have turned international money markets into "one of the hottest areas of international investment."[5] The value of currencies can swing back and forth between appreciation and depreciation, based on their trading. There has been a concern that governments and business have lost control over the value of money due to its freedom to float and be "hotly" traded in what is estimated to be a $1 trillion market. However, in the summer of 1995, successful actions by governments demonstrated that central banks and governments still do have some control over affecting currency values: The U.S. dollar soared after the central banks of the United States, Germany, Japan, and Switzerland bought dollars to drive its value higher, and the Japanese minister of finance urged Japanese institutions to weaken the yen by investing abroad. The result was a dollar that climbed over the yen for the first time in six months.[6]

KEY CONCEPT — WEAK OR STRONG MONEY?

Why do governments want to strengthen or weaken their currency? Let's use the United States as an example to explain these principles. If the United States wants to *weaken* the dollar (lower its value), U.S. goods become less expensive abroad, encouraging exports and cutting trade deficits. Increased demand for U.S. products creates jobs. Additionally, when the dollar is weaker, foreign companies will want to produce goods in the United States, creating more jobs. And as it becomes cheaper for foreign companies, they tend to invest more money in plants, creating even more jobs and spurring economic growth. A weaker dollar also attracts more foreign tourists and causes Americans to vacation at home, where it's cheaper.

The downside of a weak dollar is the danger of inflation, which can be triggered by U.S. companies raising prices in response to higher prices of foreign goods. Heavy foreign investment in the United States, however, pulls power and income away from U.S. companies and into foreign companies. Another danger is that too many U.S. goods in foreign markets can disturb other countries' economies and cause problems with international relationships. Additionally, with a weak dollar it becomes more expensive for U.S. companies to do business abroad.

When the dollar is *stronger* (increases its value), foreign goods are less expensive for Americans and travel abroad is less expensive. Plus, U.S. business has greater control over itself. But fewer exports means the loss of jobs, and lack of foreign investment means less capital for U.S. business.

Foreign exchange values also hinge on interest rates, inflation, and political conditions. If interest rates are high, foreign investors are attracted and the currency appreciates as demand grows. If interest rates are low in comparison with other countries, investors lose interest income and the currency depreciates. The level of inflation will attract or deter investors depending on the level of inflation in their countries. And finally, the governments must be stable enough to ensure investors that the value of their currency will remain intact—investors want to be able to turn foreign currency back into their own money without incurring losses.

KEY CONCEPT   CONSUMPTION

The demand for goods and services varies considerably in the short term because it is affected by income, interest rates, prices, employment, lending conditions, and foreign exchange rates. Actual consumption—spending by households on commodities and services—is divided between spending on *durable goods* (those lasting three years or more) and spending on *nondurable goods* (those lasting less than three years). Durable goods (cars, major appliances, furniture) tend to be more expensive, more volatile, and more cyclical, and tend to be purchased when the economy is in good shape. Conversely, nondurable goods (clothing and food) are less responsive to the business cycle. And services (rent, utilities, medical care), which take up half of consumer spending, are fairly stable and relatively independent of business cycles.

Regression analysis demonstrates the strong correlation between consumer spending and GDP. For every increase in real consumer spending, there is an increase in real GDP. Consumer spending tends to increase as income increases, but increases in spending do not totally keep up with increases in income because people save some of their money. "For every $1 increase in after-tax income, individuals spend 92 cents (saving the remaining 8 cents) . . . The relationship suggests that consumption spending grows at nearly three-quarters the rate of total GDP and increases by 92 cents for every dollar that disposable income increases."[7]

USE SOFTWARE AND REGRESSION ANALYSIS TO PLOT RELATIONSHIPS

With popular software, such as Excel and Lotus 1-2-3, managers can use regression analysis to estimate the direct relationship between their products and GDP. And if their products are durable or expensive, they will be more closely linked with growth or decline of GDP.[8]

KEY CONCEPT   THE ECONOMY AND INVESTMENT

Economic indicators provide important information for managers throughout the organization, but they can be especially significant to those managers contemplating capital investment proposals. Here are economic indicators that can help with investment decision making:

- *Residential construction* is considered investment in capital and is an indicator of the future direction of the economy. When residential construction peaks or valleys, it's a good bet the overall economy will soon be behaving the same way.

- *Nonresidential fixed investments* are capital investments in plant, machinery, and equipment, which enable managers to expand the company's capacity to produce. When companies invest in nonresidential fixed investments, it is an indication that they foresee profits as a result of the investment.

- *Business inventories* are "the most cyclically sensitive components of aggregate demand," and are "far more volatile than any other major component of GDP." Managers need to be on top of sales trends so that they are not taken by surprise when abrupt changes in demand take place. Excess investment in inventory or not enough investment in inventory can be damaging to profitability.[9]

ANALYZING THE MACROENVIRONMENT

The macroenvironment—those layers of context within which the organization operates—must be monitored and analyzed in order to gain competitive advantage. The world and the organizations that operate within it are in constant states of evolution. Changes in the macroenvironment impact the organization. Each of the areas of the macroenvironment is linked to the other; each affects the other and together they operate within an economic system. (See Figures 7.1 and 7.2.)

Changes in the macroenvironment impact the system as well as the company's ability to operate at an optimum level. Table 7.2 shows the areas where changes can occur in different environmental sectors and Table 7.3 lists the kinds of changes that impact the macroenvironment. Managers must judge which are relevant to the success of the organization.

MICROECONOMICS

Microeconomics provides the underpinnings of macroeconomics. Microeconomics involves the supply and demand for products and provides an explanation for how prices and quantities of products are determined, and how labor and capital are used.

One of the most basic economic problems faced by managers is how to allocate the organizations' resources in a way that will provide the most benefit to the organization. Managers must make decisions about what markets to enter and exit. For example, American

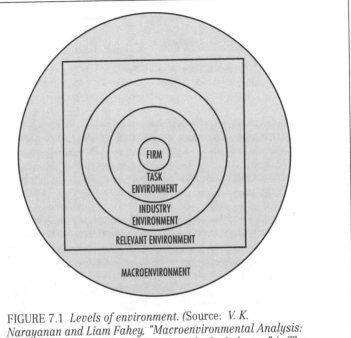

FIGURE 7.1 *Levels of environment.* (Source: *V. K. Narayanan and Liam Fahey, "Macroenvironmental Analysis: Understanding the Environment Outside the Industry," in* The Portable MBA in Strategy, *eds. Liam Fahey and Robert M. Randall [New York: John Wiley & Sons, 1994], p. 198.)*

Airlines decided not to engage in the battle for air space in the southwestern United States, because of the intense price competition and stellar performance of Southwest Airlines.[10] Japanese NEC, without a presence in the U.S. computer market, recognized the strong demand that existed and decided to enter the market in 1995 by investing in Packard Bell.[11]

Managers must also know how much of the budget should be allocated to those endeavors. Every organiza-

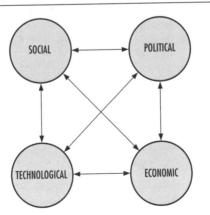

FIGURE 7.2 *(Source: V. K. Narayanan and Liam Fahey, "Macroenvironmental Analysis: Understanding the Environment Outside the Industry," in* The Portable MBA in Strategy, *eds. Liam Fahey and Robert Randall [New York: John Wiley & Sons, 1994], p. 201.)*

TABLE 7.2 MACROENVIRONMENT

Social Environment	Economic Environment
Demographics: population size, age, geographic distribution, ethnic mix, income levels	*Structural Change:* change within and across sectors and industries and in relationships among key economic variables
Lifestyles: household formation, work, education, consumption, leisure	*Cyclical Change:* upswings and downswings in economic activity, such as GNP, interest rates, infla-
Values: political, social, techno- logical, economic	tion, consumer prices, housing starts, industrial investment

Political Environment	Technological Environment
Formal System: electoral process and institutions of government, regulatory agencies	*Research:* basic research seeking knowledge (invention)
Informal System: political activ- ity outside government, like com- munity and media	*Development:* turns knowledge into prototype form (innovation)
	Operations: adapts prototype for other uses (diffusion)

Source: V. K. Narayanan and Liam Fahey, "Macroenvironmental Analysis: Understanding the Environment Outside the Industry," in The Portable MBA in Strategy, eds. Liam Fahey and Robert Randall (New York: John Wiley & Sons, 1994), pp. 199–200.

tion is confined to a degree in this decision-making process, due to budgetary constraints. Few organiza- tions have exhaustive budgets. In making these deter- minations, managers are faced with the microeconomic forces of increasing competition, technological advancements, and shifts in consumer tastes. When making decisions about resource allocation, managers must consider: the output of goods and services; the input of labor, materials, plant, and equipment; and how all the forces interact.

The supply and demand of products influence prices, which in turn influence market conditions (see Table 7.4). The government also influences the market through its power to levy taxes and impose regula- tions. For example, in the United States, the Food and Drug Administration (FDA), with regulatory authority over the pharmaceutical industry, influences prices by stipulating the amount of testing and the approval process necessary—thus affecting the time and the cost it takes to get new drugs to market. Additionally, culture plays a role. National and religious cultures drive the production of certain products. An excellent example is the influence of Christmas on the retail industry. Today, smart companies are striving to be more responsive to the demands of the market and its customers.

TABLE 7.3 ASSESS CHANGES THAT IMPACT MACROENVIRONMENT

Changes Impacting Industry

- Emergence of new products
- Sales of existing products
- Entry and exit of competitors
- Emergence of new suppliers
- Entry and penetration of substitute products

Changes Impacting Immediate Task Environment

- Demand by existing customers
- Existing competitors' strategies
- Suppliers' strategies
- Current strategies

Changes Impacting Current Strategies

- Existing products
- Existing target market segments
- How the firm competes
- Current goals

Changes Impacting Future Strategy and Execution

- Potential new products
- Potential new customers
- Potential new ways of competing
- Strategy choice criteria
- Need for new organizational structure
- Need for new operating processes

Source: V. K. Narayanan and Liam Fahey, "Macroenvironmental Analysis: Understanding the Environment Outside the Industry," in The Portable MBA in Strategy, eds. Liam Fahey and Robert Randall (New York: John Wiley & Sons, 1994), p. 213.

KEY CONCEPT — SUPPLY AND DEMAND

Microeconomics assumes that product prices and quantities react to forces in the marketplace. Consumers' demand for a product will decrease as its price increases and will increase as price decreases. This relationship is expressed in a downward sloping demand curve—the lower the price, the greater the quantity. This curve slopes for two reasons: As price increases, demand decreases because consumers can purchase other substitutes; and as price rises, the purchasing power of consumers is limited, and consumers purchase less. Conversely, producers will supply fewer products as price decreases, and more products as price increases. Therefore, the supply curve slopes up.

TABLE 7.4 SUPPLY AND DEMAND

Change in a Short Time Period	Followed by Change in a Long Time Period
Increase in *demand* causes price to rise.	*Supply increases* as new sellers enter the market and original sellers increase production capacity.
Decrease in *demand* causes price to *fall.*	*Supply decreases* as less profitable firms exit the market or decrease production capacity.
Increase in *supply* causes price to *fall.*	*Demand increases* as consumer preferences change in favor of the products relative to substitutes.
Decrease in *supply* causes price to rise.	*Demand decreases* as consumer preferences eventually change away from the product toward substitutes.

Source: *Philip Y. K. Young and John J. McAuley, The Portable MBA in Economics (New York: John Wiley & Sons, 1994), p. 153.*

The demand curve defines the number of items consumers will buy over a range of prices they will pay. The supply curve defines the number of items companies will produce over a similar range of prices. The quantity produced and the market price are determined where these two curves intersect.[12] (See Figure 7.3.)

However, there are other factors besides price that influence supply and demand, and whenever one of these other factors changes, market equilibrium is affected. Tables 7.5, 7.6, and 7.7 describe those factors.

 DEMAND ELASTICITY

Demand varies in direct relationship to price. Demand elasticity means prices stretch across a range that is determined by buyers' responsiveness. When there is a change in price, there is a change in demand.

Managers have to know how high to set the price yet remain competitive, and how low to set it and still make a profit. Demand is elastic when a reduced price attracts more consumers to purchase the product and the increase in sales compensates for the reduced price. Elasticity also includes the concept that price can be stretched only so far: After a point at the high end of the range, consumers will no longer purchase the product.

When demand is inelastic, there is little stretch. The component of price doesn't affect the demand. For instance, medical devices are expensive, but consumers who require them will pay the going price because of their tremendous need. Regardless of the price, there is

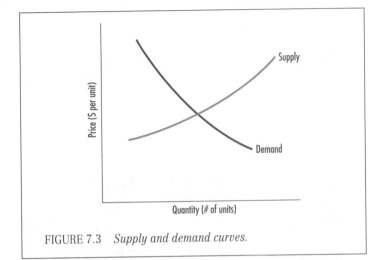

FIGURE 7.3   *Supply and demand curves.*

a demand for the product. On the other hand, less expensive items, such as food products, can also be inelastic because they, too, are necessary.

Time is another element of elasticity: The longer the time frame, the greater the potential for elasticity— demand has more of a chance to change because people have the time to choose substitute products or, over time, their attitude about the product shifts. As time passes, for instance, the price of a product falls and more people buy. Telephone answering machines and VCRs are good examples: Once they were considered luxuries by many; as the cost dropped, they became more popular and are now common household items. (See Table 7.8.)

DEMAND IS KEY TO COMPETITIVE ADVANTAGE

Shifts in demand present opportunities and threats. Companies can thrive and grow or shrivel up and die,

TABLE 7.5

Key Demand Factors	Key Supply Factors
Price	Price
Income	Cost of production
Tastes	Technology
Preferences	Weather conditions
Price of related products	Price of other seller products
Future expectations	Future expectations
Number of buyers	Number of sellers

Adapted from: *Philip Y. K. Young and John J. McAuley,* The Portable MBA in Economics *(New York: John Wiley & Sons, 1994), pp. 148–150.*

TABLE 7.6 NONPRICE FACTORS AFFECTING DEMAND

Income

When income increases, people tend to buy more products; however, if there is a negative correlation between the rise in income and a decrease in demand for a particular product, the product is considered inferior. As incomes rise, products that were once acceptable are replaced with higher-priced substitutes.

Tastes and Preferences

Consumers tastes and preferences change over time. What once was popular becomes passe. Or when consumers begin to believe they must have a product, preferences can change quickly. Sometimes price has no influence in product selection. Consumers will buy expensive products because they have an extreme need for them and, conversely, they won't buy inexpensive products they consider harmful.

Price of Related Products

When a substitute product increases in price, the other product increases in demand. Consumers once favored companies like Procter & Gamble even though they charged premium prices for their brand-name products. However, once consumers learned that generic products had comparable quality to brand names, the lower prices of generic products caused consumers to shift their preferences, increasing demand for generics and decreasing demand for brand names.

Future Expectations

When consumers expect a product—for example, a stock—to increase in price, they will be more inclined to buy it and, as they buy more, expectations among consumers grow and demand increases.

Number of Buyers

When a large group of consumers fits into a similar demographic profile, demand for products that appeal to them increases. For example, the baby boomers, due to the size of their population, have enormous impact on market demand. Senior citizens are another group with increasing clout because they are growing in number; they influence demand for products geared to the elderly.

Adapted from: *Philip Y. K. Young and John J. McAuley*, The Portable MBA in Economics *(New York: John Wiley & Sons, 1994), p. 148.*

depending on their anticipation of changes and response to conditions. In retail, consumers started buying at discount stores and curtailed buying from department stores. Stellar performer Wal-Mart recognized consumer demands for more cost-effective products and reaped the rewards, while Sears spent the early '90s keeping itself afloat. Innovative, technologically advanced Hewlett-Packard was one of the first

TABLE 7.7 NONPRICE FACTORS AFFECTING SUPPLY

Cost of Production

Production costs determine the quantity of products that can be produced relative to the profit needed by companies. Variable costs, such as wage levels and the price of materials, and fixed costs, such as plant and machinery, can cause the cost of production to rise, thereby limiting the supply.

Technology

Technology allows firms to handle inventory more efficiently and, thus, firms have the ability to handle an increased amount of inventory with a reduction in cost. Managers need to be aware of technological changes so that their companies are not caught unaware of new, appealing products being produced by competitors.

Prices of Other Products

When a product is seen as profitable, the supply of complementary products increases. Windows 95, released in August of 1995, was a catalyst for the whole industry. Computer and office supply stores, as well as manufacturers of related hardware and software, geared up for a slew of business when Windows 95 hit the market. Retailers' profits came not just from the sale of Windows 95, but from all the other complementary products that were being sold along with it.

Future Expectations

Windows 95 again illustrates this point. Other manufacturers knew there was a powerful demand building for this product and they revved up their own operations to produce hardware and software, from spreadsheets to games, to exploit the opportunities that Windows 95 would offer.

Number of Sellers

If there is only one seller in a market, a monopoly exists, and the seller has tremendous power over the supply of goods produced, as well as the price. When there is a large number of sellers, there is greater competition. There is also a greater variety of products.

Weather Conditions

When crops suffer due to weather conditions, supply is affected. If Florida or California is hit with tropical storms or drought, fruits and vegetables become scarcer items on grocery store shelves and, consequently, prices are higher.

Adapted from: *Philip Y. K. Young and John J. McAuley,* The Portable MBA in Economics *(New York: John Wiley & Sons, 1994), pp. 149–150.*

entrants into the workstation market as the computer industry shifted from mainframes to networks of personal computers and workstations. To its detriment, IBM was slow to enter the market and did not understand the shift in market demand.

TABLE 7.8 KEY INFLUENCES ON DEMAND ELASTICITY

Elastic	Inelastic
Product is a luxury	Product is a necessity
Many substitutes are available	Few substitutes are available
Price is large part of income	Price is small part of income
Long time to react to price	Short time to react to price

Source: *Philip Y. K. Young and John J. McAuley, The Portable MBA in Economics (New York: John Wiley & Sons, 1994), p. 169.*

PRICE COMPETITIVELY OR WATCH DEMAND DIE

DANGER!

Price counts. The Apple Macintosh offers a valuable lesson. Mac's easy-to-use system once differentiated it enough to justify its high prices. Mac had steep profit margins. Yet Apple refused to lower prices or license its operating systems to other manufacturers, which would have produced lower-cost imitators. When Microsoft introduced its Windows products, they were run on cheaper IBM clones, providing Microsoft with a huge share of the market that Apple had essentially given away. In 1994, Apple attempted to fight back with Power Macs, which were great products but were still priced too high, especially in light of continued price cutting by competitors. Consumers never received enough enticement to switch from Microsoft. When Windows 95 hit the market in the summer of 1995, it had all the attractive features of a Mac and more. Analysts watched to see how big a bite it took out of Apple—too big a bite could mean real trouble for the Apple tree.[13]

MARKET STRUCTURES AFFECT SUPPLY AND DEMAND

In economic theory, there are four different market structures that affect supply and demand: perfect competition, monopoly, monopolistic competition, and oligopoly (see Table 7.9). When changes take place in these structures, not only can supply and demand change but distribution channels can also be affected. In 1993, PepsiCo, which owns Kentucky Fried Chicken, Pizza Hut, and Taco Bell, faced the decline in the fast-food market. In response, PepsiCo looked for new, innovative channels to distribute its products. It started selling fast-food from carts at stadiums and special events and at outlets set up in supermarkets.[14]

TABLE 7.9 FOUR BASIC MARKETS

Perfect Competition

- Large number of relatively small buyers and sellers
- Standardized product
- Easy market entry/exit
- Players have complete information about market price
- Firms have no control over price
- Price by supply and demand
- Key characteristic is price volatility; prices move almost constantly as trade shifts supply and demand

Products: wheat, corn, pork bellies, coffee beans, financial instruments, government securities, corporate stocks, bonds, precious metals.

Monopoly

- One seller
- Power comes from being only seller
- Unique product/no close substitutes
- Market entry/exit blocked by government regulations
- Regulated monopolies set prices, but need permission from regulatory bodies

Monopolies: gas and electric utilities, cable, firms protected by patents (e.g., Polaroid's monopoly on instant cameras). Yet, demand can fall off when new products make monopoly's product less appealing, which happened with video cameras and one-hour film development. Many monopolies are in the process of being deregulated.

Monopolistic Competition

- Large number of relatively small buyers and sellers
- Differentiated product enables firms to set higher prices but price differences slight
- Relatively easy market entry/exit, yet ease makes it difficult to sustain differentiation
- Players have complete information about market prices

Small retail companies

Oligopolies

- Fairly small number of large sellers
- Standardized or differentiated product
- Relatively difficult market entry
- Players have complete information about market prices
- A few large sellers that earn majority of market's total revenue
- Larger number of smaller niche firms
- Entry difficult due to high start-up costs, well-established brand names, distribution systems
- Price set by price leader; if pricing discipline not observed, price war breaks out
- Seller's power depends on size or differentiation

Companies in manufacturing, communications, transportation

Adapted from: *Philip Y. K. Young and John J. McAuley, The Portable MBA in Economics (New York: John Wiley & Sons, 1994), pp. 154–157.*

CROWDS CROWD OUT MARKETS

DANGER! Changes in markets can happen gradually as demographics shift. And sometimes changes come suddenly with the introduction of new technologies. Understanding how supply and demand change with the markets serves as a guide to managers. When conditions change quickly, firms might appear to be entering a market with higher prices but end up finding the situation has reversed. Managers should check to see if the market can support high prices for any period of time. Once a market has been identified as profitable, firms may rush to enter, with the result that the supply increases enough to cause the market to collapse.

END POINT

Knowledge of economics can help managers view competitors differently, anticipate changes in business cycles, and price products more responsively to the demands of the market. Economics provides a way for managers to view the environment in which their business operates from a more holistic view, combining the macro and the micro and enabling managers to understand the dynamics of the system and how movement in one part affects all the other parts.

The third section of this book ties together the organization's functions and examines strategies for positioning the company to gain greater competitive advantage. It takes a more detailed look at two major functions of the organization—manufacturing and marketing—and it discusses the monumental impact information technology has on almost every aspect of business.

MORE READING

Bach, George L. *Economics.* Englewood Cliffs, N.J.: Prentice-Hall, 1987.

Casler, Stephen D. *Introduction to Economics.* New York: Harper-Collins, 1992.

Davidson, James Dale, and Lord William Rees-Mogg. *The Great Reckoning.* New York: Simon & Schuster, 1993.

Fahey, Liam, and V. K. Narayanan. *Macroenvironmental Analysis for Strategic Management.* St. Paul, Minn.: West Publishing Co., 1986.

Fahey, Liam, and Robert M. Randall (eds.). *The Portable MBA in Strategy.* New York: John Wiley & Sons, 1994.

Hall, Robert, and John Taylor (eds.). *Macroeconomics: Theory, Performance, and Policy.* New York: Norton, 1993.

Hirshleifer, Jack. *Price Theory and Applications.* 4th ed. Englewood Cliffs, N.J.: Prentice-Hall, 1988.

Keat, Paul, and Philip Young. *Managerial Economics: Economic Tools for Today's Decision Makers.* New York: Macmillan, 1992.

Kennedy, Paul. *Preparing for the Twenty-First Century.* New York: Random House, 1993.

Keynes, John Maynard. *The General Theory of Employment Interest and Money.* London: MacMillan Press Ltd., 1936, reissued 1973.

McAuley, John. *Economic Forecasting for Business.* Englewood Cliffs, N.J.: Prentice-Hall, 1986.

Silk, Leonard. *Economics in Plain English.* New York: Simon & Schuster, 1978.

Young, Philip K. Y., and John J. McAuley. *The Portable MBA in Economics.* New York: John Wiley & Sons, 1994.

Functions and Strategies:
Making Business Work

If I always appear prepared, it is because before
embarking on an undertaking, I have meditated
for long and have foreseen what might occur. It is
not genius which reveals to me suddenly and
secretly what I should do in circumstances unex-
pected by others; it is thought and meditation.

Napoleon Bonaparte

Information Technology:
The New Engine of Business

In the 1800s, the railroads were the engines pushing the economy, transporting goods and people in ways that had not previously been experienced. Manufacturing reigned after the railroads, but the service economy began to usurp it in the 1980s. As the twenty-first century approaches, information technology (IT) is becoming the new engine that drives the economy, and the train looks a whole lot different. IT, like an explosive, nonstop express, has taken over and the effects of its power can be felt around the globe.

In today's Information Revolution, the capture and release of information is critical to success. The speedy availability of information is reshaping the way business operates and the way society functions. The kinds of goods and services produced in an economy impact how companies conduct business and reflect how the society itself performs. IT is quickening the pace of life, shrinking the world, and collapsing time. Knowing how to use it effectively is crucial. This chapter looks at ways in which managers can harness the power of IT and use it to enhance competitive advantage.

KEY CONCEPT — INFORMATION TECHNOLOGY REVOLUTIONIZES ECONOMIES

In recent years, IT growth has been compounding, and its future staggers the imagination. Growth has been phenomenal. Inside the United States, "business and consumer spending on high-tech equipment accounts for some 38 percent of economic growth since 1990."[1] In 1993 alone, "countries around the world installed more than 7.4 million miles of fiber."[2] In 1995, the chip market had "its third straight year of 30 percent growth,"[3] and worldwide chip sales are expected "to rocket from $110 billion in 1995 to $273 billion in 2,000," with "61 percent of that growth outside the

US."[4] "Corporate purchases of package software rose from $7.4 billion in 1983 to $51 billion in 1994."[5]

 DIGITAL AGE BRINGS VIRTUAL WORLD

The information age has brought with it a new universal machine language, whose digital elements unite people around the world in a new IT culture. Companies around the globe use IT to perform daily operations and, through the strategic use of IT, make themselves more competitive.

As the world has evolved, inventions have determined the direction of the future. This was true for the printing press, the steam engine, and the electric motor. The degree to which the invention influences the future is a reflection of its power. The computer is the most powerful invention yet. Its ability to turn simple digits into deep reservoirs of information and to communicate that information in a way that increases human knowledge holds untold possibilities for the future. The computer imitates life. It virtualizes business, "byting" into almost every facet of business life: It speeds up activities, restructures power, and makes information more dynamic. (See Table 8.1.)

Digital images are creating *virtual* worlds, recreating the real world in a computerized form. In *virtual communities,* people with similar interests chat in groups in virtual rooms, or meet in pairs to "talk" in privacy. Yet, while conversing in this virtual room, one person might actually be in Maine and the other in Monaco. Time and space lose significance in a virtual world, and all kinds of possibilities emerge. Ross Controls, a valve manufacturer highlighted in Chapter 9, has gained enormous competitive advantage due to the virtual products it creates in conjunction with its customers. The product doesn't exist, until the customer and a Ross Controls team member sit down at the computer and turn on the computer-aided-design (CAD) program to design a new valve that meets the customer's latest requirements.

 TECHNOLOGIES DEMAND CHANGE

LANs, WANs, ISDNs, ATMs, SONETs, chips, and microprocessors are everywhere. But if an organization doesn't know how to change itself to absorb the alphabet soup of telecommunications or the elemental digits of computerization, the benefits of IT will remain elusive. Table 8.2 supplies a glossary of useful terms.

IT IMPROVES BUSINESS

IT has propelled progress, driven innovations, stimulated wealth, and lured investments. Business spending on IT—those nonresidential fixed

TABLE 8.1 THE IMPACT OF DIGITAL TECHNOLOGY

Organizational Structure

Using electronic, networked systems, information crosses boundaries quickly, creating new organizational structures that extend beyond functional departments, strategic business units, divisions, or even the company itself.

Human Resources

Information technology provides workers with the ability to operate out of virtual offices, allowing greater flexibility in work schedules. Although some workers have lost their jobs due to technological advances, the digital world has driven others to upgrade their skills. IT stimulates the need for more training and education.

Relationships

Databases and networks enable customer service representatives to provide instant answers and speedy, specialized customer service. Using information technology, products can be customized to meet customers' needs. This supports the development of partner relationships between companies and their customers and results in higher levels of customer satisfaction. New partnerships are formed between companies and suppliers as information is shared along the distribution chain, and organizations realize the value of working together.

Manufacturing Operations

Information technology reduces cycle time, product defects, and manufacturing costs, and speeds interactions with customer and suppliers in both manufacturing and service companies. Computer-integrated-manufacturing (CIM), computer-aided design (CAD), and the advancement in chip technology enables the creation of a wider variety of innovative products.

Marketing and New Products

Using vast market research databases, marketing departments can pinpoint customers' wants and needs with great specificity, segmenting markets with more and more precision. IT has enabled companies to track customers on a one-to-one basis, opening the way for customized products and the development of long-term relationships with valued customers. This trend has fostered linkages between marketing, R&D, and manufacturing as cross-functional teams design and manufacture customized products.

Strategic Planning

Information technology drives progress, productivity, and profit, and can be a significant strategic factor for gaining competitive advantage.

investments in machinery and equipment that enable companies to expand capacity—accounts for half of all nonresidential investment. Recent studies show that companies investing in computer technology get significant returns on their investments.

TABLE 8.2 TECHNOLOGY TRANSLATED

AI: Artificial intelligence. Computers provide a means for finding solutions by facilitating the analysis of problems. AI can evaluate markets and environments and can identify core problems and offer solutions.

ATM: Asynchronous transfer mode. Digital switching and transmission technology, which mixes and sends voice, data, and video traffic at incredibly high speeds over a single line.

Bridge: Links two LANs so they can share data.

Broadband: Transmission of voice, data, and video at speeds higher than 2 million bps.

CAD: Computer-aided design. Used primarily by architects and engineers to design and draw detailed blueprints for buildings, machinery, cars, planes, etc.

CAM: Computer-aided manufacturing. Enables manufacturers to produce goods on a 24-hour basis using robots.

CASE: Computer-aided-software engineering. Used to create special software programs.

CIM: Computer-integrated manufacturing. Using computers to assist in manufacturing processes enables manufacturers to be flexible and transform the way they produce goods.

Client/Server: Network of PCs in which one computer is the central repository (server) for programs and files that can be shared by other computers (clients).

DRAMS: Dynamic random-access memory chips. Stores 64 million bits of information.

EDI: Electronic data interchange. Enables the transfer of information, such as invoices, shipping orders, and payments, between computers of different companies.

Ethernet: LANs that allow networking products from different vendors to share information.

ISDN: Integrated services digital network. High-capacity digital service used in telecommunications that turns standard copper phone lines into high-speed digital links which can send voice and data at the same time.

Intelligent Hubs: Circuit boards that enable PCs to exchange information over LANs.

LAN: Local-area network. A system within an organization that links computers, allowing them to share information. LANs carry everything from e-mail to videoconferencing.

Packet Switching: Breaks data into smaller packets, moves it through a network using different routes, and then repackages data back together.

Router: A sophisticated bridge connecting LANs that use different standards. Routers move data outside the LAN via modems and gateway computers.

SONET: Synchronous optical network technology. High-speed transmission architecture that exploits the bandwidth of fiber-optic networks, sending signals simultaneously over two different paths.

> **TABLE 8.2 (Continued)**
>
> **TCP/IP:** Transmission Control Protocol/Internet Protocol. A language of the electronic world that is being used for everything from mainframes to LAN equipment.
>
> **WAN:** Wide-area network. Transmits signals from a LAN to a distant LAN via public or private lines.
>
> **World Wide Web:** An Internet service connecting users with various sites, allowing them to retrieve hypertext and graphics.

Economist Erik Brynjolfsson and Lorin Hitt, from MIT's Sloan School of Management, studied 367 *Fortune* 500 companies between 1987 and 1991. Their findings indicate that after depreciation, companies have a 67 percent return on their investment in IT.[6] It takes less capital to improve business productivity through investments made in IT than it does through investing in plants and heavy equipment. For example, telephone companies can "boost the carrying capacity of their existing fiber-optic cables by simply upgrading the electronics . . . without having to go through the expensive process of digging up old cables and installing new ones." IT also increases efficiency while it lowers prices: "The price of information technology equipment has dropped by 23% over the past five years."[7]

Brynjolfsson and Hitt's study also indicated that IT led to improvements in customer service and the quality of products. Additionally, IT has increased the variety of products, while lowering costs. The fax machine is an example: In 1986, 200,000 fax machines were sold; by 1995, the number had climbed to 5 million.[8] Sales in 1994 totaled $2 billion,[9] yet "average fax machine prices dropped 28%" since 1991.[10] Additionally, the huge increase in demand for fax machines created increased revenues for complementary products such as paper, toner, and telephone service.

 IT: POWER AND SPEED

Progress in IT has been extraordinarily rapid. What's in today might well be out tomorrow. Huge vacuum-tube computers introduced in the 1950s can't compare with the capabilities of the pocket calculators of the '90s. And the fiber-optic cables of the '90s are "an improvement of 170,000% over the phone cables laid across the Atlantic in the late '50s."[11]

Power and speed are IT's hallmarks. Intel Corporation's microcomputer chip, first introduced in 1971, changed the electronics industry forever. Ten years later, the 286 became an industry standard, and in less than another decade, the 486 was performing 50 times faster. The Pentium, Intel's latest version, "processes 219 million instructions per second" and the P6, which will be the sixth generation of the chip, "is expected to perform twice as fast."[12]

NETWORKS CHANGE BUSINESS ENVIRONMENT

Networks enable companies to do business continually on an anywhere, anytime basis. They link up information, providing companies with a vast resource of knowledge from which to make strategic as well as tactical everyday decisions.

At Digital Equipment Corp., well known for its expertise in networking, almost everyone has a workstation or terminal that is hooked into a worldwide network. Within Digital's culture of individual freedom and responsibility, workers share ideas and provide project feedback via the network, which supports a horizontal style of management. For example, back in 1986, the company's CDA software project was field-tested using the network. The project team believes that 90 percent of the bugs were uncovered through input provided by reviewers entering their comments into electronic notepads in the system.[13]

Texas Instruments Inc., a billion-dollar IT company that makes digital signal processors, provides another example of a high-tech company reaping the rewards of networking. Texas Instruments has 17 cutting-edge fabrication plants (*fabs*) in countries around the world that are plugged into a worldwide IT system. Networked software keeps work distributed to *fabs* throughout the system. Additionally, engineers in Dallas can check on the chip technology in any of the *fabs*. For example, engineers in Texas can fix problems in the Philippines and "reprogram the computer-controlled production line by the time the morning shift arrives the next day." This high level of efficiency "has improved on-time delivery from 77% to 96% since 1990."[14]

With its network, Del Monte Corp. gets "daily inventory reports electronically from grocers," who need only "one and a half weeks of inventory on hand, compared with the four weeks worth they used to warehouse to avoid shortages."[15] By restocking grocers' shelves as soon as products fall to a minimum level, Del Monte helps grocers save thousands of dollars in warehousing costs.

Kao, the leading Japanese soap and detergent maker, is known for VAN, its sophisticated, value-added network, which provides frontline managers access to information across the organization. The system not only gives engineers technical information and marketing people consumer information, but it enables data to be compared, providing the company with valuable knowledge that is used to create products consumers want.[16]

WAL-MART: RETAILER WITH A NOTEWORTHY NETWORK

Star The retailing industry is especially affected by networking: One of the key factors in Wal-Mart's success has been its ability to innovate using a sophisticated IT system that enables it to capture point-of-purchase sales information store by store, compile it, and send it back to management and suppliers. The way information is electronically handled allows Wal-Mart to manage inventory, ordering, and shipping with the highest levels of efficiency. Managers can foresee emerging patterns, forecast sales trends, and determine demand; thus, they can act more quickly than competitors. The detailed, store-by-store, department-by-department sales data support decentralized management, enabling store department heads to decide on their own how to meet revenue and growth goals.

The IT system also links suppliers into the network, creating a seamless, fast procurement and distribution process. Suppliers receive daily information, enabling them to alter their own manufacturing schedules. Additionally, by partnering with suppliers, like Procter & Gamble, "Wal-Mart has all but eliminated the need for manufacturers' sales reps selling at the store level."[17]

Wal-Mart exemplifies an innovative company that harnessed the power of information technology and combined it with excellence in customer service to provide a new way of operating. Its ability to leverage IT has led to its position of leadership in the retail industry.

TiP TRAIN PEOPLE TO USE INFORMATION AND TECHNOLOGY

Teaching people how to manage and communicate information is a key to competitive success. Providing training and education in how to use both the technology and the information it supplies gives the organization the competitive edge it needs in a new, knowledge-based world.

Regardless of the type of high tech used by a company, it is the human factor that determines how well IT is utilized. How people use information is crucial to success. Information that is hoarded and not disseminated impedes people within the organization from gaining valuable knowledge. But too much information, not properly assimilated and understood, can be just as bad. All the information in the world can get siphoned through a company's network, but if the culture doesn't support the sharing of information, it won't be of help to the people who need it most.

WITHOUT GOOD NETWORKS, NEGLIGIBLE NET PROFIT

Lack of timely information impedes effective decision making. Information must circulate to the right people at the right time. Even high-tech companies can have trouble practicing what they preach. IBM's PC business exemplifies the profitability problems a high-tech company has when it can't get its own networks in order.

G. Richard Thoman, head of IBM's troubled PC business, is in the process of turning red ink to black. In 1994, the PC division had "an estimated $1 billion operating loss," which stemmed from a variety of factors: The business "didn't have a coordinated information system . . . had absolutely no timely data on its operations . . . and could gather results only on a monthly basis at best." In one location alone there were "223 incompatible computer systems." When Thoman came on board, he "couldn't even tell whether he had laptops or desktops tied up in inventory." Now "new computer systems pump out daily status reports" and "inventory turns over every 60 days."[18] And the numbers are starting to lose their crimson shade.

NETWORKS HELP THE LITTLE GUY

Networks support the concept of virtual organizations. With the freedom of the network, employees no longer have to work out of central or regional offices. At Cyrex Corp., a small Texas manufacturer of semiconductors, "all 20 U.S. salespeople work from their homes, fully equipped with cellular phones, notebook PCs, and pagers . . . and a real-time order-processing system."[19] The IT this high-tech firm uses enables it to compete with companies that have 10 times the number of salespeople. Additionally, being networked saves on the cost of maintaining offices. And small companies as well as large can plug into online databases that provide market research and business opportunities.

IT AND BUSINESS STRATEGY

IT is shaping business operations of the future. No longer is it simply a means to enhance efficiency. IT is a fundamental means of creating and maintaining competitive advantage. The greatest benefits from IT seem to come when existing organizational strategies, structures, and processes are altered in conjunction with IT investments, rather than just merely adding new IT systems to the old pile of organizational components.

N. Venkatraman, a scholar in strategic management and information technology, firmly believes that the real power of IT lies in "restructuring the relationships in the extended business networks to leverage a broader array of competencies."[20] He provides a number of questions that managers can ask themselves as they consider the strategic role of IT. (See Table 8.3.)

Table 8.4 provides insight into the influence of IT at the level in which it is applied within the organization. Each level provides potential benefits but is dependent on the organization's ability to exploit the opportunities presented at that level.

Much depends on whether managers see IT as a source of opportunity or are threatened by the changes it can bring about. Along with IT comes the need to change organizational structures, reporting relationships, and performance measurements. The degree to which IT can

---

TABLE 8.3 IT QUESTIONS FOR SENIOR MANAGERS

Level 1 Localized Exploitation

What are the criteria for success in applying a particular IT system? What changes in performance criteria should accompany a particular application?

Level 2 Internal Integration

What is the rationale for internal integration? How does the business process resulting from integration compare to the best in class?

Level 3 Business Process Redesign

What is the rationale for the current organizational design? What are its strengths and weaknesses? What significant changes in business processes are happening in the market? What is the cost of maintaining the status quo?

Level 4 Business Network Redesign

What is the rationale for the current approach to business network redesign? What are its strengths and limitations? Should interfaces be common or proprietary? What are the potential functions for the IT applications? Is there a coherent strategy to the business network, or is the network simply composed of isolated strands of relationships? What are the opportunities for restructuring the business network?

Level 5 Business Scope Redefinition

What role does IT play in influencing business? What role does IT play in business relationships within the extended business network? Should IT competence come from inside or outside the company?

Source: N. Venkatraman, "IT-Enabled Business Transformation: From Automation to Business Scope Redefinition," Sloan Management Review (Winter 1994, vol. 35., no. 2), pp. 73–74.

TABLE 8.4 FIVE LEVELS OF IT-ENABLED TRANSFORMATION

Level 1   Localized Exploitation

IT, such as toll-free numbers, order-entry systems, inventory control systems, and e-mail, applied to isolated systems usually provides little change in business strategy and can be easily imitated by competitors. Without proper performance measurements, levels of change in performance, relative to the changes in technology, can never be accurately tested. IT applications at Level 1 can reduce cost and quicken response, but there is little differentiation in the marketplace. In order to create competitive advantage, managers need to add value to each application.

Level 2   Internal Integration

Internal integration has two components: (1) Interconnectivity and interoperability of different systems operating through a common platform, and (2) interdependence of business processes across functions. Companies tend to focus more on interconnectivity than interdependence, but both components are important and need to be used. Stressing one without the other won't provide competitive advantage.

Level 3   Business Process Redesign

IT should not simply be laid on top of existing processes; it should be used as a strategic lever for business process design. IT functionality can alter basic processes, such as centralization vs. decentralization, line vs. staff, and coordination vs. control. Redesigning needs to be approached rationally and systematically. Companies must understand their competitors' processes as well as their own before they undertake huge changes.

Level 4   Business Network Redesign

Process linkages in design and manufacturing provide the potential for differentiation and expand business network redesign. But electronic data interchange (EDI) by itself does not. Simply sharing information with customers and suppliers or processing transactions electronically does not provide competitive advantage. It does, however, provide the organization with increased administrative efficiency, just as inventory movement provides operational efficiency by streamlining inventory levels in the supply chain. Only when IT enhances decision making or provides distinctive value-added services does the IT become strategic. When partners in these exchanges can leverage the competencies in the shared network—for example, by saving the company from vertical integration—then competitive advantage is gained.

Level 5   Business Scope Redefinition

More flexible, fluid networks of joint ventures, alliances, and partnerships are replacing hierarchical economies of scale, vertical product-line extensions, and vertical mergers and acquisitions. Managers must demonstrate how the use of IT applications enhances coordination and control of business processes inside with business processes outside the organization. IT should enhance the ability to combine core competencies so that they have greater appeal to customers. The IT infrastructure should support efficient coordination and control.

Source: N. Venkatraman, "IT-Enabled Business Transformation: From Automation to Business Scope Redefinition," Sloan Management Review (Winter 1994, vol. 35, no. 2), pp. 73–74.

be leveraged to provide competitive advantage depends on an organization's ability to envision the future and "to create an appropriate organizational environment."[21]

IT ALONE AIN'T STRATEGIC

No single IT application in and of itself is strategic. It only becomes strategic according to the way it is used. One of the most well-known IT systems—American's Sabre System Computer Reservation System—becomes strategic, not by easing the seat reservation process alone, but when the information it provides is used to make more knowledgeable decisions about scheduling, pricing, and promotion.

IT PROVIDES ADVANTAGES BEYOND EFFICIENCY

For years, firms often used IT for the sole purpose of making their administrative functions operate more efficiently. But as Venkantramen points out, the company must investigate all the ways in which IT can be exploited for competitive advantage. For example, many firms have 800 numbers: It's the level of service provided in meeting the customers' needs when they call that sets the organization apart.

At Honeywell, when a customer calls a dedicated customer service representative, rather than ringing busy, the call is automatically routed to another member of the customer service team. This provides customers with someone familiar with their needs.

Many firms now electronically process their invoices, but it's how innovatively they use their new systems that counts. "BP America Inc., for example, the U.S. subsidiary of British Petroleum Co., is setting up a system that will process at least 40% of the 440,000 invoices it receives each year electronically. The switch will do more than saving on man-hours and paperwork: BP expects to be able to eliminate duplicate purchases and negotiate bulk rates."[22]

It's what companies do with information that counts. Ryder System Inc., a $4.2 billion transportation company, "captures every bit—and byte—of information on its trucks electronically," making "scheduling the company's 8,500 technicians and 162,000 trucks simpler, inventory tracking and parts ordering more efficient, and reports to fleet customers far more detailed." The company estimates "the $33 million investment in new computer systems will pay for itself in two years."[23]

Computer-aided design (CAD) changed the competitive environment for Flower and Samios, a small Australian architectural company (see sidebar), providing opportunities it hadn't expected. Table 8.5 lists benefits that can be derived from using this form of technology.

Small Company, Big IT Star: Flower and Samios

Flower and Samios increased business 400 percent and grew from being a $20 million company to being a $100 million company because the architects put down their pencils and picked up a mouse. In 1987, the firm did not own a computer; in 1992, it had invested $240,000 in information technology.

The firm's principals were originally attracted to the use of computers when they lost a bid due to the difference between their pencil-sketched presentations and the 3-D computer images presented by another firm. The use of computer-aided-design (CAD) technology ultimately changed the entire way the company conducted its business. As well as changing roles and skills in the company—staff assumed greater responsibility for projects and relied less on draftspeople and external specialists—changes spurred competitive advantage by improving customer service, supplier relationships, and design capabilities.

Flower and Samios' decision to go high-tech was tactical, not strategic: The principals turned to IT in response to a perceived threat from competitors. They originally used IT as a presentation tool, but as they became adept at using the CAD systems on their new Macintoshes, their skills grew and the structure of the firm changed. Fewer people were needed, and only those people who were willing to devote themselves to both learning and using the technology were hired or kept in the firm. As the level of proficiency with technology grew, more sophisticated equipment was purchased. Gradually, the benefits of using the technology became more apparent and new opportunities for creating value-added services for customers emerged. IT became more than a tool; it became "embedded in every aspect of the firm's operations." The strategic fit that developed in five years evolved "from an incremental tactical implementation of technology which ultimately transformed the business."

Flower and Samios Technological Steps to Success

- All employees, including senior officers, were required to master and use the new technology.

- IT investment costs were spread over time across projects, limiting the need for scarce capital and allowing costs to be absorbed by overhead in projects.

- Only off-the-shelf hardware and software were purchased, supporting an easier learning process and enabling the technology to become part of the core business process without having to rely on

(Continued)

(Continued)

outside, expensive technical assistance. This also kept management in the driver's seat, even though the technology drove the business.

Source: *Philip W. Yetton, Kim D. Johnston, and Jane F. Craig, "Computer-Aided Architects: A Case Study of IT and Strategic Change,"* Sloan Management Review *(Summer 1994, vol. 34, no. 4), pp. 57–67.*

KEY CONCEPT — IT CAN DRIVE BUSINESS STRATEGY

IT can drive changes in business strategy in small as well as large companies, creating new structures, roles, and processes.

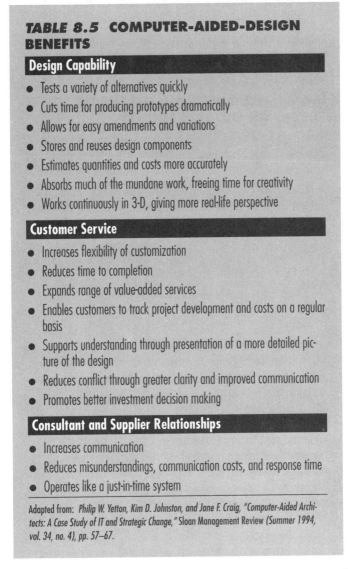

TABLE 8.5 COMPUTER-AIDED-DESIGN BENEFITS

Design Capability

- Tests a variety of alternatives quickly
- Cuts time for producing prototypes dramatically
- Allows for easy amendments and variations
- Stores and reuses design components
- Estimates quantities and costs more accurately
- Absorbs much of the mundane work, freeing time for creativity
- Works continuously in 3-D, giving more real-life perspective

Customer Service

- Increases flexibility of customization
- Reduces time to completion
- Expands range of value-added services
- Enables customers to track project development and costs on a regular basis
- Supports understanding through presentation of a more detailed picture of the design
- Reduces conflict through greater clarity and improved communication
- Promotes better investment decision making

Consultant and Supplier Relationships

- Increases communication
- Reduces misunderstandings, communication costs, and response time
- Operates like a just-in-time system

Adapted from: *Philip W. Yetton, Kim D. Johnston, and Jane F. Craig, "Computer-Aided Architects: A Case Study of IT and Strategic Change,"* Sloan Management Review *(Summer 1994, vol. 34, no. 4), pp. 57–67.*

IT dramatically reshaped the business strategy and vision of Flower and Samios. This company's experience demonstrates how incremental mastery of IT, and the strategic applications that emerge from its use, can transform business processes and create competitive advantage. Once IT became embedded in the firm's operations, the company was able to assess new strategic options made available through the technology. IT enabled the company to operate with lower costs and provided it with the ability to offer higher-quality and more unique customer service, which helped to differentiate the firm from its competitors.[24]

TAILOR TECHNOLOGY AND WORK WITH ENVIRONMENT

It cannot be stressed enough: Each business decision must be made in light of the context within which the organization operates, and that includes choosing and integrating IT into business processes. Although some companies, like Flower and Samios, successfully used off-the-shelf technology, often full advantage is not achieved without carefully tailoring technology to fit the organization.

THE QUESTION: GO INSIDE OR OUTSIDE FOR IT?

Deciding how to build information systems and incorporate IT into business is never easy. Issues to keep in mind when making IT decisions include:

- *Changing requirements*—How flexible does the system have to be to handle unforeseen future changes? What are the emerging technologies that might provide better advantage?

- *Strategic service it provides*—How significant is it? Is IT a core element of strategy?

- *Knowledge levels*—What facets of IT does the organization have the ability to handle efficiently internally? Does it have the level of expertise needed to manage outsourced contracts?[25]

In large companies, a system that maximizes flexibility and control and that allows suppliers inside and outside the company to compete will provide the best choices for decision makers.

In smaller companies, using a combination of both internal and external resources can also be the best approach. Hiring an outside consultant who doesn't totally understand the business can be a mistake, but so can total reliance on an insider who doesn't have full technological knowledge. Choose third-party suppliers with knowledge of hardware and software who will build the system and then stay around to make sure things are working properly. And build systems that are bug-free, and offer a full selection of easy-to-get software and peripherals.[26]

INTEGRATE TECHNOLOGIES

In world-class firms, technology is fully integrated and accessible to almost everyone in the organization. In a study of 900 North American manufacturing firms conducted by Deloitte & Touche and the University of North Carolina, world-class manufacturers differentiated themselves as leaders through the integration of technology. They had greater facility in using knowledge-based integrating technologies such as artificial intelligence, computer-aided design (CAD), computer-aided engineering (CAE), and local-area networks (LANs).[27]

IT COMPANIES: INNOVATION AND DEMAND

IT has set the world spinning. In addition to looking at the use of IT within companies, it's worthwhile to take a glimpse at companies that produce high-tech products: These companies adopt a variety of creative strategies in order to succeed in a highly competitive market. They turn profits even when their products are inexpensively priced, and sometimes they actually offer their products for free.

In 1993, for example, Computer Associates International Inc. gave away its accounting software Simply Money, "on the theory that favorable word of mouth would outweigh the trivial expense of making the diskettes—and persuade customers to buy upgrades and related programs." Likewise, Nintendo Co. "charted a business model in which the game consoles would be given away to consumers at cost, or even below, to boost sales of software."[28]

As chips get smaller, faster, and cheaper, the range of possible products increases. As this drama unfolds and chips become denser and capable of holding more and more information, products become almost limitless and many can be produced in huge volume. Markets have at times been swamped with inexpensive, quality products. Yet, high-tech product gluts seem to occur on a temporary basis, shifting with the response from the marketplace. Demand in IT is incredibly elastic. IT drives creativity and competition: As volume increases and the market becomes deluged with products, companies must provide customers with additional, innovative benefits in order to attract their attention. Value-added elements, such as the establishment of relationships with customers and suppliers or the ability to differentiate products above the level of a commodity, become the factors that determine success.

In the early '90s, for instance, Intel had a strong hold on the PC microprocessor market, so in order to compete, smaller companies like Cirrus Logic Inc., LSI Logic Corp., and VLSI Technology "took aim at so-called chip sets that added sound and visual effects for PCs and on emerging-device areas, such as digital set-top boxes, that link up to the Information Superhighway."[29] Smaller, faster chips can perform a great range of functions. California-based C-Cube Microsystems created "a $25 compression chip that squeezes audio and video information so that a full-length movie will fit onto a single compact disk." And LSI Logic Corp. hopes that by the year 2000, it will "be looking at 50 million transistors on a chip, and almost any electronic system will fit on it."[30]

COMBINE HIGH VOLUME WITH LOW PRICES AND BE GENEROUS

Being generous pays off. When markets are overflowing, it makes sense to give customers inexpensive add-ons. By giving the customer the opportunity to experience complementary products, a company opens windows for future conversation.

KNOW THE MARKET

In order to win, understand the present market and the technological future. Provide clear value to customers and recognize potential customers.

LEARN HOW TO MASS-CUSTOMIZE PRODUCTS

With the ability to meet the specific requirements of customers, companies can establish niches for themselves and build customer loyalty in this high-volume, low-price IT market. Companies that develop agile manufacturing processes (discussed in the next chapter) can gain competitive advantage.

COMMITMENT LEADS TO SUCCESS

Developing new technologies is not easy. It takes time, effort, money, and commitment. Persistence pays. During the 1970s, AT&T had enough of a cash flow to pursue the development of fiber optics, but it wasn't committed. Corning, on the other hand, stuck to its plan for 15 years, investing $100 million in the development of fiber-optic technology, a strategy which now provides the firm with a hefty portion of its profits. Likewise, Pfizer gave up on computerized tomography (CT) scanners, while GE's medical systems unit hung in. GE's efforts paid off: In 1994, the unit's revenues reached about $3.5 billion. In order to maintain the high level of commitment necessary to complete IT goals, IT must be an essential component of the organization's long-term strategy.[31]

ANALOG DEVICES, INC.: COMMITTED TO CHIPS

Large, bureaucratic companies that suffer when success leads to complacency are not alone. Even smaller companies in the fast-paced, high-tech world can become overconfident. By the late 1980s, when the electronics industry experienced a slowdown, Analog Devices, Inc., a Massachusetts-based manufacturer of electronic components, had a quarter of a century of success under its belt. Expecting to continue reaping the rewards it had in the past, the company was caught off guard when quality became a significant issue and the Japanese began to prosper in semiconductor areas once dominated by Americans.

Founder Ray Strata became committed to quality and continuous learning. In 1990, the company lost money for the first time in its history, but Strata hung in and continued to improve processes: After instituting total quality management (TQM) techniques (see Chapter 9), the company cut its chip failure rates from over a thousand parts per million to approximately 40. It also produced in higher volume and sold at a far lower price: Chip volume, which had run in the thousands, was running in the millions, and chips, which once sold for $50 each, were selling for $1 to $2. Analog adjusted to the market changes and Strata's commitment paid off: In 1995, the company experienced 20 percent growth and its earnings rose 60 percent. With sales of $900 million, Strata wants sales to reach $2 billion by the year 2000.[32]

FAILURE TO EXPLOIT IT CAUSES LOST OPPORTUNITIES

DANGER! Over and over, IBM's past failure to exploit the computer market is highlighted by pundits. Whether that failure was due to the company's inability to adhere to core beliefs or to adapt to changing markets or to poor vision, the point that should not be lost is that it failed to exploit opportunities, paid a dear price, and the road to recovery took years.

MERGERS MATTER

KEY CONCEPT The way technologies and companies merge in the future will hold keys to competitive advantage. In the digital age, technologies are cross-breeding, giving birth to new generations of products and industries that are unpredictable and unlimited in the scope and possibilities they offer.

The entertainment world provides a powerful example of the vast empires being built through mergers and acquisitions driven by companies' strong desires to marry technologies. When Walt Disney Co. acquired

Capital Cities/ABC in the summer of 1995, it was called a marriage of "software and hardware." ABC's technology gives Disney entrance into approximately 93 million homes in the United States. While Disney gets access to television networking and publishing, ABC gets access to films, music, parks, resorts, and consumer products, as well as telecommunications—Disney has a partnership with three Baby Bell regional phone companies to provide video programming and interactive services. The $19 billion acquisition was the largest in the broadcasting industry and the second largest in U.S. history—that is, until Time and Turner announced their engagement in September that same year. The merger of Time Warner, Inc. and Turner Broadcasting Systems, Inc., will generate annual revenues of $19 billion. Their products will range from *Time* magazine and *Sports Illustrated* to CNN and Warner movies. Their combined news-gathering resources will be incredible and the impact on the industry will be profound—the products and profitability born of the results of technological mingling are yet to be fully determined.[33]

Other acquisitions that are driven by a desire for the technological dowry the marriage brings are exemplified by IBM's acquisition of Lotus. IBM Chairman Louis Gerstner, Jr., wanted Lotus' Notes, a leader in "groupware," a fast-growing sector of the industry. This sophisticated software enables computers to share data, text, and graphics. Part of Notes' attraction is that it is not a stand-alone software: It combines networking and database technology. Additionally, Lotus has 10,000 business partners—big and small—in the form of consultants, software developers, and service providers. For every $1 of revenue Lotus generates, $5 is generated in revenue for partners. With IBM's marketing power, Notes can possibly become even more of a leader, generating income IBM wants.[34]

 BREAKUPS MATTER, TOO

Rather than bigger being necessarily better, size may be so cumbersome that the time and cost it takes to manage and coordinate may outweigh the benefits. At the same time that Turner and Time were making plans to marry, AT&T was making plans to split. AT&T found its vast proportions hampered its flexibility and impeded it from moving as nimbly as it would like. Streamlined into three separate companies—telephone services, credit cards, and cellular services; telephone equipment makers; and computer suppliers—AT&T believes it can take better advantage of growth opportunities in the information industry with a more focused approach. Restructuring itself from being America's primary telephone company into three companies, amid a field of competition, has enormous implications for the telecommunications and computer industries as well as for AT&T itself.[35]

END POINT

The world is different because of technology. And it will continue to change. Almost every aspect of a company is affected. Manufacturing processes have been undergoing an overhaul as managers use high-tech machines to make operations run more efficiently. Marketing, too, has been impacted. In fact, IT has been a major force in bringing manufacturing and marketing—two traditionally disparate functions—closer together. The next chapter examines some of those changes and discusses how functional barriers are gradually being taken down as marketing works more closely with R&D and manufacturing to provide greater value to the customer in this highly technological and market-driven business world.

MORE READING

Davenport, Thomas H. *Process Innovation: Reengineering Work Through Information Technology.* Boston: Harvard Business School Press, 1991.

Edsomwan, Johnson A. *Integrating Innovation and Technology Management.* New York: John Wiley & Sons, 1989.

Frederickson, J. W. (ed.). *Perspectives on Strategic Management.* New York: HarperBusiness, 1991.

Goodman P. S., et al. (ed.). *Technology and Organizations.* San Francisco: Jossey-Bass, 1990.

Huber, G. P., and W. H. Glick (eds.). *Organizational Changes and Redesign.* New York: Oxford University Press, 1993.

Keen, P. W. *Shaping the Future: Business Design Through Information Technology.* Boston: Harvard Business School Press, 1991.

Kochan, T., and M. Useem (eds.). *Transforming Organizations.* New York: Oxford University Press, 1992.

Kunda, G. *Engineering Culture: Control and Commitment in a High-Tech Corporation.* Philadelphia: Temple University Press, 1992.

Lacity, Mary C. *Beyond the Information Systems Outsourcing Bandwagon: The Insourcing Response.* New York: John Wiley & Sons, 1995.

McKinnon, Sharon M., and William J. Bruns. *The Information Mosaic.* Boston: Harvard Business School Press, 1992.

Monger, Rod F. *Mastering Technology.* New York: The Free Press, 1988.

Quinn, J. B. *Intelligent Enterprises.* New York: The Free Press, 1992.

Rogers. E. *Diffusion of Innovations.* New York: The Free Press, 1983.

Scott-Morton, M. S. (ed.). *The Corporation of the 1990s: Information Technology and Organizational Transformation.* New York: Oxford University Press, 1991.

von Hippel, E. *The Sources of Innovations.* New York: Oxford University Press, 1988.

Wang, Charles B. *Techno Vision: The Executive's Survival Guide to Understanding and Managing Information Technology.* New York: McGraw-Hill, 1994.

Zuboff, S. *In the Age of the Smart Machine.* New York: Basic Books, 1988.

M&M: Manufacturing and Marketing

Manufacturing and marketing, historically at odds, are finding they have more in common. In recent years, the competitive, market-driven environment has caused them to become more appreciative of each other. Manufacturing makes the product, and marketing promotes, sells, and distributes it. In the past, marketing was the only one of the two that concentrated on the customer, determining customers' wants and needs and creating the means for attracting customers' attention.

Now manufacturing is experiencing a shift toward a *service* orientation, toward meeting and exceeding customers' requirements by including them into the design and production of products. Mass customization—products specifically designed to meet individual customers' requirements using mass-production techniques—has surfaced and is growing as companies strive to compete in a vastly changed market. Manufacturing, with its new customer focus and reengineered processes, is emphasizing proximity to the customer, finding ways to facilitate customer feedback, and maintaining greater flexibility in its production processes.

At the same time, the significance of marketing, with its knowledge of customers, markets, and products, is being recognized as an essential part of all functions and as a strategic link between them. This chapter examines the principles of manufacturing and marketing and some of the cutting-edge ways companies are using both in today's competitive marketplace.

KEY CONCEPT — BUSINESS PROCESSES, NOT FUNCTIONS, PROVIDE FOCUS

The organizational focus has shifted outside the company to the customer, and a business-process, or systems-based, approach is being employed. Functional "silos" that once epitomized the independence of corporate departments are acknowledging some of their interdependencies, and the limitations of their vertical structures are being recognized. Using a new configuration, activities are being reorganized and functions are joining together to meet customers' requirements.

In traditional organizations, companies grouped similar activities and tasks together according to function and essentially organized them to assist with the internal operations of the organization. Now, however, a systems perspective has emerged that takes a broad, holistic view: It sees how the company is linked with the market and its customers, and it sees the way value is linked throughout the entire system—how activities upstream are responsible for the quality of performance downstream.[1] What happens in one area of business affects the whole system; therefore, when all areas work together, the end result is better performance for the company. When manufacturing and marketing work hand in hand with R&D to fulfill the organization's strategic goals, the results can be truly rewarding.

KEY CONCEPT — CAPACITY IS KEY IN BOTH MANUFACTURING AND SERVICE INDUSTRIES

Capacity is a key determinant of productivity: It shows how well management matches all its resources—capital, materials, equipment, and people—in both the manufacturing and service industries.

The end result of operations is productivity: the yield of goods made or services provided in relation to the resources employed in producing them. In other words, how efficiently and cost effectively the organization utilizes its resources to produce products and services determines its level of productivity.

PRODUCTIVITY DOES NOT MEAN VOLUME

DANGER! Productivity does not mean simply producing a huge volume at low cost. Productivity at its best means performance. Large numbers of inferior products that don't meet customers' standards or requirements are not going to provide competitive advantage. In managing manufacturing operations, the goal is to produce and deliver a variety of quality goods in the most efficient, cost-effective way possible.

KEY CONCEPT — MATERIALS: TOO MUCH OR TOO LITTLE

The challenge for managers is to find the right balance of inventory, to determine how much should be on hand and available at any given time so that capacity is not influenced negatively. Being caught without enough materials or without the proper materials can impede production, bring it to a halt, or result in the manufacture of flawed goods. Having too much material, as demonstrated in the chapter on accounting, can also be an impediment to productivity—too much inventory, an asset that affects liquidity, can be costly and negatively impact cash flow. Three critical functions must be considered in handling materials: acquisition, storage, and logistics. (See Table 9.1.)

Theories about managing inventory are, like everything else in the business world, undergoing change. In the classical model, the cost generated by inventory was offset by the advantages it provided in solving sales and distribution problems. If finished goods sit on shelves, they are readily available to sell and can be quickly used in response to an increase in demand; thus, the case was made for making sure plenty of inventory was available. New theories, however, such as *just-in-time* (JIT) manufacturing (see Table 9.2) are based on radically reducing inventories. This theory balances the cost of inventory against the benefits derived from accumulating it.

CAPITAL AND CAPACITY

Capital impacts capacity. Every organization is limited by the amount of capital it will make available to invest in plant and technologies.

Some manufacturers limit capital investment as the best means of staying healthy—even when things look good. Clark Equipment Co., an Indiana manufacturer of heavy equipment, had earnings in 1994 that "grew 114

TABLE 9.1 FUNDAMENTALS OF MATERIALS

Acquisition

Development and maintenance of vendor relationships, and evaluation of the quality of goods and the process of procurement.

Storage

Determining the proper level of inventory; maintaining the minimum amount necessary without running short.

Logistics

Managing distribution from the supplier, within the organization, and to the customer. This requires knowledge of transportation methods and distribution channels.

Adapted from: Linda G. Sprague, "Operations Management: Productivity and Performance," The New Portable MBA, eds. Eliza G. C. Collins and Mary Anne Devanna (New York: John Wiley & Sons, 1994), p. 210.

TABLE 9.2 MANUFACTURING PROCESSES

Assembly Line

A product-dominated process. Both machine power and people power are arranged in a fixed, ordered sequence, which moves continually and uniformly. The labor is unskilled and the work is broken down into small, repeated tasks. The flow of production is smooth, logical, and efficient, but lacks flexibility. The capacity for an assembly line is determined by the bottleneck: the point at which the line is most likely to slow or break down.

Batch Flow

A compromise configuration in which a unique product is manufactured. But due to economical considerations, a *batch,* rather than just one of the items, is made. Batches have a tendency to result in higher levels of inventory because production is not based on real requirements. Batch flow is a compromise between a job shop and the assembly line.

Continuous Flow

The principle is the same as the assembly line, but the flow is truly continuous because the material is actually fluid and travels down a pipeline, not an assembly line. The bottleneck literally comes at the point where the pipe is the most narrow.

Flexible Manufacturing Systems (FMS)

Computer-controlled tools and material-handling systems are integrated and centrally monitored and scheduled. FMS works most efficiently when making a large variety of parts in small batches. Flexible manufacturing has appeal because product life cycles are declining and customers' preferences for customized products is increasing. This drives manufacturers to produce a greater variety in shorter time and increase the utilization of equipment.

Job Shop

A process-dominated configuration, with no standard, sequential flow pattern, in which expertise is grouped. Theoretically, the same product is never made twice; each product proceeds through the area its own way or in a "jumbled flow." Specialized equipment and highly skilled workers are located in the same space, enabling higher utilization of equipment and better control over work and training. Management, planning, and inventory control are more difficult, yet there is more flexibility.

Just in Time (JIT)

Parts go through each manufacturing step, depending on a daily demand-pull schedule. This process reduces inventories and cycle times, and can be applied across industries. It encourages skills in solving problems on the factory floor, incrementally improves processes, and speeds response time.

> ### TABLE 9.2 (Continued)
>
> #### Lean Production
>
> Lean production, as opposed to mass production, is based on the concept of continuous improvement, or *kaizen* as it is known in Japan, and a learn-by-doing approach. It is an integrative approach that stresses efficiency, teamwork, simplification, flexibility, reduction of waste, and speed in the production process. Production occurs in multiple, small lots instead of huge, high-volume runs. Workers are trained in a variety of skills, and jobs are rotated frequently. Lean production also emphasizes communication and feedback throughout the distribution chain.
>
> #### Manufacturing Cell
>
> A grouped job shop in which each cell makes a particular part, which travels through the cell in one direction. All the equipment needed to make the part is kept within the cell. With accurate analysis of the process, cell manufacturing reduces material handling and setup time; thus, it reduces cycle time as well as inventory levels. Cell workers must have varied skills to handle the different machines, but they also experience repetition of tasks. To maintain cell integrity over time requires continued analysis.

percent to $62.8 million, on sales of $947 million, up 37 percent." Yet, it outsourced production that could "be brought back in-house when the boom passes." It felt safer "to lose some sales at the peak in order to reduce the amplitude of the cycle."[2]

Weyerhaeuser Co. is another manufacturer cautious about adding capacity. Even though the paper industry is experiencing a boom (expected to last until 1997), the company "announced only one new paper-plant expansion in 1994." Instead, it is concentrating on "improving the yield plants get from each log, streamlining production to squeeze more out of current plants." CEO John W. Creighton's goal is to "improve operating income . . . to provide more cushion for the next downturn."[3]

Other companies take riskier routes. Ford, determined to move out of its number two position and overtake General Motors, "will spend upwards of $20 billion on increased capacity and new models by the decade's end."[4]

TiP USE CAUTION INVESTING IN CAPACITY

As a general rule, companies have discovered that it's wiser to be cautious about adding capacity: It may be better to lose sales during present good times than to invest in capacity that's not needed in the future. Both machines and people are difficult to dispose of once they have been incorporated into the organization. Cash not spent on capital outlays provides a cushion of protection for the organization. However, wise investments in smart technology can lead to cost savings over time through more efficient manufacturing. The bottom line: Plan carefully and invest wisely.

TECHNOLOGY: MAN AND MACHINE

In manufacturing, "technology" includes both man and machine. Equipment that can't be operated is of no use. Likewise, people without proper equipment won't be as productive as they could, and full capacity will never be reached. Therefore, an important element in the productivity equation, and the challenge for managers, is to provide workers with the training to develop skills and to match those skills with the necessary machinery and equipment. This means managers must determine how much capital to invest in people power and how much to invest in machine power in order to reach the desired level of capacity throughout the production process.

Capital outlays have often supported investment in machine power rather than people power, especially as processes have been reengineered. Investment in high-tech, highly efficient machines generally means fewer workers are needed for a given level of output. However, the people who do work in the production process are being called on to develop new, sophisticated skills. The point emphasized here is that determining the proper balance between man and machine is crucial; when that balance and high levels of productivity are reached, profits will increase and the company will become healthier.

TOTAL QUALITY MANAGEMENT (TQM)

TQM focuses on the customer and emphasizes teamwork and participatory management as a means of motivating employees and stimulating innovation and improvement. By constantly examining and upgrading systems and processes, companies can incrementally and constantly improve over time.

Based on the concept of continuous improvement, TQM is a proactive approach to manufacturing, used in some way by almost all manufacturers. It has its origins in quality control circles (QCCs) used in Japanese manufacturing. QCCs were originally used as morale boosters, emphasizing employee involvement. In the early '60s, Matsushita started using the technique for managing production. TQM, which incorporates some of Frederick Taylor's theories of scientific management, has been used to counteract low productivity, poor products, bureaucratic paralysis, and problems with employees. Workers are trained in the use of statistical quality control measurements and in ways to analyze production and distribution to improve both efficiency and quality.[5] In the United States, the much-sought Malcolm Baldrige National Quality Award is based on principles of TQM. The quality cycle—Plan-Do-Check-Act—continuously sets higher goals and is a fundamental component in many TQM programs.[6]

KEY CONCEPT: THE FLEXIBILITY OF AGILE MANUFACTURING

It has already been said that flexible companies gain competitive advantage in turbulent and highly competitive environments. That need to be flexible also applies to manufacturing. Operations management must be able to switch gears and adjust manufacturing processes to market demands—to ramp production up or down, to provide a wider variety of products, or to service customers more quickly. Essentially, flexibility means management must configure its production system to reflect its strategic choices in competitive situations. It might choose one type of configuration at one point and another at a different point.

However, making a factory flexible is easier said than done. And measuring improvements in flexibility can be just as tricky. David Upton, an associate professor at Harvard Business School, studied the flexibility of 61 North American manufacturers and came up with some enlightening discoveries:

- The correlation between the degree of computer integration and flexibility is slight.
- Small plants are not necessarily more flexible than large plants.
- Newer, bigger processes were typically better able to perform quick changeovers than older, smaller machines.
- Experienced workers can impede a plant's ability to be flexible.
- Goods produced don't necessarily reflect flexibility, but potential products do; if a factory has the capability of efficiently making something it hasn't made before, it has a degree of flexibility.
- One or two specific features won't make a factory flexible—it's the designed alignment of features to provide a particular type of flexibility that's important.[7]

Interestingly, Upton's most significant finding is that flexibility depends more on people than on machines. "Operational flexibility is determined primarily by a plant's operators and the extent to which managers cultivate, measure, and communicate with them. Equipment and computer integration are secondary."[8]

In order for managers to be successful in transforming their plants into flexible factories, managers need to

TABLE 9.3 CHANGES IN MANUFACTURING

Manufacturing is calling for a new way of managing operations. Although variations depend on the particular industry and business strategy, there are some generalities that can be made:

- Workers should be skilled and trained in multiple tasks.
- Inventory is held to a minimum.
- Time is of the essence.
- Products are varied and customized.
- Product development is handled by multifunctional teams.
- Manufacturing plants are smaller, but smarter.
- Equipment is organized in cells.
- Knowledge counts. So do relationships.
- Customers and suppliers link more closely with manufacturing.
- Communication is significant.
- Information networks are expanding.
- Service—customer satisfaction—is being sold, not goods.
- Value and service determine price.

determine the form of flexibility desired (for example, the ability to produce varied products or the ability to shift rapidly from one production mode to another), the type of equipment and the kind of skills people need to operate the equipment, and the training they will require.[9]

NOTHING'S EASY

New methods are never easy. Table 9.3 lists the major changes taking place in manufacturing. Each requires adjustment. And when ideas are imported from one culture to another there are always additional problems. JIT might work well in Japan but have greater problems in the United States due to differences in the macroenvironment. Product variety and shortened cycle times put additional stress on the organization's capital and physical equipment and place greater demands on suppliers. Flexibility also puts workers under stress, as they must learn new skills and become more adaptable to a constantly changing work environment.

THE ESSENCE OF TIME

Another key standard of performance is cycle time—how long it takes from the time a company receives an order from a customer to the time the product is delivered. In manufacturing, the faster the goods are produced, the more efficient the manufacturing process. Timing involves scheduling: determining the order in which activities should be carried out, and the time it will take to carry them out. Scheduling also includes coordinating activities with resources, making sure that necessary materials and equipment are available when needed. (See Table 9.4.)

Process maps and *flow charts* are used to track progress and pinpoint bottlenecks or areas where flow can be improved. These tools examine how operations are carried out, the sequence of actions, and which sequences provide more value than others. When processes are analyzed for efficiency, as in reengineering, the question "Why?" is continually asked. Additionally, in the evaluation process, rather than concentrating on the effects, managers need to search out and discover the root cause of problems, to work with facts, not opinion, and to have the freedom to raise all kinds of questions.[10]

LEVERAGE MANUFACTURING

To fully leverage manufacturing, don't think of JIT, TQM, and FMS as ends, but consider how they will be the means to develop new skills and new capabilities

---

TABLE 9.4 SCHEDULING METHODS

Aggregate Scheduling

Created in conjunction with the capacity plan, it establishes the overall long-term capability of the organization.

Master Scheduling

Combines real orders with forecasts to assign work over specific, shorter time periods.

Dispatching

Matches supply and demand at the point services or products are provided or manufactured.

Queue Managing

Work-in-process inventory control that attempts to minimize the amount of time in a queue or line.

Material Requirements Planning (MRP)

(Also known as Manufacturing Resources Planning.) Most widely used computerized production-scheduling tool that is based on forecasts of future demand, production lead times, and real-time data from the shop floor. It combines product data with parts available and lead times needed. MRP facilitates scheduling by helping to determine when parts should be ordered and when manufacture of parts should begin.

Adapted from: Linda G. Sprague, "Operations Management: Productivity and Performance," The New Portable MBA, eds. Eliza G. C. Collins and Mary Anne Devanna (New York: John Wiley & Sons, 1994), pp. 222–223.

that will provide competitive advantage in the future.[11] Using each technique independently provides the company with a particular type of advantage. Decide which will offer the company the most valuable capabilities. Some studies have shown that when all three are strategically combined, utilization rates increase by 26 percent and workspace decreases by 34 percent.[12] At the same time, these techniques aren't right for every manufacturer. The main rule to remember is to use what works best within the context of the environment.

DEVELOP A MANUFACTURING STRATEGY

Manufacturing adds value by enabling companies to make better products than competitors. Get beyond thinking of choices among cost, quality, and flexibility that just provide short-term solutions. Long-term success will come from constantly looking for ways to differentiate from competitors. Apply improvement programs to longer-range goals and develop operating capabilities that will provide competitive advantage. Robert H. Hayes and Gary P. Pisano, two Harvard Business School professors, offer two basic steps to manufacturing competitiveness:

1. Target one or two manufacturing areas in which to excel that add value to the organization. These must be areas the customer considers valuable and they must be hard for competitors to duplicate.

2. Develop a plan for identifying valuable capabilities. Bring in and train workers in skills needed to develop targeted capabilities.[13]

LOCATION IS STRATEGICALLY IMPORTANT

Although new manufacturing trends tend to reduce the number of workers employed (implying lower labor costs), these new methods require a highly skilled workforce, which means workers must be trained and educated. Generally, "engineers outnumber production workers three to one" in these systems.[14] Additionally, even production workers must have multiple skills to handle a variety of complex machines and equipment. Hard mathematical skills are needed as well as softer interpersonal communication skills.

This demand for an educated workforce implies the need for manufacturing facilities to be located in areas populated by skilled workers. In addition to finding areas with easy access to the right kind of employees, other crucial factors should also be considered. Table 9.5 provides additional guidelines for managers in determining manufacturing locations.

TABLE 9.5 DETERMINING MANUFACTURING LOCATIONS

Assess Global Locations

- Examine how firm competes
- Forecast evolution of global market
- Review internal constraints on resources
- Synthesize impact of these factors on manufacturing strategy

Assess Regional Locations

- Political and market access requirements
- Degree of risk
- Regional demand
- Production parameters

Assess Potential Sites

- Hard and soft production activities for each location
- Size of facility, production flow
- Supplier and distribution activities

Adapted from: A. D. MacCormack, L. J. Newman III, and D. B. Rosenfield, "The New Dynamics of Global Manufacturing Site Location," Sloan Management Review (Summer 1994, vol. 35, no. 4), pp. 69–80.

KEY CONCEPT — USA: A MANUFACTURING RENAISSANCE

The United States has an outstanding infrastructure as well as excellent academic resources, and manufacturers are beginning to recognize and appreciate these benefits. JIT manufacturing requires more interaction and dependence on suppliers; therefore, sophisticated infrastructures, especially in transportation and communications, are essential.

The trend toward decentralizing manufacturing and locating smaller plants in regional markets with sophisticated infrastructures is growing, and the United States is a prime location. The huge mass production plants that helped companies achieve large economies of scale are shrinking, and new, smaller manufacturing operations are germinating, particularly in American soil. Sony is manufacturing in Pennsylvania because "the US is the world's largest TV market . . . and the closer Sony gets to its customers, the less it has to spend on shipping." Sony also drew on local resources: "nearby Carnegie Mellon University helped Sony engineers build a robot that automatically fine-tunes the televisions before shipping."[15] Other Japanese companies, like Honda, Nissan, and Toyota, manufacture in the United States for similar reasons.

Agile or flexible manufacturing seems to be drawing some manufacturing operations back onto industrialized shores because of the advantages it provides. Some companies are finding that the savings in labor costs from offshore manufacturing no longer outweigh the savings in distribution costs from manufacturing closer to customers and the advantages derived from close collaboration on customized products.

In fact, contrary to doomsday forecasts about manufacturing, since 1993, "manufacturing productivity has soared 4.9 percent annually."[16] In a September 1995 letter to the editor of *Business Week*, Jerry J. Jasinowski, president of the National Association of Manufacturers, wrote, "Manufacturing productivity grew by an average of 2.4 percent from 1985 to 1993, six times the productivity growth elsewhere in the economy. Meanwhile, prices of manufactured goods have risen an average of only 2.4 percent a year since 1981, half the rate of services. And in the past five years, exports of U.S. manufactured goods grew at an average annual rate of more than 10 percent."[17]

KEY CONCEPT — USE DEVELOPMENT PROJECTS AS CHANGE AGENTS

Manufacturing can be a strategic force when development projects are used to build capabilities. Even when development projects don't meet their objectives, they can pave the way for new products and new expertise.

In the 1980s, Digital Equipment Corporation's RA90 high-density disk drive project did not reach the high goals that management had set for it: By the time it reached the market in 1988, it was two years late, the cost had doubled, and the industry had quickly moved to smaller drives. But through knowledge acquired in striving for breakthrough innovations, such as the development of an electromechanical drive system and a thin-film head, the project improved DEC's competitive position, providing it with new capabilities and the expertise it needed "to become a leader in disk drives."[18]

Hitachi-Seiki, a leading supplier of flexible manufacturing systems, failed in its early efforts to create computerized equipment for sequencing machining tasks. Yet, each major project the company tackled since 1972 provided it with rich learning about the capabilities and skills it needed to attain its goals—it needed engineers with the skills to write software, and it learned to take a systems approach to problem solving, combining functional perspectives and skills.[19]

Because development project teams are microcosms of an organization, they can help the organization to learn. Projects work under time and budget constraints that can highlight the strengths and weaknesses of the organization's culture, structure, and systems. Development projects are tools that can be used to develop knowledge and skills and to attain and maintain market positions.[20]

Multifunctional teams help in the development of new products. At IBM, new products are now being created "by teams from research, design, procurement, logistics, and manufacturing—all working side by side." The new strategy is working: "The Butterfly subnotebook moved from a lab project to a finished product in 18 months—a record for IBM."[21]

KEY CONCEPT — PROTOTYPING TECHNOLOGIES

Prototypes are powerful tools that monitor and guide projects. (See Table 9.6.) They offer structure and discipline, provide a mechanism for improving products, and present a means for learning, which can be passed on to others inside and outside the organization. When prototypes are used early in a development project, they can provide invaluable support because critical decisions affecting most of the cost of products are made during the initial stages of the development project.[22]

When manufacturing products, companies must also manufacture the machines and parts needed to make the end product. For instance, "for every part that goes into a car, Ford figures it must design and build 1,200 others." Prototypes help guide manufacturing processes, but building them can be time consuming and costly. New technologies, such as CAD processes and rapid prototyping machines, enable prototypes to be made at "warp speed." "Ford has become a world leader in the field of rapid prototyping," which can "mean time savings of 60 percent to 90 percent," and "cost savings—generally between 50 percent and 70 percent per part."[23]

KEY CONCEPT — MANUFACTURING AND MARKETING: A NEW MIX

Modern marketing defines, develops, and delivers value to customers. In the globally networked company of the twenty-first century, marketing's function is to keep the entire organization as well as its partners and alliances "informed about the target customer's ever-changing definition of value."[24] Marketing can provide the vital link that connects manufacturing, R&D, and sales with valuable information on the customer.

Profitability in this new approach to marketing, not sales volume, is the focus. The only way to ensure long-term profitability is to provide the customer with superior value. "The customer's willingness to pay is the ultimate test of the value that has been created."[25] "Marketing's new role is to translate the overarching business strategy ('What business are we in?') into process performance that will ensure the highest possible sales to the most valuable customers."[26]

Viewing the organization from a holistic perspective, marketing and manufacturing are strategically con-

TABLE 9.6 PROTOTYPES AS TOOLS

Prototypes

- Provide a common language
- Offer a focal point for understanding
- Speed the launch of products
- Result in higher-quality products
- Help fulfill a product's intended purpose

Prototypes consist of

- A series of representations
- Early mock-ups
- Computer simulations
- Subsystem models
- System-level engineering models
- Production process models

Test prototypes to ensure they

- Get closer to the desired product
- Are available to everyone
- Satisfy customer expectations
- Can be manufactured with available capabilities

Prototypes fail when they

- Are not built early enough
- Don't focus on the entire system
- Don't test the right process
- Are not tested widely in the field

Reprinted by permission of Harvard Business Review. An exhibit from "How to Integrate Work and Deepen Expertise" by Dorothy Leonard-Barton, et al. (September/October 1994). Copyright © 1994 by the President and Fellows of Harvard College, all rights reserved.

nected. Market research plays a role in forecasting. It helps to set the direction for the development of products and define the business by identifying market demands, trends, and customers' preferences. "Good products develop from a close-up, day-to-day understanding of customer needs and dissatisfactions."[27] In fact, market-oriented planning is now being used by many companies in the process of drawing up their financial and strategic plans—it helps the company understand the customers' perceptions of value and assists in defining the products that manufacturing will produce. Its concepts and information are being used as the basis of decision making as managers seek to incorporate the customers' perspectives into everything that is done. Marketing also plays a vital role in distributing products to customers, targeting the best channels to use.

DESKJET PRINTER: RESULT OF MINGLING M&M AND R&D

At Hewlett-Packard, the DeskJet project was created to "to get the company to start looking to other functions besides design engineering for creative solutions." The DeskJet, a low-cost, inkjet printer with the high-quality resolution of a laser printer, was successful because marketing, manufacturing, and R&D worked in support of each other as they sought project goals.[28]

HP's printer division faced declining market share as it was squeezed between costly, high-quality laser printers on one end and low-priced dot-matrix printers at the other. In order to avoid being squashed, it designed and built new capabilities that enabled it to produce a unique, competitive product as well as establish a new market position for itself. It established a new segment in the printer market, increased market share, and laid the foundation for a new family of profitable products for HP.[29]

Manufacturing, marketing, and R&D communicated with one another about customers' requirements, adopting nontraditional practices—*engineers went to the malls to listen to customers' desires.* Moreover, manufacturing's early involvement pushed the building of crucial prototypes and kept the project moving on target at a fast pace. All three functions colocated to the same spot. Working together facilitated communication and the integration of work. With true alignment between the functions, the DeskJet team was guided by a common understanding of the project's goals and was able to make daily decisions from the perspective of the project as a whole.[30]

CULTURAL BARRIERS CAN IMPEDE MINGLING

Strategic plans that include dramatic change, such as mingling manufacturing, marketing, and R&D, can hit blockades that will alter or impede the plans. The major barriers are: turf—the change may threaten a manager's role, identity, or power base and will be resisted; and communication—disparate functions might think and interpret information differently.

CREATE SHARED UNDERSTANDING AND SPACE

Shared language and understanding have to be supported and developed. One way is through developing good communication skills, which are essential to crossing functional boundaries. Another is to provide a common work area where people can have easy access to each other. Even with high-tech networks, when projects are being developed and large physical separations exist, communication is restricted. Sharing space supports collaboration. Additionally, the workspace should be within easy access of other resources that might be needed.[31]

R&D: COLLABORATION PAYS OFF

Tighter budgets generally mean tighter cost controls on R&D. But recently, smart companies—even when they are fierce competitors—have been compensating for lack of funds by collaborating with each other on "*precompetitive*" R&D. Collaboration not only spreads costs across companies, but it spreads risk and generates ideas while avoiding a duplication of efforts.

Companies are crossing borders to join in the game: "IBM, Siemens and Toshiba . . . are teaming up to develop the 256-megabit memory chips," and Hewlett-Packard and Canon are working together on laser printers even though they are archenemies when it comes to ink-jet printers. And companies are collaborating within borders. IBM, Motorola, and Apple Computer developed the PowerPC chip, which rivals Intel's microprocessor; so "Intel struck back, announcing a venture with Hewlett-Packard." Even "GM, Ford Motor, and Chrysler have formed 12 consortiums on such topics as electric-vehicle batteries, parts recycling, and better crash dummies."[32]

Big companies are linking with small, and business units within large corporations are blending their R&D talents. When innovative 3M Corp was developing its Never Rust soap pad, it "brought together experts from its adhesives, abrasives, coating, and nonwoven technologies.[33]

CULTURE CAN CAUSE COLLABORATION PROBLEMS

Managing cross-company—especially cross-national—R&D projects can be difficult. Miscommunication and turf battles can create major problems. In addition to good communication skills, commitment by all the parties is a key to success.

UNDERSTAND MARKETING TOOLS

As marketing becomes more integrally related with other functions, it's important for managers to have an understanding of the basic tools and concepts. See Tables 9.7 and 9.8.

MARKET SHARE VERSUS CUSTOMER SHARE

New marketing theories are stressing *share of customer* as opposed to share of market. With the share-

TABLE 9.7 BASIC MARKETING MIX TOOLS: FOUR P'S

Product

Goods or services offered for sale to the customer that help the organization to achieve its goals. Issues include product features, quality, and reliability. Activities include development of the product, such as planning and R&D, and activities afterwards, such as installation, service, and maintenance. Emphasis is now on customer service and satisfaction throughout the exchange process.

Price

How much the product costs—the money exchanged for the product. Issues surround determination of how much to charge. Customer must perceive the benefits of the product to be greater than the price in order to purchase the product. Companies either lower prices or increase value, or perception of value, to entice customers to buy.

Place

Distribution—getting the product where customers can purchase it. Issues include inventory, transportation, and location. Current emphasis is on being close to customers in order to meet customers' needs more efficiently. Place should be convenient to the customer. Information technology, however, is affecting "place" as more products are being marketed in "space."

Promotion

Communication—includes advertising, sales promotion, sales, and public relations.

of-customer approach, *one-to-one* marketing is used. Its goal is to develop a greater understanding of the individual customer, using interactive communication in order to get a greater share of business from the company's most valuable customers.

Market share, on the other hand, is the percentage of money customers spend on a company's product compared to the total amount spent on all products in the same category. Marketing plans generally contain goals to achieve a particular amount of market

TABLE 9.8 BASIC MARKETING STRATEGY

- Define the segments and the requirements of the target audience.
- Define the values and benefits, and position the product.
- Determine the right price for the product.
- Determine how the product will be delivered to the market.
- Create a communication strategy that raises targeted consumers' awareness and persuades consumers to buy the product.

share using marketing tools like promotion and discounting.

In the early 1970s, the Boston Consulting Group devised a matrix to help determine how successfully products from specific strategic business units (SBUs) are positioned in terms of growth and market share. The matrix was designed to give managers a quick and clear way of seeing the mix of the company's portfolio of products, and to help in devising marketing strategies to support that mix. Table 9.9 demonstrates the matrix approach to understanding market share and growth, and Table 9.10 describes strategies to use with the Boston Consulting Group's matrix model.

TECNOL: SMALL COMPANY WINS MARKET SHARE

Star

Texas-based Tecnol Medical Products Inc. unexpectedly found itself competing for market share with giants like Johnson & Johnson and 3M. And even more surprising, it found a way to win. In 1984, Tecnol started making medical face masks, which "sold as low-priced commodities." Looking for a niche market, the company seized the opportunity presented by the AIDS epidemic and started making "specialty masks that shield health-care workers from infection." In the process, it became "the top mask supplier to U.S. hospitals . . . with 60 percent of the $71 million U.S. hospital market. Tecnol dwarfs 3M's 21 percent share and Johnson & Johnson's 10 percent."[34]

TABLE 9.9 BOSTON CONSULTING GROUP MARKET SHARE MATRIX

	High Market Share	Low Market Share
High Market Growth	**Star:** High-share, high-growth businesses or products that generally need a lot of investment to secure their rapid growth.	**Question Marks:** Low share in high-growth markets that require investment just to hold their market position. The question is whether to put more cash into them to improve share, to phase them out, or to leave them alone.
Low Market Growth	**Cash Cow:** High-share, low-growth businesses or products, usually well established, that do not need a lot of investment to maintain their market share.	**Dog:** Low share in low-growth market. They may have enough cash to support themselves, but they are in a position that is below the average.

TABLE 9.10 FOUR STRATEGIES

Four basic strategies for exploiting the strengths of the portfolio can be applied to make the organization as healthy as possible.

Build

Help question marks grow into stars. Invest in order to improve quality. Spend on promotional campaigns to increase consumer interest, or cut prices to attract more sales.

Hold

Do what is necessary to maintain customer loyalty and to protect cash cows and stars that have good market positions.

Harvest

Reap as much profit as possible from cash cows, dogs, or question marks when they are weak, before divesting of them. Reduce R&D, promotion, customer service, and any excess spending on these products, "milking" them of their potential to generate cash.

Divest

When dogs and question marks are dying, don't use extraordinary means to save them—drop them in order to use cash that supported them to support more profitable products.

Source: *Alexander Hiam and Charles D. Schewe,* The Portable MBA in Marketing *(New York: John Wiley & Sons, 1992), p. 33.*

By creating a niche for itself, Tecnol has been able to fight the big guys. Learn from Tecnol and gain market share by:

- Choosing the right market and anticipating rapid changes
- Incrementally modifying a standard product
- Designing a variety of models
- Continually innovating
- Investing in R&D
- Developing manufacturing expertise
- Expanding products and alliances

KEY CONCEPT

SEGMENTED MARKETING AND DIFFERENTIATED PRODUCTS

Market segmentation is the process of analyzing and identifying groups of customers. The market is divided so that customers can be specifically targeted with products that appeal to their tastes and preferences.

Segmented marketing contrasts with mass marketing, which appeals to large groups of consumers and is primarily used to sell standardized goods—for example, orange juice, gasoline, sugar. Mass marketing uses mass media, such as TV and billboards, and works well when a large group of people generally have the same basic wants and needs. However, using mass media can be expensive, and competitors can devise marketing strategies that have greater appeal.

The manipulation of information in vast computer databases has made segmented marketing possible. More and more detailed information provides marketers with thinner and thinner slices and more complex mixes of variables on consumers. Identified segments can be targeted for particular products and marketing strategies can be specifically designed to appeal to each segment. For instance, a discount clothing store specializing in women's business attire can identify the age, income, and employment status of women in its geographic region and develop a marketing strategy to appeal to those women. (See Table 9.11.)

Segmentation considers how particular buyers respond to product offerings and marketing communications. Some buyers may be price sensitive and purchase only products with the lowest prices. Others may be service sensitive and deal only with companies that offer easy, speedy service and high levels of help.[35] (See Table 9.12.)

TABLE 9.11 SIX STEPS TO SEGMENTATION

1.

Determine market boundaries in accord with business strategy.

2.

Determine which segmentation variables will be most useful.

3.

Collect and analyze segmentation data, identifying customers with the same wants and needs.

4.

Draw a profile of each segment with variable information to form a picture of buying behavior.

5.

Target the segments by looking for the best opportunities that come from matching the company's resources with those opportunities.

6.

Design a marketing plan that best highlights the product features and creates the image that will appeal to the targeted segment. Determine the best method for reaching that group.

Source: *Alexander Hiam and Charles D. Schewe, The Portable MBA in Marketing (New York: John Wiley & Sons, 1992), pp. 217–219.*

TABLE 9.12 SEGMENTATION VARIABLES

Demographics

Age, gender, race, ethnicity, marital status, family size, family configuration, education, occupation, income

Geographics

National, regional, local, urban, suburban, rural, climate, population

Psychographics

Values, beliefs, attitudes, opinions. Can be segmented by religion, culture, socioeconomic status, political preferences, occupation, interests, hobbies, and any affiliations that provide insight into tastes and preferences.

Behaviors

Brand loyalty, usage rate, perceived benefits, application, buyer readiness

Additionally, using segmentation, companies can differentiate a line of products. For example, a company manufacturing beer can segment the market to determine who likes ale, who likes beer, and who prefers light beers. Using this information, it can formulate strategies to reach each group. The full line supports the company, while the differentiated products appeal to special segments of the population, enhancing the company's ability to be profitable. Segmented marketing tends to be more costly due to the diverse marketing campaigns utilized for each segment, but segmenting the market and differentiating products also tends to increase total sales. (See Table 9.13.)

TABLE 9.13 WAYS TO DIFFERENTIATE

Product	Segments
Technical breakthroughs	Underserved markets
New ingredients	Global markets
New functions	New segments
Better physical attributes	

Price	Distribution
Better value	New channels
Higher volume inducements	In-store services
Deeper discounts or special deals	Company-owned outlets

Adapted from: *Robert T. Davis, "Marketing Management: Becoming a Market-Driven Company," in* The Portable MBA, *eds. Eliza G. C. Collins and Mary Anne Devanna (New York: John Wiley & Sons, 1990), p. 184.*

KEY CONCEPT · DEVELOP VALUE THROUGH ONE-TO-ONE MARKETING

The trend in marketing has been toward more and more segmentation and has moved from mass marketing to segmentation to customized, one-to-one marketing. Using information technology, marketers can track the individual buying patterns of millions of potential customers, one by one.

One-to-one marketing gives companies the opportunity to develop relationships with selected customers who will provide the company with the most profit. By individually addressing those customers and using interactive methods for communicating with them (for example, the Internet and interactive TV), companies can build loyalty and long-term relationships. By *dialoguing* with the customer, either electronically or personally, the company finds out what the customer wants and needs.

Levi Strauss exemplifies a company using IT to market customized products. It now offers customized jeans that are precisely tailored to the unique dimensions of each customer. Customers try on sample jeans and then sales clerks feed measurements into a CAD program on the computer. The system sends the measurements directly to the factory where fabric is cut and jeans sewn. This personalized service adds only $10 to the bill. Rather than remaining a mass-produced piece of clothing, the custom-fit jeans turns into a *dialogue* with the customer, an *interactive experience,* and Levi Strauss gathers highly specific information on the customer that can be used in the future.[36]

One-to-one marketing (also known as *relationship marketing*) differs dramatically from mass marketing, which measures success through market share and which is often short-term. The measure of success with one-to-one marketing is the quality and duration of the relationship with the customer. "The new marketer will gauge success by the projected increase or decrease in a customer's expected future value to the company." Additionally, marketing that relies on relationships with loyal customers tends to have lower costs and is "less vulnerable to the ups and downs of economic cycles."[37]

TIP · START AT THE VERY BEGINNING— WITH THE CUSTOMER

Marketers are bringing consumers and their ideas into the development process. By going directly into the marketplace and discovering what consumers want in a product, a new, truly interdependent relationship is developed with the customer.

Philips NV, a Netherlands-based electronics company, developed a new on-line children's product by sending designers, psychologists, and sociologists to brainstorm with children and parents in several European countries. Philips was looking for ideas for an interactive product. With feedback from this first wave of research, the company developed a product and then retested it on the same group before putting it into production. Using this marketing/design methodology, the company was able to create and refine product features, giving the product greater appeal and potential in the marketplace.[38]

Working with consumers from the very beginning raises interest and awareness of the consumers involved. Bringing them into the development process early helps to establish a base of potential clients and starts to build a sense of loyalty even before the product hits the market—because customers helped design the product, they are more naturally interested in it.[39]

 ## POSITION TO SHAPE PERCEPTION

Use positioning to shape the perceptions of customers—to have them perceive the product in a particular way. For example, if a company identifies customers who are sensitive to price, the company can position itself as offering quality at the lowest possible prices, such as Hewlett-Packard did with the DeskJet. It offered customers a printer with the high-quality resolution of a laser, but the low cost of an inkjet.

Apple provides another example. It was positioned as having the most user-friendly computers on the market, but this position is now being threatened by what Microsoft purports to be the friendliness of Windows 95. Because of the proliferation of Microsoft, it will be interesting to watch how Apple responds and whether it alters its marketing strategy to enhance other dimensions of its product line to reposition itself.

Table 9.14 outlines steps to take to find the best market position.

 ## BUNDLING PRODUCTS CAN HELP MARKETERS

When devising marketing strategies, companies sometimes bundle products to take advantage of the demand for one product to increase sales of another, or to increase sales of both. For instance, most computer companies often bundle software and peripherals in with the sales of PCs.

SERVICE REQUIRES MORE THAN A SMILE

For customers sensitive to service—such as strategic alliances and partners—the company must provide the level of service required to maintain a good relationship. Marketers should identify issues significant to the

Stellar Performer: Ross Controls
Virtual Manufacturer

Ross Controls, a privately owned, medium-sized manufacturer of pneumatic valves and air-control systems, provides an excellent example of a company that has been enormously successful establishing learning relationships with its customers. Founded in 1921, the company was a leader in its industry until the late 1960s when competition from abroad began to cut into its profit margins. By the '80s, it was facing grave financial and managerial challenges. It couldn't compete on a price basis with competitors who were manufacturing offshore, so it began to look for new ways to gain competitive advantage.

Led by then-COO, Henry Duignan, it adopted a model of operating that stemmed from the tradition of the village, whereby the best craftspeople produced goods that met the particular needs of the villagers. The blacksmith "mass-produced" horseshoes and then altered them to custom-fit each villager's individual horse. The baker prepared dough for dozens of loaves of bread, but set aside some of the dough to make special loaves which called for additional ingredients to meet the requests of specific customers. Ross Controls decided it could do the same. Using automation, it could mass-produce pneumatic valves and then work with customers to custom-design valves, altering them to meet customers' specific needs. Thus, it could develop special relationships and interact personally with customers, building trust and loyalty that would help it compete on a level other than price.

This mass-customized approach, known as *Ross/Flex Service*, accounts for 20 percent of sales and has grown 1000 percent per year since it was first initiated in the early '90s. The other 80 percent of sales comes from standardized catalog products. Yet as sales for customized products grow, so do sales for standard products: For every dollar of custom products sold, Ross Controls now sells $1.50 of standard products—customers realize it's easier to buy standard valves from a company that's providing them with personalized work.

Ross works hand-in-hand with customers throughout the manufacturing process, visiting customers' plants to see how they use pneumatic systems, continually seeking product feedback and upgrading and refining design elements. The company has established a library of design components, which it constantly adds to as new designs are created. Through the use of computer technology and its store of design components, it can create tooling instructions, producing revised designs in less than 24 hours, and can deliver a prototype in 72 hours. Working closely with customers enables Ross to keep on top of changes, essentially enabling it to manufacture at the point of sale. Design, manufacturing,

(Continued)

(Continued)

and delivery have become one process, and the average delivery order time has been cut from as much as 16 weeks down to 24 hours. High-tech robotic and computer numerically controlled machines (CNN) provide 24-hour-a-day production capability: About 98 percent of Ross' orders now meet customer delivery schedules.

As it builds learning relationships, Ross Controls uses its own growing database of knowledge as well as the knowledge of its customers. This has required a cultural shift, as the manufacturer is no longer selling a product but rather a process in which the customer is a major participant. This new relationship also requires higher levels of trust between the company and the customers. With subjective manufacturing, cost is uncoupled from the seller and the competition: Profit margins stem from the relationship developed between seller and buyer. The future success of both becomes linked.

In making the changes that are required to shift to this new type of manufacturing, Ross Controls recognized the need to educate its workers and to assuage their fears about losing their jobs. Plant workers involved in making standardized products were especially threatened by the success of the customized work. Ross Controls guaranteed them that no one would lose jobs due to technological advances—workers would be retrained in operating the new technology and working with the new robotics required for this type of manufacturing.

Ross Controls adopted a team approach for its customized products. Customers interact with a team of "integrators" who are responsible for working with them through the entire process—from determining initial needs to reviewing the product for upgrades to designing refinements using computer-aided design. Teams receive intensive one-year training so they can handle all aspects of this process.

The end result of all this training, trust, and teamwork is a "virtual product"—a product that doesn't really exist until the customer needs it. It's a far better product because it's created to meet the precise specifications of the customer who helps design it. Once a customer pays for the initial design and prototype, modifications are made without charge, and the product is constantly refined and modified as needs change. The product becomes the customer's, and Ross becomes the manufacturing arm—the "virtual company"—costing the customer far less in the long run. Ross Controls' end goal is to have customers eventually design their own valves using technology available through Ross.

Ross Controls' loyal customers give it a large percentage of their business. By thinking smart, educating workers, using sophisticated technology, and learning from its customers, Ross Controls shows that smaller companies can compete in a global market if they put their knowledge to work.

Sources: *Interview with Ronald J. Heilner, Director of Communications; corporate material.*

customer, establish ways to measure service, and define the rewards that will be received when goals are reached.[40]

PRODUCT LIFE CYCLE

Like people, products go through developmental stages in the course of their lives: They are created or introduced into the world, go through a process of growth and maturity, and then decline before they die. In the introductory stage, growth is slow and profits are minimal. If the product is accepted, it grows and expands with the success of the marketing strategies used. In maturity, growth and profits level off until the product begins to decline. Decreasing sales and profits will eventually cause the product to be pulled from the market.

As products grow and mature, customers tend to become more knowledgeable, and the level of service the marketer provides needs to shift with the changes in the customers' attitudes and behaviors.

Different pricing strategies are used at the various levels in a product's life cycle. Figure 9.1 shows how price strategies change as products mature.

TABLE 9.14 SEVEN STEPS TO THE BEST MARKET POSITION

1.
Determine which markets the product serves—a product can meet the needs of more than one market.

2.
Identify primary and secondary competitors.

3.
Determine how consumers make choices to meet their own needs.

4.
Learn how competitors are perceived.

5.
Identify gaps in market positions—spots not occupied by competitors.

6.
Select position desired and design promotional plan and strategy that will carry intended message to consumers.

7.
Continually monitor and adjust position as necessary.

Source: Alexander Hiam and Charles D. Schewe, The Portable MBA in Marketing (New York: John Wiley & Sons, 1992), pp. 226–227.

PRICE: HOW MUCH TO CHARGE?

The product has been born. It's ready to be introduced. The market is ripe. How much should it cost? Price depends on the demand in the market, the competition, and the cost it takes to make the product. The lowest price that can be set is known as the *floor*, and the highest price the *ceiling*.

The floor is determined by how much it costs to produce and market the product. In order to make a profit, the price of a product must be set high enough to cover the expense of making it, including the fixed and the variable costs. The ceiling is determined by the demand for the product. Finding the optimum price between the floor and the ceiling depends on a number of factors. Detailed pricing strategies are beyond the scope of this chapter, but finding a balance between the two forces can be critical for long-term success. The most common formulas that managers turn to for assistance in pricing are outlined as follows.

The *unit cost of a product* is determined by dividing the total number of units to be produced by the total cost. For example, if fixed and variable costs total $100,000 and the company produces 50,000 product units, the cost of one unit is $2.

$$\text{Unit cost} = \frac{\text{fixed costs} + \text{variable costs}}{\text{number of units}}$$

With *cost-plus pricing,* a markup is added to unit cost, providing the company with a particular profit or rate of return on sales. To find the cost-plus price, the cost is divided by 1 minus the desired rate of return on sales. If a company wants to make 20 percent return on a product that costs $2, the cost-plus price is $2.50. ($2/(1 – 0.20) = $2.50).[41]

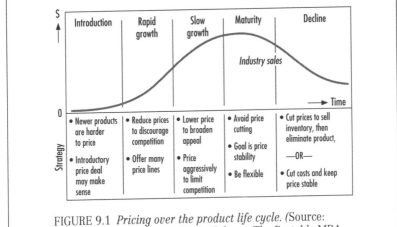

FIGURE 9.1 *Pricing over the product life cycle.* (Source: *Alexander Hiam and Charles D. Schewe,* The Portable MBA in Marketing *[New York: John Wiley & Sons, 1992], p. 310.)*

$$\text{Cost-plus price} = \frac{\text{unit cost}}{1 - \text{desired rate of return}}$$

With *markup pricing,* a standard markup is added to the estimated cost of the product by each of the entities on the distribution chain. In other words, the wholesaler adds a markup before selling to the retailer, who adds a markup before selling to the customer.[42]

With *target pricing,* the selling price is supposed to provide a specific rate of return, but only if a specific volume is sold. This method does not take demand into account and it assumes that the volume it specifies will be sold. If a company targets price with the assumption that 25,000 units will be sold, and only 15,000 sell, it may end up with a negative ROI. The formula is:

$$\text{Selling price} = \frac{\text{total costs} \times \text{desired rate of return}}{\text{number of units}} + \text{unit cost}$$

When companies use *marginal-cost pricing,* they sell "an additional unit of a product for the extra cost of producing that unit," charging less than the average total cost. *Demand-based pricing* operates on the principles of supply and demand outlined in Chapter 7—as price is reduced, demand goes up. In contrast, *premium pricing* demonstrates that "for some products, higher prices bring higher sales volume."[43] Sometimes, high-priced products can establish upscale niche markets for themselves.

Generally, "the average total cost of a product declines steadily as more units are produced." This *economies of scale* results from an increase in production volume and experience. This principle drives companies' desire for market share. With greater volume, lower costs can be passed on to the customer. This strategy works best "with products entering the rapid growth stage of the product life cycle."[44]

Break-even analysis is used to determine how many units of a product a company has to sell in order to cover all the costs of production, and how much profit the company will make as volume increases after it reaches the break-even point. In calculating breakeven, it is important to differentiate between fixed and variable costs. Fixed costs don't change with the level of activity or output, while variable costs do. For example, the costs associated with a toy manufacturer's plant and machinery are fixed costs. Variable costs include the purchase of raw materials. "The amount by which the selling price exceeds the average variable cost is the 'contribution margin' per unit of product sold. When the amount of product sold reaches the point where the total contribution margin covers all the fixed costs of a product, the firm breaks even."[45]

Let's assume, for example, that a toy manufacturer must decide how many toys to produce. Let's further assume that fixed costs of machinery, plant, utilities, and wages are $100,000, and that the variable cost per unit of plastic and other materials is $5, and the toy sells for $15. To find the *break-even point,* the total fixed costs are divided by the price minus the variable cost per unit. The manufacturer's break-even point is 10,000 toys (100,000/10).

$$\text{Break-even quantity} = \frac{\text{total fixed costs}}{\text{price} - \text{variable cost per unit}}$$

WORK TOWARD BUILDING TRUST THROUGH UNDERSTANDING PRICE

When pricing is the only consideration, selling the product becomes merely a transaction. Companies today are looking for ways to build relationships; therefore, managers should work toward repeated transactions so that trust can build through the course of interactions. In a "zero-sum" game that focuses on negotiating over price with price-sensitive customers, one side loses and the other wins. When marketers gather feedback directly from customers, they are able to determine the best pricing strategy, enabling price to work in everyone's favor.[46]

KEY CONCEPT — DISTRIBUTION: THE RIGHT TIME AND THE RIGHT PLACE

Distribution, the system of delivering products to markets and into customers' hands, generally entails passing the product through a linked chain of intermediaries. The efficiency of distribution not only adds value to the product, but it cuts costs as well. Distribution is effective when it utilizes time and place efficiently, ensuring the product is in the right place at the right time. A distribution channel congested with competitors can prevent a product from being where it should be, when it should be. How products are distributed can be just as important as other factors and can add value to products, providing that ever-important competitive edge.

Two key intermediaries in the distribution chain are retailers and wholesalers. Retailers sell directly to customers. Wholesalers distribute products to commercial or professional users—to retailers or to other manufacturers, or to government and other large institutions. As well as distributing products, wholesalers also buy and sell products. Intermediaries also include market researchers, transportation companies, warehouse and storage companies, financial institutions providing credit, sales and promotion services, and various management services. These intermediaries are used because they can provide services more efficiently or effectively than the manufacturer.

As products move down the distribution chain (see Figures 9.2 and 9.3), exchanges are made in the form of goods, money, and information. In order to make the flow smooth and avoid breakdowns, communication must be excellent. One role of marketing is to facilitate that communication, promoting products to all the intermediaries as well as to the end user. The process of promoting products through the distribution chain is known as *push/pull.* In a *push strategy,* each member promotes the product to the next company on the chain, persuading it to accept the product; thus, the product is *pushed* through the channel. In a *pull strategy,* the marketer successfully uses promotional and advertising tools that stimulate demand for the product; thus, intermediaries want to accept the product in order to satisfy their customers. This *pulls* the product through the chain.

PUSH

PULL

REMEMBER INFORMATION TECHNOLOGY MAKES TIME REAL

Information technology enables all the members of the distribution change to be even more closely linked to each other, to receive information simultaneously, and to get information in real time or as close to real time as possible, even when distribution points might be scattered around the globe.

Honeywell's Customer Satisfaction Department, highlighted in Chapter 4, illustrates this point: Honeywell had to educate the distributors and wholesalers in

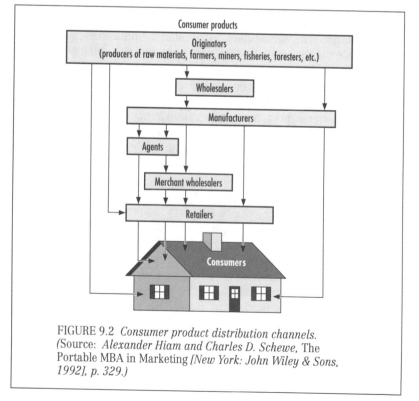

FIGURE 9.2 *Consumer product distribution channels.* (Source: *Alexander Hiam and Charles D. Schewe,* The Portable MBA in Marketing *[New York: John Wiley & Sons, 1992], p. 329.)*

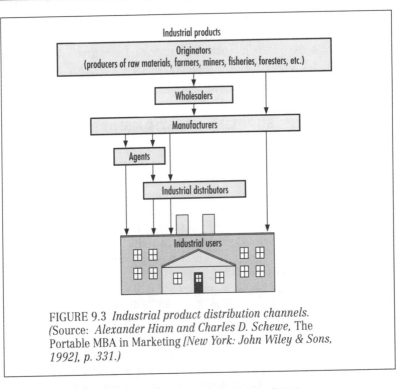

FIGURE 9.3 *Industrial product distribution channels.*
(Source: *Alexander Hiam and Charles D. Schewe,* The
Portable MBA in Marketing *[New York: John Wiley & Sons,*
1992], p. 331.)

its distribution chain about the benefits of IT. But once
those customers learned how to access and use Honeywell's database, they were able to track their shipments
themselves, saving time and freeing customers and service reps to work on ways to make the distribution system even more efficient.

FEDERAL EXPRESS: DISTRIBUTING
EXPERTISE

Star   Federal Express' strategy is built around customer
value, and its business processes are organized
around the customer. Like Honeywell, Federal
Express provides customers with specifically developed software and computer terminals, allowing customers to track delivery themselves. The network
provides customers with real-time information about
where their products are en route to their destinations.[47]
Every process is designed to provide fast and reliable
delivery of customers' packages. Rather than building on
existing operations and using traditional ways of sorting
and delivering mail, Federal Express re-created the way
it did business. It centralized shipments out of its hub in
Memphis, purchased and operated its own airplanes,
and used information technology to help it handle distribution and logistics in a whole new way. In the process,
it created new markets for itself. It also demonstrated its
ability to adapt continually. In 1990, when market
research and feedback showed the company that customers' expectations had increased as customers grew
more sophisticated, Federal Express realized it needed to

begin concentrating more on lowering cost. So, it re-evaluated its strategy and realigned its business processes to meet its customers' changing requirements. Now, for a lower price, customers can have packages delivered the next afternoon, rather than before 10 A.M.[48]

DEVELOP SUPPLIER RELATIONSHIPS

Industrial marketing now involves strategic alliances formed by just-in-time (JIT) supplier relationships. In these relationships, the basic concept is to make the supplier an extension of the customer.

The parties agree upon a planned delivery schedule of "defect-free merchandise." This tight scheduling allows the manufacturer to reduce costs by reducing levels of inventory, and both parties become dependent on each other and move to a win/win position as they cooperate to achieve mutual goals—the speedy delivery of quality products.[49] These relationships are ongoing and gener-ally take place between a retailer and a supplier. The parties "agree on objectives, policies, and procedures for ordering and physical distribution of the supplier's prod-ucts." Their purpose is "to achieve some of the efficien-cies of vertically integrated systems without common ownership." They provide both parties with greater flexi-bility than they would have operating alone.[50]

TRUST IS CRITICAL; SO IS COMPARABLE COMPENSATION

The organizational cultures of both parties must be in sync. Reward systems and performance measures must be compatible to ensure that both parties are equally motivated and compensated for their efforts. And trust must be developed so that the relationship can be nurtured and built; otherwise, the relationship is doomed to fail.[51]

PROMOTION: PERSUADING THE PUBLIC

The goal of promotion is to raise awareness of the product with the targeted audience and to demonstrate the value and benefit of the product, prompting the consumer to buy. Promotion informs, persuades, and reminds. It creates messages that are intended to elicit specific responses that stimulate people to buy, influ-encing the shape of the demand curve and removing the impact of price from purchasing decisions. (See Figure 9.4.)

Promotion comes in a variety of forms—the most obvious is advertising. Advertising is a paid-for, imper-sonal method of promotion that is strictly a one-way form of communication. It has the benefit, however, of control. Marketers create the message and deliver it in a

Stellar Performer: Wal-Mart
Innovative Marketing and Distribution

In 1962, when Sam Walton established his first large-scale, rural discount store, he reinvented mass-market selling, countering industry beliefs that retail volume can't be built in small towns. He met his 1977 goal of becoming a $1 billion company and, by 1992, Wal-Mart was the largest retailing organization in the world. In 1994, sales totaled $82.5 billion. The company has over 2,000 discount centers, over 200 supercenters, and, in an expansion beyond the traditional market, it opened over 428 discounted membership stores known as Sam's Clubs.

Wal-Mart's marketing strategy supports its procurement and distribution strategy. Because the everyday prices are low, there are no special promotions, which means there is a predictable movement of products, allowing for a controlled inventory and speedy delivery cycle times. Plus, it handles 85 percent of its distribution. Its fleet of 2,000 trucks restocks store shelves twice a week. Suppliers ship directly to one of Wal-Mart's 20 national distribution centers, eliminating intermediate suppliers and local distribution centers. Shipments leave distribution centers in less than 24 hours, increasing inventory turnover.

The company works in partnership with key manufacturers like Procter & Gamble (P&G). As mentioned earlier, Wal-Mart's sophisticated information network not only provides it with vital information, but also enables it to share that information with suppliers. P&G can gather data to help it determine whether products should be refined or if there are opportunities for niche products. Sharing sales information also helps both companies control inventory. P&G knows when it needs to replenish its line, saving Wal-Mart from having to warehouse excess stock, and saving costs.

In comparison to its competitors in the industry, Wal-Mart has 20 percent lower gross margins, lower overhead, 30 percent higher net margins, twice as high returns to shareholders, and it pursues 20 percent annual growth.

Sources: James C. Collins and Jerry I. Porras, Built to Last: Successful Habits of Visionary Companies (New York: HarperBusiness, 1994); Carl Horowitz, "Boon or Boondoggle?" Investor's Business Daily, 24 May 1995 (America Online: Investors Business Daily, 1995); Tim R. Furey and Stephen G. Diorio, "Making Reengineering Strategic," Planning Review (July/August 1994).

planned and systematized way. It has reach and frequency—it can reach a large number of people and can be repeated over time in well-planned sequence using a variety of media. But it's inflexible and can be costly, and it's hard to match response with specific ads. The main channels used by advertising are TV, radio, billboards, and print advertising in newspapers, magazines, and journals. The challenge of advertising is to draw the attention of the consumer despite the "noise" in the environment—the numerous distractions and messages that people are bombarded with on a daily basis.

Direct mail has become a popular form of advertising that is more easily measured. It differs from mass-media advertising in a number of ways, but its major distinction is that it is interactive. It offers the customer something definite, gives the customer all the information necessary to make a decision, and provides a means for the customer to respond—for example, with an 800 number or a business reply card.

In addition to advertising, marketers use personal sales as well as other promotional tools, including event sponsorship, discounts, contests, coupons, premiums, and public relations.

The characteristics of the product, its stage in the life cycle, and the nature of the market affect the way marketers develop their strategies. Depending on the objectives, marketers use careful analysis and planning and combine tools to create the marketing mix that will bring the results they are seeking.

END POINT

As the business world changes, alliances once viewed as unlikely will become more accepted and appreciated. Managers with enlightened perspectives, able to see beyond the status quo, will constantly be innovating and improving on the standard way of operating.

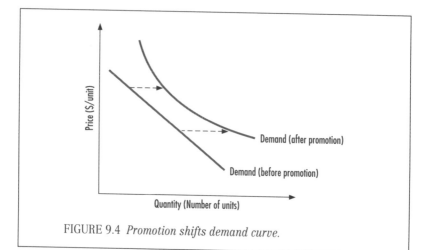

FIGURE 9.4 *Promotion shifts demand curve.*

Productive manufacturing and effective marketing require people to collaborate and learn from each other in the development of products, in meeting and foreseeing the needs of customers, and in the creation of market strategies. Formulating strategy, however, is not an easy process since there are so many variables to consider. The next and final chapter discusses a variety of strategic approaches for today's leading-edge managers.

MORE READING

Davidson, William, and Bro Uttal. *Total Customer Service: The Ultimate Weapon.* New York: Harper & Row, 1989.

Harrington, James H. *Business Process Improvement.* New York: McGraw-Hill, 1991.

Hayes, R. H., and S. C. Wheelwright. *Restoring Our Competitive Edge: Competing through Manufacturing.* New York: John Wiley & Sons, 1984.

Imai, M. Kaizen. *The Key to Japan's Competitive Success.* New York: McGraw-Hill, 1986.

Ishikawa, K. *Guide to Quality Control.* Tokyo: Asian Productivity Organization, 1976.

Juran, J. M. *Juran on Planning for Quality.* New York: The Free Press, 1988.

Kenney, M., and R. Florida. *Beyond Mass Production: The Japanese System and Its Transfer to the U.S.* New York: Oxford University Press, 1993.

Kotler, Philip. *Marketing.* Englewood Cliffs, N.J.: Prentice-Hall, 1987.

Levitt, Theodore. *The Marketing Imagination: New, Expanded Edition.* New York: The Free Press, 1986.

Miller, J. G., A. DeMeyer, and J. Nakane. *Benchmarking Global Manufacturing: Understanding International Suppliers, Customers and Competitors.* Homewood, Ill.: Business One Irwin, 1992.

Pine, Joseph B. II. *Mass Customization: The New Frontier in Business Competition.* Boston: Harvard Business School Press, 1993.

Ries, Al, and Jack Trout, *Positioning the Battle for Your Mind.* New York: Warner Books, 1986.

Schewe, Charles, and Alexander Hiam. *The Portable MBA in Marketing.* New York: John Wiley & Sons, 1992.

Settle, Robert, and Pamela Alreck. *Why They Buy: American Consumers Inside and Out.* New York: John Wiley & Sons, 1986.

Skinner, W. *Manufacturing: The Formidable Competitive Weapon.* New York: John Wiley & Sons, 1993.

Stanton, William J. *Fundamentals of Marketing.* New York: McGraw-Hill, 1991.

Vollmann, T. E., W. L. Berry, and D. C. Whybark. *Manufacturing Planning and Control Systems.* 3d ed. Homewood, Ill.: Business One Irwin, 1992.

Webster, Frederick E., Jr. *Market-Driven Management: Using the New Marketing Concept to Create a Customer-Driven Company.* New York: John Wiley & Sons, 1994.

Womack, J. P., D. T. Jones, and D. Roos. *The Machine That Changed the World: The Story of Lean Production.* New York: Harper Perennial, 1991.

Zeithaml, Valarie A., A. Parasuraman, and Leonard A. Berry. *Delivering Quality Service: Balancing Customer Perceptions and Expectations.* New York: The Free Press, 1990.

Strategic Thinking:
It's All About Moves

In order to win in the marketplace, managers must make choices about how they are going to leverage the strengths of their organizations. Strategy is like a game. The opponent's position is always considered as the player weighs possibilities about the outcome of moves. Intelligent players always try to stay one step ahead of their opponents by anticipating what actions are going to be made and how those actions will impact the game. Armed with foresight and knowledge, adroit players can quickly determine the best move to make at each step of the contest.

However, business strategy is far more complex than any board game or any game played between two teams. The business playing field holds a dynamic mix of players, products, and possibilities. All of the facets of the organization as well as the conditions of the market enter into the decisions about what strategies to choose. This chapter examines the principles of strategic management and outlines significant areas that today's manager must consider: innovation, core competencies, value creation, growth, restructuring, reengineering, and global strategies.

KEY CONCEPT PRINCIPLES OF STRATEGIC MANAGEMENT

In today's competitive environment, skillful corporate players anticipate a wide variety of factors: technological advancements, global playing fields, new players, new products, new market sizes, new customers, and competitors' strategies, to name a few. Not only must managers anticipate these events, but they must then make decisions about which aspects of the organization to leverage against what's happening in the market. If the wrong choices are made, managers lose opportunities and give their opponents a competitive advantage.

Table 10.1 provides a guide for managers to use in the process of developing strategic plans for their companies. Table 10.2 provides questions for managers to answer as they tackle each element of strategic planning. And Table 10.3 points out what innovative companies do to achieve leadership positions in the market.

TiP THE STRATEGIC GAME NEEDS GOALS

Goals give players a reason for playing. They are the targets the company is aiming for, the desired outcomes it wants, the rewards it is seeking. Without goals, players will lose interest, attentions will scatter, the game will die down. Additionally, goals help managers to coordinate activities and motivate other players to play well.

TiP THE OUTCOME DEPENDS ON ALL THE MOVES

Not only big choices, but small choices that get made every day have cumulative power and determine success.

TiP IT'S TRICKY, BUT IT'S NOT ROCKET SCIENCE

Know the organization's present position. Know the competition's position. Know where the organization wants to go and what resources it has to get there.

TABLE 10.1 SUCCESSFUL STRATEGIC MANAGEMENT

- Analyze the industry, the micro and macroenvironment. Assess how these factors impact the organization in the present and how changes might influence the organization in the future.
- Identify the organization's strengths and weaknesses; its core competencies and capabilities; and its vulnerabilities, constraints, and limitations. Include culture, leadership, infrastructure, technology, and processes in the analysis.
- Exploit opportunities. Take risks. Be entrepreneurial. Innovate.
- Develop core competencies with values that will satisfy and draw customers.
- Link external factors—the scope of the market and the company's position—with internal factors—core competencies and resources.
- Integrate long- and short-term planning, setting long- and short-term goals.
- Leverage the linkage between the organization and the marketplace as effectively as possible by anticipating changes and designing, implementing, and continually adjusting strategy to those changes.

TABLE 10.2 ISSUES AND QUESTIONS FOR STRATEGIC MANAGEMENT

Corporate Scope

Business scope: What business is the firm in?

Stakeholder scope: Who can it leverage to attain goals?

Business scope relatedness: How should businesses in the corporation relate to each other?

Change scope by: Merging, acquiring, divesting, forming alliances, aligning or opposing stakeholders, internally developing?

Strategic issues: What businesses to invest, retain, reduce, divest?

Strategic challenges: How to add value? How to create synergy?

Business Unit Scope

Product: What range?

Customer: Who? What do they need?

Geographic: Where?

Vertical: Linkages with suppliers and customers?

Stakeholder: Who can it leverage?

Change scope by: Adding/deleting customers or products? Moving into or out of geographic area? Aligning or opposing stakeholders?

Strategic issues: What products to invest, retain, divest? What relationships with stakeholders to develop?

Strategic challenges: How to identify and exploit opportunities and create strategy?

Competitive Position Dimensions

Product line width: Breadth of line

Product features: Style, design, size, shape, "bells and whistles"

Product functionality: Performance, reliability, durability, speed, taste

Service: Technical assistance, repair, hot lines, education about use

Availability: Distribution channels, bulk purchase, speed

Image and reputation: Brand name, high-end product, quality

Selling and relationships: Sales force that can detail many products; close ties with distribution channels; historic dealings with large end users

Price: List, discounted, price performance comparisons, price value comparisons

Marketplace Goals

Vision: Future position?

Businesses: What primary and secondary businesses to enter, stay, or leave?

TABLE 10.2 (Continued)

Position: What rank of marketplace leadership?

Products: For each line, what market share? For how long? What types of new customers? Which competitors to beat?

Differentiation: What type?

Stakeholders: What reward is created for organization's customers, shareholders, owners, employees, government, society?

Adapted from: *Liam Fahey, "Strategic Management: Today's Business Challenge," in The Portable MBA in Strategy, eds. Liam Fahey and Robert Randall (New York: John Wiley & Sons, 1994), pp. 9–21.*

EXPLOIT OPPORTUNITIES AND INNOVATE

Experts claim success in the future will come from an organization's ability to learn and innovate. Smart managers think beyond the market as it exists and see different ways of doing things. A useful technique is to envision which products, bundled together, will provide greater value for customers and opportunities in the marketplace. Services and products created through innovation offer tremendous opportunities for growth.

Through innovative strategies, companies can change industries in a number of fundamental ways: Market boundaries can be reinvented by drastically changing price and performance or by changing spatial boundaries. ATMs, for example, have altered the dynamics of the banking industry, voice messaging has impacted the telecommunications industry, and the Internet is changing marketspace dramatically.

TABLE 10.3 INNOVATIVE MARKET LEADERSHIP

- Creates new vision for the industry's future
- Introduces new products
- Builds linkages between unrelated products
- Extends product lines and modifies existing products
- Drives change in understanding and use of products
- Serves the most demanding and challenging customers
- Drives technological changes
- Creates or identifies new functionality for products
- Develops new forms of service, distribution, and delivery

Source: *Liam Fahey, "Strategic Management: Today's Business Challenge," in The Portable MBA in Strategy, eds. Liam Fahey and Robert Randall (New York: John Wiley & Sons, 1994), p. 36.*

Markets can also be altered by moving products from niche to mass markets—the now widespread availability of cellular telephones provides an example. Markets also change shape as industries merge or break down. The acquisition of ABC by Disney and the merger of Time and Turner give these companies enormous power to re-create the entertainment industry, a $400 billion economy with 2.5 billion workers, in ways that are probably yet to be imagined.

KEY CONCEPT — MASSIVE PARALLELISM: AN INNOVATIVE MOVE

Massive parallelism, using sophisticated technology and high degrees of cooperation, creates products that customers have not yet envisioned. It operates on the principle of staying ahead of the game, of imagining the future and enhancing productivity by helping functions work together simultaneously.[1]

With massive parallelism, cross-functional teams innovate by developing product concepts and by making forecasts about business and possible technologies. Functional areas like manufacturing and marketing can immediately begin formal planning, while manufacturing creates an infrastructure that will support the new product traits. By the time the product is clearly defined, manufacturing is ready to go, and adjustments are made as the process proceeds. This calls for excellent communication between team members and information systems, allowing adjustments to be entered and specs updated. Everyone involved is informed of progress and adjustments at the same time.[2]

Using massive parallelism, a company can take its core products and create new generations by forecasting better designs or new applications. For instance, at 3M, a concept definition team found that "a dry laser imaging technology already in use internally at 3M could be commercialized to meet doctors' demands for faster and more cost-efficient systems." Massive parallelism enables 3M to cut in half the time it takes to get new products to market. 3M is now planning ways to apply parallelism to multiple parallel projects in an attempt to stay ahead of competitors it knows will imitate its innovative successes. 3M, spotlighted earlier as a stellar innovator, has true stretch goals: Its managers are now striving to generate 30 percent of sales from products that have not been on the market for more than four years. 3M's use of massive parallelism demonstrates how a company can anticipate customers' needs to fully exploit opportunity.[3]

KEY CONCEPT — STRATEGY: DEVELOP CORE COMPETENCIES

Core competencies—areas in which firms have specific expertise beyond their competitors—provide competitive advantage. A company's competencies include its combined knowledge, skills, and values. By achieving depth in several targeted areas of competence, a company provides itself with the rich, solid ground from which innovative products and services can spring.

The core competencies of companies like 3M, Sony, and Motorola have sustained their growth and helped them to succeed. Generally, companies cannot maintain excellence in too many core competencies. When a company focuses on a few core competencies, the organization tends to tighten up, values sharpen, and the focus shifts outward, linking more directly with customers' needs.[4]

Core competencies require the "management of complex, iterative processes . . . and the integration of learning in many parts of the organization," and they necessitate combining the ability to bundle multiple technologies with market intuition and customer knowledge. For example, Canon's core technical competencies are "miniaturization and mechatronics"—Canon can design and manufacture small, complex electromechanical devices well. These give birth to core products like lens systems and laser engines, which in turn are basic components of products valued by Canon's customers—its cameras, camcorders, copiers, and laser printers.[5]

Table 10.4 points out questions companies can ask to identify their core competencies.

KEY CONCEPT — CORE COMPETENCE LEADS TO CORE PRODUCTS

In order to develop new business, companies must look at competition from three levels: core competence, core

---

TABLE 10.4 THREE QUESTIONS TO IDENTIFY CORE COMPETENCIES

1.

Is it a significant source of competitive differentiation? Core competencies should provide distinct value and benefit to customers.

2.

Does it transcend a single business? Core competencies should provide access to a variety of markets.

3.

Is it hard for competitors to imitate? It should be difficult for others to learn how the firm does what it does.

Source: C. K. Prahalad with Liam Fahey and Robert M. Randall, "A Strategy for Growth: The Role of Core Competencies," in The Portable MBA in Strategy, eds. Liam Fahey and Robert M. Randall (New York: John Wiley & Sons, 1994), p. 261.

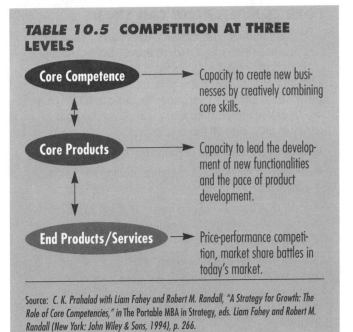

TABLE 10.5 COMPETITION AT THREE LEVELS

Core Competence → Capacity to create new businesses by creatively combining core skills.

Core Products → Capacity to lead the development of new functionalities and the pace of product development.

End Products/Services → Price-performance competition, market share battles in today's market.

Source: C. K. Prahalad with Liam Fahey and Robert M. Randall, "A Strategy for Growth: The Role of Core Competencies," in The Portable MBA in Strategy, eds. Liam Fahey and Robert M. Randall (New York: John Wiley & Sons, 1994), p. 266.

products, and end products and services (see Table 10.5). If core competencies become the basis for the company's portfolio of businesses, then managers will have greater ability to envision new applications for those competencies.

Canon's competencies, for example, give the organization the "opportunity for gaining economies of scale in core products"—its lens systems and laser engines have multiple uses across the organization, providing the company with an "ability to anticipate new functionalities and leverage technical resources."[6] Canon operates like a biological process: The company is "a constantly evolving line of businesses." The company tries to beat the competition by giving birth to products that give new life, while making the last product obsolete.[7]

Canon uses its core competencies for its own core products, but it also sells core products to other companies. To compete in the future, not only will companies have to build market share for end products and services, but they will have to develop dominance in core products, which provide the basis for new product opportunity.[8]

When core products are used profusely within an organization, they plant seeds for new ideas—new ways they can be used or applied. Kao leveraged its knowledge of fine powders and coating technology to expand from being number one in Japan's soap and detergent industry to also being number two in the cosmetics industry, and now it is using its competency in coatings to establish itself as a leading manufacturer of floppy disks.[9]

CORE COMPETENCIES CAN ERODE

DANGER! When building core competencies there are also pitfalls that should be avoided. Brian Marsh, Head of Planning Consultancy for Shell International Petroleum in London, advocates making sure margins are sufficient to keep regenerating competencies by avoiding "erosion, emigration, and emulation." Without regeneration, core competencies can:

- Erode over time and depreciate in value

- Be copied by competitors, eliminating competitive advantage

- Emigrate because of consumer and environmental changes, becoming "yesterday's breadwinners" and no longer yielding value

Marsh believes the customer is of ultimate importance, stating, "if you want to enhance your core competencies you have to start thinking like your customers." He suggests identifying core competencies by discovering what clients like about the company and what competitors perceive to be weaknesses.[10]

CREATE COMPETITIVE SPACE

Create competitive space by utilizing core competencies and leveraging resources to "invent" businesses. Make sure this competitive space provides the strategic architecture needed to develop new business by building a structure for recognizing opportunities. Additionally, separate from past perceptions of the market and focus on functionalities, not present products and services.[11] The organization must innovatively seek out new competitive spaces, constantly preparing itself for future competitive positions.

EDS exemplifies a company that works to develop future potential on a continual basis, even when it is presently successfully positioned. (See sidebar.)

KEY CONCEPT — CREATING VALUE

In order to create value for the future, companies must improve operational performance, while adapting and reshaping their business portfolios and their assumptions about the marketplace. At the same time, they need to create strategies and use their resources to develop new markets and businesses. Business leadership in the future will belong to companies that create value by identifying and exploiting new business opportunities.[12]

Companies create value when they deliver products or services that provide them with profit margins greater than their competitors'. Margins count because they provide fuel for reinvesting in the company's competencies and resources. AlliedSignal's Lawrence

EDS: Star Company Seeks White Space

Electronic Data Systems Corp. (EDS), a Texas-based information systems and management consulting firm, asks the right questions, adopts a futuristic mind-set, and actively seeks new competitive space as it plans a growth strategy to carry it into the next century.

In 1992, EDS experienced its "30th consecutive year of record earnings" and had $8.2 billion in sales, yet it aggressively looked for more ways to grow and is presently seeking to reach a goal of $25 billion in sales.

In 1993, over 150 managers, led by EDS visionary chairman Lester Alberthal, the Leadership Council, and a Corporate Change Team met in Dallas to lay the foundation for future strategies that would pave the way to achieving such huge goals. Managers from around the world came in separate "waves" to attend the Dallas meeting, analyzing "white space opportunities," examining possible alliances, and looking into the kinds of skill sets that would be required as the company set out on its journey. Each wave tackled specific issues, benchmarking EDS's competencies against competitors and investigating possible new competencies to build. Over 2,000 people ended up participating in the year-long strategy development process.

The result of all this strategic planning was the vision of a broader, more creative role for EDS in the industry and a new competitive strategy that called for the company to "globalize, informationalize, and individualize." EDS is looking beyond its historical position as a "business-to-business company" to individual consumers. It is aggressively seeking new markets, new alliances, and new capabilities. Its goal is to mass-customize its products and services, providing individual customers with the products, services, information, and knowledge they need.

In 1995, EDS' revenues climbed to $10.05 billion and it demonstrated its leadership ability to structure space with the acquisition of A. T. Kearney: It merged its own management consulting division with Kearney to form an independent subsidiary of EDS that will be one of the world's largest management consulting firms. In addition, as GM proceeds with its plans to spin off EDS, the company will achieve greater flexibility, giving it even more energy to expand its competitive space.

Sources: Interview with Cathy Meister, EDS representative; Maria Shao, "GM will spin off EDS unit," The Boston Globe (8 August 1995), pp. 39–40; Gary Hamel and C. K. Prahalad, "Competing for the Future," Harvard Business Review (July/August 1994), pp. 127–128.

Bossidy thinks margins are critical and stresses the need to benchmark the margins of the organization's competitors on a daily basis. When his company misses a planned goal, he claims it's often because markets weren't read correctly or forecasts were wrong. And, he claims, "a real professional maintains margins. . . . I regard it as an obligation to do what you have to do to make your margin commitments."[13]

Every element of the organization must be considered in creating value. In large corporations, the parent can add value as ABB does by linking businesses into a global network, "rationalizing production across countries, cross-selling products, sharing technical developments, and transferring best practices," or as Canon does by supporting cross-fertilization of technologies and product teams in its business portfolio.[14]

Table 10.6 offers some questions for managers to ask as they examine the value of their business portfolios.

Table 10.7 illustrates how value can be evaluated: Structural issues like cycle time, systems, and productivity must be synergistically combined with product portfolios and distribution channels, and strategically leveraged in order to determine which future direction will bring value to customers and success to the organization.

RESTRUCTURING STRATEGIES

Many companies have included restructuring in their strategic plans in an attempt to gain efficiency by cutting excess waste. Restructuring creates lean companies, reducing the size of the organization. But for many people, restructuring translates into a simple,

---

TABLE 10.6 STRATEGIC QUESTIONS FOR CORPORATIONS AND BUSINESS UNITS

Find value or lack of value by asking the right questions:

- What are the major parenting opportunities in this business?
- Will local managers underperform without the help of a parent? Why?
- Would this business be worth more to someone else than to us? Why?
- What are the critical success factors in this business?
- Are these factors similar to or different from the other businesses in the portfolio?
- Does the parent's culture impede success factors for the unit?

Source: Marcus Alexander, Andrew Campbell, and Michael Goold, "A New Model for Reforming the Planning Review Process," Planning Review (January/February 1995), p. 19. This table is reprinted from Planning Review (Jan/Feb 95) with permission from The Planning Forum, The International Society for Strategic Management and Planning.

TABLE 10.7 VALUE CREATION SCORECARD

Managing the performance gap

Organizations must improve performance across a variety of dimensions: quality, cost, cycle time, productivity, and profitability.

Managing the adaptability gap

Organizations must anticipate industry changes and initiate and manage industry transformation, which is different from improving, enhancing, or being the best in what exists.

Managing the opportunity gap

Organizations must create new businesses, pioneer new markets, and discern and communicate strategic direction.

PERFORMANCE GAP	+	ADAPTABILITY GAP	+	OPPORTUNITY GAP
Restructure		*Reshape*		*Revitalize*
Quality		Portfolio choices		Growth
Costs		Product mix		New business
Cycle time		Channels		development
Logistics		Price-performance		New market
Head count		New business		development
Productivity		model		Strategic direction
Administrative systems				Resource leverage

→ **Value Creation** ←

Source: C. K. Prahalad with Liam Fahey and Robert M. Randall, "A Strategy for Growth: The Role of Core Competencies," in The Portable MBA in Strategy, eds. Liam Fahey and Robert M. Randall (New York: John Wiley & Sons, 1994), pp. 253–254.

yet scary, word: *downsize*. Restructuring trims, sometimes brutally, the fat from the belly of the company, cutting people from the structure, carving out layers from the middle of the organization. Restructuring also cuts processes, severing any strategic business units or divisions that are underperforming and not helpful to the body of the company.

Because it entails layoffs, restructuring is never easy. It can be devastating for those losing jobs and it can be traumatic for those who retain employment in a newly structured setting and environment. As job security is shaken, so is employee loyalty.

In *Competing for the Future*, Gary Hamel, professor of strategic and international management at the London Business School, and C. K. Prahalad, professor of business administration at the University of Michigan in Ann Arbor, claim that "restructuring seldom results in fundamental business improvements. It buys time . . . can raise a company's share price, but improvement is almost always temporary." Downsizing deals with past mistakes instead of with future markets. It tries to correct old errors instead of trying to leap forward with new ideas that will enhance competitive positioning in the future. The authors claim data show that stock prices for firms that restructured increased for a short time, but then declined below where they were at the time of downsizing.[15]

Hamel and Prahalad blame most layoffs at large U.S. companies on senior managers who let their economic engines—their growth margins and profitability—run out of gas. It's up to managers, they say, to make sure the engines of their companies are primed, and it's up to managers to avoid the potholes ahead that will damage their engines.[16]

STAY HEALTHY, NOT THIN

Some experts say senior management should shift its restructuring focus from how people leave (what kinds of incentives and severance are provided) to who leaves and who is left. For success in the future, competent, loyal employees will be needed to implement new strategies. The focus should be on "positioning the organization for the future, not implementing a downsizing."[17]

Hamel and Prahalad want firms to cure their "corporate anorexia," believing it's better to be healthy than thin. They believe senior managers can get a better handle on whether their companies are positioned to grow and can begin to discover ways to increase the flow of revenue in the future, providing needed profitability and diminishing the need to downsize.[18]

Restructuring, they say, has often been a destructive force that "has destroyed lives, homes, and communities in the name of efficiency and productivity."[19] Rather than cutting people, assets, and investments, corporations should build, by focusing on the future and ways to increase revenue streams.

KEY CONCEPT — GROWTH STRATEGY

More than just downsizing, companies need to invest in the future by focusing on ways to create opportunities to grow their businesses. Without a doubt, many companies have cut the size of their payrolls, but many successful companies did not rely on trimming alone.

Merrill Lynch & Co.'s profits rose by cutting staff in one area while increasing staff in other areas. "By reducing the number of support staff and increasing the number of revenue-building brokers, investment banks, and traders, revenue per employee has jumped more than 70 percent since 1990." In 1993, "profits rose by 46 percent to $1.4 billion, as sales climbed 24 percent to $16.6 billion. And market value is up 17 percent, to $8.3 billion."[20]

Companies like GE and Intel strive to achieve strength in market value from commitment to sustained growth and improved productivity. Keeping in line with GE's vision to be number 1 or 2 in all of its businesses, managers are expected to improve sales or profits annually—just matching last year's work is not sufficient. This aggressive approach seems to work: GE, the model of a "modern diversified giant," topped *Business Week's Top 1000 Companies* in 1994, "as GE's market value climbed by a hefty 25 percent, to almost $90 billion."[21]

In the mid-'80s, when Intel CEO Andy Grove was faced with huge losses, rather than mandate immediate layoffs, he implemented a 125 percent solution: He asked employees to work 10 extra hours a week without pay. When that wasn't enough, he asked them to take a 10 percent pay cut. But finally, he gave in to the numbers and downsized. At the same time, the company began an aggressive drive of improvement, backed by the belief that it should "destroy its old products with its next products." Like GE, its philosophy seems to work: In 1993, profits rose 115 percent and sales rose 50 percent, while market value went up 18 percent.[22]

To help focus energy on growth, Table 10.8 provides a half dozen questions for managers to ask as they develop future strategies for success, and Table 10.9 offers a dozen questions for managers to ask in an attempt to maintain that focus by identifying management's strengths and weaknesses.

BREAK NEW GROUND

Innovate and be constantly willing to alter and upgrade processes and systems and try new ideas.

Wal-Mart, number one in the retail industry, succeeded because Sam Walton continually embraced change, wasn't afraid to make mistakes, and wasn't afraid to break new ground. Walton set up operations where they hadn't been before. The company continues to debunk myths, forging ahead as it continues providing customers in rural and suburban settings with a wide range of low-cost products. Although it has its opponents, studies have shown that when Wal-Mart enters an area, real per-capita income in the area rises, the area's trade increases by 15 percent, and the trade area doubles in radius.[23] Others tried to do what Sam Walton did, but he succeeded by innovating and reinventing.

ORGANIZATIONS ARE ORGANISMS

When growth is impeded, either because of internal malfunctioning or because of external forces or trauma, development is retarded. This is true for humans and it's true for organizations. When development is hindered, the organism doesn't function as it

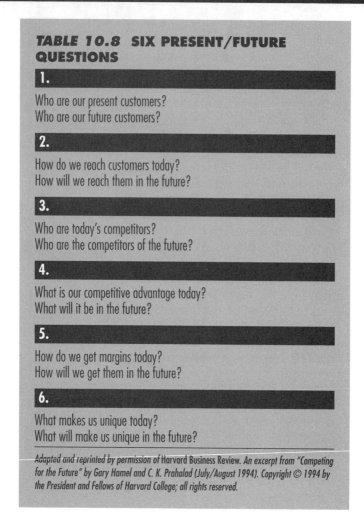

TABLE 10.8 SIX PRESENT/FUTURE QUESTIONS

1.

Who are our present customers?
Who are our future customers?

2.

How do we reach customers today?
How will we reach them in the future?

3.

Who are today's competitors?
Who are the competitors of the future?

4.

What is our competitive advantage today?
What will it be in the future?

5.

How do we get margins today?
How will we get them in the future?

6.

What makes us unique today?
What will make us unique in the future?

Adapted and reprinted by permission of Harvard Business Review. An excerpt from "Competing for the Future" by Gary Hamel and C. K. Prahalad (July/August 1994). Copyright © 1994 by the President and Fellows of Harvard College; all rights reserved.

was designed to and it becomes more difficult for it to reach its fullest potential.

DEVELOP STRETCH GOALS

Western companies are discovering the more organic approach to growth used by the Japanese. They are beginning to learn how to regenerate themselves so they can evolve and grow to meet the demands of the twenty-first century.

The Japanese have demonstrated they know how to aggregate their core competencies to reach stretch goals and, in the process, stimulate internal growth. Sony's core values led to its core competence in miniaturization, a major feature of its wide range of products. In the late 1950s, when Sony changed its name from Tokyo Tsushin Kogyo, it was a small company, but it took a giant step toward becoming a global company. Not only did the company want to change its image with an easier-to-pronounce name, but it wanted to improve the image of Japanese products from being perceived as "cheap" to being regarded as high quality.

TABLE 10.9 TWELVE QUESTIONS FOR FUTURE GROWTH

1.

How much time do we spend on external rather than internal issues?

2.

How much time do we spend thinking about the kinds of changes that will take place in the next 5 to 10 years?

3.

How much time do we spend building a shared perspective of the future?

4.

Is our strength operational efficiency or innovation and growth?

5.

Are we continually catching up, or are we getting out in front?

6.

Has our transformation agenda been set by competitors or by our own foresight?

7.

Do competitors view us as a rule maker or rule follower?

8.

What new core competencies will we need to build?

9.

What new product concepts should we pioneer?

10.

What alliances will we need to form?

11.

What nascent development programs should we protect?

12.

What long-term regulatory initiative should we pursue?

Adapted and reprinted by permission of Harvard Business Review. An excerpt from "Competing for the Future" by Gary Hamel and C. K. Prahalad (July/August 1994). Copyright © 1994 by the President and Fellows of Harvard College; all rights reserved.

At the time, no one in the world was using transistors for radios, but founder Masaru Ibuka was sure that radios capable of fitting in people's pockets would be widely accepted around the globe. "Being a pioneer and doing the impossible" are core values at Sony, and the norm is to never give up once a commitment has been made, an attitude that "pervades all the research and development work."[24]

Competitive strategies must create a stretch for the organization. With stretch goals, the energies of the organization are forced to focus on developing internally at the same time they stimulate innovative perspectives of the marketplace. An example repeatedly used to exemplify stretch goals is NASA's Apollo program to put a man on the moon. Not only did the goal include reaching the moon, but the time limit for achieving such stellar performance was a short decade. Everyone had to work together, utilizing all resources available. The strengths of the system were put into play. Stretch goals lead to better use of resources as managers must think creatively about how to leverage every possible resource.

PARTNERING STRATEGIES

Reputations can be ruined by choosing the wrong partner. And more than love at first sight, business partnerships require compatibility and the desire to work together toward future goals, even over bumpy roads. Acquisitions, mergers, alliances, and partnerships offer companies ways to grow and can be beneficial to both large and small companies. But anyone who has gone through divorce recognizes the importance of selecting the right partner.

In establishing alliances, identify areas of similarity and differences and define the compatibility of partners in terms that reveal the value each partner brings to the relationship. Being able to accommodate each other is important. And there needs to be an acknowledgment and understanding of the other's *core cultural identity*. This calls for greater self-awareness: Managers must understand the assumptions others hold—only then can they modify their own behaviors or begin to change those assumptions.[25]

Almost like a prenuptial agreement, companies entering partnerships need to make it clear how economic benefits will be distributed and how the system of governance will work. Life and business change. Variables that could influence the relationship should be flagged and it should be determined ahead of time how future problems will be negotiated. Additionally, ways to modify internal systems—to transfer learning and to exploit external conditions—should be built into the agreement.[26]

NEC: GROWTH THROUGH ALIGNMENT

Star

NEC, a Japanese leader in telecommunications, computers, and semiconductors, grew from being a $3 billion company in 1980 to being Japan's top computer company. The excellence of NEC's strategic architecture enabled it to grow at an astounding rate. For 15 years, the concept of converging computers and communications (C&C) has been the central supporting logic behind NEC's strategy. C&C provided broad-based support for NEC's diverse business portfolio. It offered the company "consistency and direction" that guided decision making and resource allocation across the organization on issues involving "markets, customers, and technologies." Its R&D budget was smaller than competitors', yet it generated growth by carefully aligning with numerous firms that reinforced its technological base.[27] In 1995, it springboarded into the U.S. by investing $170 million in 20 percent of Packard Bell Electronics, the United States' largest seller of personal computers.[28] NEC uses external alliances extensively, learns from those alliances, and uses them to leverage its own resources.

PULL TOGETHER, NOT APART

The energy required for successful growth demands that the whole organism operate in sync. If one part of an organization is pulling in one direction and another part is pulling in a different direction, the organization will be weakened and will not have the strength that is needed for growth. Within the organization, goals and visions for the future must be shared.

CHECK OUT ASSUMPTIONS

Assumptions and conventions that the company and the industry take for granted can be misleading and harmful. Managers can help their organizations identify assumptions and create dialogue about them. Unless assumptions are brought to the surface and discussed, decisions can be made on erroneous presumptions.

David A. Nadler, author of *Organizational Architecture: Designs for Changing Organizations* and coauthor with former Xerox CEO David T. Kearns of *Prophets in the Dark: How Xerox Reinvented Itself and Drove Back the Japanese,* has witnessed the wide variety of assumptions that can emerge from a group: During a major Xerox strategic project, the team was examining various investments and, in the course of their discussions, 18 different assumptions surfaced. Moreover, there was strong disagreement on nine of them.[29] If those assumptions had not risen to the surface through good communication, the project would have been negatively affected due to lack of shared understanding about important elements on which decision making rested.

On a broader level, Southwest Airlines, headed by visionary chairman Herb Kelleher, questioned a whole industry's assumption that the hub-and-spoke network works best. Instead of following the traditional flight pattern, Kelleher focused on pairing high-volume cities such as Dallas–Houston, San Francisco–Los Angeles,

Stellar Performer:
Southwest Airlines
Industry Challenger

In CEO Herb Kelleher's vision, Southwest doesn't compete only with other airlines; it competes with cars and buses. Ticket prices between some California cities, where it has 50 percent of the intrastate market, are so low they almost rival the price of gas.

Southwest's highly desirable purpose is to get people where they want to go as quickly and as cheaply as possible. But Herb Kelleher's no-frills strategy also makes it feasible. The airline has the lowest cost structure in the airline industry: 7.2 cents to fly one seat-mile. It flies only Boeing 737s to reduce cost on fuel, maintenance, and parts. Everything in the system is simplified, built around efficiency, low cost, and quick turnaround times. There are no meals, no advanced seat reservations, no connecting flights, and travel is "ticketless." With its no-frills service, it is able to provide its customers with competitively lower prices.

Southwest utilizes all its assets. It was the first airline to win the Triple Crown—best on-time performance, lowest complaints per customer, and fewest lost bags per passenger—for a full year. It has clearly defined, integrated business processes that drive its competitive advantage in the marketplace. Southwest has consistently outperformed the industry in annual revenue growth, operating profits, flights per aircraft, passengers per employee, and employees per aircraft.

In recent years, the company has expanded geographically, acquired Morris Air Corp., increased its fleet to 197 planes, and now serves 45 airports. The workforce has risen in number: It now employs 17,000, a 97 percent increase over the last four years. But despite such rapid growth, Southwest takes time to select new employees carefully; it is committed to making sure its employees fit into its friendly, highly cooperative, team-oriented culture.

Herb Kelleher, irreverent and humorous, lives and models his vision, personally interacting with his employees at all times of the day and night. He also makes sure his senior managers spend at least one day a quarter working outside their departments with employees in the field. Resourceful and determined, Kelleher is a figure to contend with in the industry.

Other carriers are trying to emulate his successful strategy. In 1994, United became a major competitor with the creation of a California executive shuttle that not only offers comparably low fares, but also provides a few perks, such as first-class and assigned seats. A fierce competitive war has ensued, and Southwest's first-quarter earnings in 1995 showed the airline's poorest performance in three years. But the

(Continued)

(Continued)

strength of Herb Kelleher, Southwest, and its culture are well known. It will be interesting to watch as new battle lines are drawn and new strategies implemented. Even though the war is on, Southwest's profits are expected to grow in the future. As Herb Kelleher said in a February 1995 *Business Week* article, "When you have this tremendous flux in the outside world, you don't want to get 'fluxed' yourself."

Sources: Tim R. Furey and Stephen G. Diorio, "Making Reengineering Strategic," Planning Review (July/August 1994), pp. 9–10; Jay A. Conger, "Leadership for the Year 2000," in The New Portable MBA, eds. Eliza G. C. Collins and Mary Anne Devanna (New York: John Wiley & Sons, Inc., 1994), pp. 403–404; Susan Chandler and Eric Schine, "Not Bad, for a Dumb Idea: United's Shuttle Has Put Southwest on Notice," Business Week, 20 February 1995 (America Online: McGraw Hill, 1995); Wendy Zellner, "Southwest," Business Week, 12 February 1995 (America Online: McGraw Hill, 1995); Wendy Zellner, et al., "Go-Go Goliaths," Business Week, 13 February 1995 (American Online: McGraw Hill, 1995); Wendy Zellner, Eric Schine, and Susan Chandler, "Dogfight Over California," Business Week, 15 August 1994 (America Online: McGraw Hill, 1994).

and Chicago–Saint Louis, and flying into second-tier airports which are less congested and therefore speedier. Southwest's innovative strategies have produced a no-frills airline that, for the past decade, "has been the only corporation in the U.S. airline industry to consistently turn a profit." In addition, it revolutionized the airline industry by serving as a model.[30] (See Stellar Performer.)

STRATEGY INVOLVES LEARNING

KEY CONCEPT
Some experts believe the organization's ability to learn is a key factor in developing the insight needed for successful strategic planning. Learning encompasses the ability to acquire new knowledge and put it to work, and to gain new perspectives that challenge the status quo. For the learning to be effective, the process must be an iterative one; that is, the organization becomes involved in a continuous process, always reflecting on knowledge it has gained from experience and looking for ways to use that knowledge to improve.

Learning organization expert Peter Senge stresses the personal aspect of learning and the need for managers to follow five special *disciplines* in order to gain competence. (See Table 10.10.) These disciplines operate together and must be integrated and approached holistically to enable managers to see the reality of their organizations and, thus, learn how to develop strategies to improve and change.

In Table 10.11, James Brian Quinn, author of *Intelligent Enterprise*, lists intelligent ways for organizations to leverage their resources to position themselves strategically.

TABLE 10.10 LEARNING ORGANIZATION'S FIVE DISCIPLINES

Systems Thinking

A conceptual framework to help make the patterns operating within the whole system clear and, thus, easier to change.

Personal Mastery

The organization's spiritual foundation whereby individuals focus their energies and deepen their vision, enabling them to see reality objectively.

Mental Models

Deeply held assumptions that influence both how individuals perceive what happens around them and how they act.

Building Shared Vision

Organizational members share the same picture of the future and are genuinely committed to achieving it.

Team Learning

The organization cannot learn unless teams learn—team members learn to think together through *dialogue*, a communication technique in which members suspend assumptions, and through understanding how their own patterns of interaction can interfere with learning.

Source: From The Fifth Discipline by Peter M. Senge. Copyright © 1990 by Peter M. Senge. Used by permission of Doubleday, a division of Bantam Doubleday Dell Publishing Group, Inc.

TABLE 10.11 KEY ATTRIBUTES OF THE INTELLIGENT ENTERPRISE

- Focus on knowledge-based activities, not products.
- Develop core competencies ("best-in-world capabilities") in selected activities.
- Continuously upgrade and improve these capabilities.
- Benchmark other activities: Consider outsourcing unless "best" or "strategic."
- Focus on the customer, the employee, and the shareholder.
- Adjust measurement and reward systems to reflect this focus.
- Establish a learning culture at the personal, team, and enterprise levels.
- Leverage knowledge through employee education and training, and through the development of sophisticated databases and networks.
- Disaggregate organizations; restructure around the task.
- Utilize worldwide best-in-class resources.

Source: James Brian Quinn, "Building the Intelligent Enterprise: Leveraging Resources, Services and Technology," in The Portable MBA in Strategy, eds. Liam Fahey and Robert M. Randall (New York: John Wiley & Sons, 1994), p. 225.

SCENARIO PLANNING: A LEARNING TOOL FOR STRATEGIC PLANNING

Scenario planning provides a dynamic way to create strategies by helping managers to imagine multiple possibilities for the future and to challenge conventional ways of thinking. The goal is to identify strategically relevant themes and possible outcomes in order to determine strategic direction. Scenarios establish a shared framework that sharpens perceptions about changes and opportunities, while at the same time encouraging diverse views to emerge.

Some companies—in particular, Royal Dutch/Shell—have used scenarios for years. Scenario planning compensates for predicting extremes. It expands possibilities yet controls going after the impossible. Scenarios serve as a framework for honest dialogue and constructive debate. Working on scenarios helps participants focus their thoughts, while stretching their imaginations. It's good to invite outsiders, such as major customers, suppliers, and consultants, to join with managers in using this tool in order to get a really diverse, but more accurate, perspective of possibilities.[31]

By breaking information into pieces and possibilities, managers have a better way of seeing how elements interact under certain conditions. Once relationships become clear, other tools, such as quantitative models, can be developed. Scenarios are valuable for their subjectivity and ability to go beyond objective data. This creative process, which is framed into narratives, enables managers to examine lots of data in digestible chunks and helps them to consider possibilities that might otherwise have been overlooked. This tool is different from computer simulations, which identify patterns among millions of possible outcomes. It is also different from contingency planning, which provides an alternate plan if something goes wrong with a primary plan, and it is different from sensitivity analysis, which examines what happens if one variable in a plan changes, while all other variables remain stable. Scenarios can examine the effect that a number of changing variables have on a system.[32] (See Table 10.12.)

Experts that support the use of futuristic tools claim that "relying solely on analysis produces paralysis," especially when the organization needs to stretch itself and creatively leverage its resources. By "inventing the future," managers can break away from data and analysis and take a mental leap forward.[33] (See Table 10.13.)

REENGINEERING BUSINESS PROCESSES

Reengineering business processes has strong appeal. It is estimated that in 1995 "U.S. companies will spend

TABLE 10.12 DEVELOPING SCENARIOS

1. Set time frame and define scope of products, markets, geographic area, and technology. Determine the knowledge of greatest value for the future.

2. Identify major stakeholders' current roles and interests and define how and why they have changed over time.

3. Identify basic trends in macroenvironment and their effect on the above.

4. Identify key uncertainties—outcomes that might affect all of the above, and identify any relationships among the uncertainties.

5. Construct initial scenario themes and identify extremes by grouping all positives together and all negatives together.

6. Check for consistency and plausibility.

7. Develop learning scenarios, which are tools for research.

8. Identify research needs.

9. Develop quantitative models.

10. Evolve toward decision-making scenarios to be used to test strategies and generate new ideas.

Source: *Paul J. H. Schoemaker, "Scenario Planning: A Tool for Strategic Thinking,"* Sloan Management Review (Winter 1995), pp. 28–30.

$36 billion on reengineering," and that figure is "expected to grow by 20 percent a year."[34] In Europe, "75 percent of companies have implemented at least one reengineering initiative," and the market is expected to grow 38 percent a year until 1998. Over a third of the companies in both Europe and the United States use reengineering to cut costs, and over half use it to cut cycle times and increase productivity.[35]

Management gurus James Champy and Michael Hammer introduced the concept to the public in their 1993 best-selling book, *Reengineering the Corporation.*

TABLE 10.13 USES OF SCENARIO PLANNING

- Building vision
- Generating options when levels of uncertainty are high or when quality of strategic thinking is low
- Analyzing significant changes taking place in an industry
- Developing a common language and framework
- Assessing different opinions that all have merit
- Assessing the robustness of core competencies
- Evaluating investment proposals

Source: *Paul J. H. Schoemaker, "Scenario Planning: A Tool for Strategic Thinking,"* Sloan Management Review (Winter 1995), p. 27.

Reengineering calls for fundamentally and radically rethinking and redesigning the organization's basic business practices and processes—customer service, product development, organizational culture, and order fulfillment—to bring about dramatic improvements in performance. Its goal is to improve productivity, quality, and customer satisfaction while cutting costs. Reengineering unifies the basic tasks of doing business "into coherent business processes." It doesn't attempt to "fix," as restructuring does, but starts over from scratch. "At the heart of business reengineering lies the notion of *discontinuous thinking*—identifying and abandoning the outdated rules and fundamental assumptions that underlie current business operations."[36]

In reengineering, "Why?" is the biggest question. Michael Hammer says, "In plain language, it means reinventing how an organization does its work."[37]

Because companies are made up of people working together, Champy and Hammer attribute the cause of corporate problems to people who are not performing as they should. "The difference between winning companies and losers is that winning companies know how to do their work better." Part of the problem, they claim, is that people focus on tasks, not on processes. No one oversees an entire process from start to finish; therefore, no one is responsible for it. It's difficult to tell where or why something went wrong, and no one is empowered to make changes to the overall process. The fragmentation of the process leads to performance problems. The organization needs to change the structure of its approach to work, and, rather than organizing around tasks, the company must organize around process.[38] (See Tables 10.14 and 10.15.)

DO IT RIGHT OR IT WON'T WORK

DANGER! Like anything else in life or the business world, if something isn't done properly, it's not going to be successful. If steps are missed, if the project is approached carelessly, or if major errors are made in implementation, then it's a setup for failure. Table 10.16 indicates some of Hammer and Champy's "musts" to follow in the process of reengineering and some common errors to avoid.

REENGINEERING IS NOT TQM

Avoid confusion. Reengineering has come under sharp criticism. But Hammer claims it's because reengineering gets confused with other management fads. Reengineering is not TQM. TQM works to enhance and improve existing processes, while reengineering "discards old processes, replacing them with entirely new ones." A key difference between the two is in approach: "Reengineering is typically focused top-down . . . aims to achieve a

TABLE 10.14 REENGINEERING CHARACTERISTICS

- Tasks are integrated and compressed into one, with one person or one team being responsible for "an end-to-end process."
- Work is compressed vertically and horizontally and decision making becomes part of the process.
- Process steps flow in natural order rather than in an artificial linear sequence.
- Processes have multiple versions and economies of scale.
- Work shifts across organizational boundaries and is performed where it makes the most sense.
- Checks and controls are reduced.
- Reconciliation is minimized, cutting back external contact points in a process.
- A case manager provides a single point of contact.
- Hybrid centralized/decentralized operations are prevalent.

Source: *From* Reengineering the Corporation *by Michael Hammer and James Champy. Copyright © 1993 by Michael Hammer & James Champy. Reprinted by permission of HarperCollins Publishers, Inc.*

quantifiable business result in a short period of time. On the other hand, TQM is typically broad-based, highly participative, and bottom-up."[39]

 REENGINEERING IS NOT RESTRUCTURING

Reengineering is not the same as restructuring: It doesn't set out to fix things. Yet, like restructuring, it

TABLE 10.15 CHANGES IN REENGINEERED COMPANIES

- Work units change from functional departments to process teams.
- Jobs change from simple tasks to multidimensional work.
- Roles change from controlled to empowered.
- Job preparation changes from training to education.
- Compensation and the focus of performance measures change from activity to results.
- Advancement criteria change from performance to ability.
- Values change from protective to productive.
- Managers change from supervisors to coaches.
- Organizational structures change from hierarchical to flat.
- Executives change from scorekeepers to leaders.

Source: *From* Reengineering the Corporation *by Michael Hammer and James Champy. Copyright © 1993 by Michael Hammer & James Champy. Reprinted by permission of HarperCollins Publishers, Inc.*

TABLE 10.16

Reengineering Musts

- Have strong leadership
- Identify and examine processes
- Create a top-notch, cross-functional team
- Shoot for breakthroughs, rather than aiming for improvements
- Break with traditions and assumptions
- Use information technology creatively
- Develop an implementation plan to deliver results quickly
- Pay attention to the needs of diverse constituents

Common Errors in Reengineering

- Focusing on consequences rather than the process itself
- Neglecting values and beliefs, and everything but process redesign
- Settling for minor redesign; fixing instead of changing
- Quitting too soon or dragging the effort out
- Going from concept to implementation without testing
- Placing constraints and keeping some parts off-limits
- Allowing culture to prevent start of reengineering process
- Trying to make reengineering happen from bottom up alone
- Skimping on resources devoted to reengineering
- Burying reengineering in middle of the corporate agenda
- Dissipating energy across too many projects
- Trying to keep everyone happy

Sources: Michael Hammer and James Champy, Reengineering the Corporation (New York: HarperBusiness, 1993), pp. 200–213; Interview with Michael Hammer, Business Week Online, 26 April 1995 (America Online: McGraw-Hill, 1995).

usually entails the loss of jobs. Therefore, it can be disruptive and painful because it does call for dramatically "doing more with less." Both Hammer and Champy are adamant that reengineering is not the same thing as downsizing. In a fiercely competitive world, reengineering enables companies to survive. Hammer admits, "Sometimes some jobs are lost in the short term, but it is better than seeing the company go under and lose all its jobs. In the long term, reengineering generates growth and new jobs, and the jobs it creates are bigger and better and more rewarding."[40]

 REENGINEERING IS HARD WORK

Hammer firmly believes reengineering works, but cautions that is not a "magic fix . . . it's hard work, but it pays off." Since 1992, Hammer has trained over 10,000 people in 1,000 companies and sees that the number one problem that companies have is managing change. "When you reengineer, you change jobs, careers, compensation, ways of working, and everything else all at the same time. This is not easy to live through, and many people try to pretend that they don't need to change."[41]

Unfortunately, there are corporations that have tackled reengineering and failed. Champy claims the key problem in these failed efforts is management itself. Harking back to the role of leadership, Champy writes in his new book, *Reengineering Management,* that it will be difficult to redesign work successfully unless the fundamentals of management are changed. Managers, he now maintains, need to have leadership skills (like those described in Chapter 1) in order to succeed; they need to let go of control and enable employees and teams to make decisions. "Senior managers must lead . . . then orchestrate or enable the brightest and best in their organization to do the actual redesign work." He has come to see how important it is to value both the hard issues of strategy as well as the soft issues of culture.[42]

Hammer agrees it takes committed leadership at the top, but sees problems arising from the middle managers who have "the most to lose in the short term." These managers "have to be persuaded to let go of the old and embrace the new."[43]

Painful though it is, downsizing seems to help companies when it is included as just one part of an overall strategy that focuses on improving productivity. Many of the companies highlighted in *Business Week's 1000* list in 1994 reexamined their management and manufacturing processes, and reinvented themselves by cutting *and* improving.

Hamel points out there must be a "balance between hope and anxiety." Reengineering is going to mean the loss of some jobs, and employees know it. Therefore, management has to be able to demonstrate that some great good is going to be the end result. The sacrifice of jobs has to be balanced by creating opportunity or by reinventing something that is going to provide growth and benefit to the remaining organization. Companies must begin to uncover their "hidden wealth" and discover resources that have not been used. By leveraging these neglected resources, companies can generate excitement about the future. For example, some companies might find hidden wealth in managing the linkages across companies better, in combining skills and expertise from several separate businesses.[44]

CONCEPT

REENGINEERING NEVER ENDS

Both Hammer and Champy are optimistic about the future of reengineering and see it as a continuing process.

Champy sees the process of reengineering as just beginning. In a 1995 interview, he said, "We are only into the first two years of what I believe is a 10-year cycle of major change in how we do our work and run our companies." Companies often have no choice but to change, and people can be motivated to participate if they understand the reasons why the company is changing its processes. Reengineering should help companies grow again, attain high performance standards, and create a good place to work.[45] In Hammer's new book, *The Reengineering Revolution,* he writes about the continual process of change, emphasizing that "after reengineering comes more reengineering."[46]

KEY CONCEPT — GLOBAL STRATEGIES

There is no question—the world is shrinking. Globalization is becoming part of business, for both large and small companies. "In 1990, the total of all measured goods and services sold in international trade was $4.5 trillion."[47]

In the so-called *borderless* world of the global market, information, products, capital, ideas, and labor are moving more freely across national boundaries, providing opportunities for companies to grow in size and capability, to expand their markets, and to manufacture their products more cost effectively.

In the next century, it is predicted that borders will become even more amorphous. Kenichi Ohmae, author of *The Borderless World* and *The End of the Nation-State,* claims that, rather than nations, "natural economic zones," such as the Growth Triangle of Singapore and the Indonesian Islands, or San Diego and Tijuana, will be the key focal areas for business. These economic zones have the "ability and determination to put global logic first," and those which comprise emerging economies offer enormous opportunities for growth and investment. These areas welcome companies that will invest, build, produce, and employ in their areas, because business investment means access to low-cost, high-quality products as well as employment and an improved quality of life for the people who live there.[48]

Ohmae's theory goes on to predict the demise of nation-states, but whether or not those predictions prove to be correct, as emerging nations develop, they will most certainly demand the services and products that have reached levels of maturity in well-developed nations. As the new millennium approaches, there will be more cross-border collaboration and more firms will realize the opportunities afforded through the development of a global strategy.

KEY CONCEPT — COMPETITIVE ADVANTAGE IN GOING GLOBAL

Experts agree the smartest companies tend to develop their full potential by operating on a global level, by uti-

Racing Strollers: Small-Sized Reengineering Star

Small companies can reengineer, too. Racing Strollers, the 12-year-old creator and manufacturer of three-wheel strollers for joggers, is a leader in its market, with $7 to $8 million in sales. However, CEO Mary Baechler became concerned when competitors started manufacturing offshore and selling similar strollers at far lower prices. Baechler knew she had to do something, but she also admitted that she was "not going to be the low-cost provider."

After Baechler was introduced to the concept of reengineering, Racing Stroller's operations went through a thorough inspection, as the company looked for ways to improve processes. Some of the findings indicated that time and money were being wasted in a variety of ways. The company was conducting 100 percent inspections on its vendors, and, due to the company's rapid growth and time constraints, when goods arrived flawed, Racing Strollers, desperate for the parts, couldn't afford to lose time, so it accepted poor products and made repairs themselves. Over time, vendor relationships started rolling downhill because the game rules weren't clear.

In the reengineering process, Racing Strollers clarified product standards to vendors. Now when products arrive flawed, they are stamped as rejects and rapidly returned. Rejects are clearly labeled regarding problems, enabling vendors to improve their own processes. The company's manufacturing process has been simplified: Instead of 100 percent inspection, the company has only one person inspecting on a sampling basis, and everyone is happier.

Other tedious and unnecessary steps were discovered throughout the company: In receiving, purchase orders were getting logged into several books before they ever made it to the computer; in production, boxes were stapled closed, then opened at shipping time, only to be restapled again. Since new processes have been implemented, costs per unit have dropped by $2 to $3, and sales have increased, which Baechler attributes to being able to ship on time. In previous years, when spring came, regardless of planning or the amount of inventory built up, the company found it almost impossible to stay ahead of orders. Now that 100 percent inspection has been eliminated, the company has been able to stay on top of orders, and inventory levels have dropped dramatically, saving the company thousands of dollars.

As Baechler and her senior management team explored the way the company carried out its work, they continually asked: "Why are we

(Continued)

(Continued)

doing it this way?" And they discovered that, although there might originally have been good reasons for doing something a particular way, for
the most part the reasons had long since disappeared.

Due to reengineering, the company is financially healthier than ever
and employees are rewarded through profit sharing. Baechler says, "It
took a tremendous force of will to change, and staying on schedule was
difficult." But she also says that running her company has been "the
most fun she's ever had."

Source: *Interview with Mary Baechler; Mary Baechler, "First Steps," Inc. (May 1995), pp. 27–28.*

lizing the best suppliers in the world, or by benchmarking against the best companies in the world, either in
their industry or in a particular function.

Going global gives firms a "unique competitive advantage." Michael Porter, Harvard Business School professor and author of *The Competitive Advantage of
Nations,* claims the choices that firms get to make in
locating their activities (for example, locating R&D in one
country, but assembling products in another country)
and the ways in which they coordinate those activities
give firms competing globally a competitive advantage
over firms operating domestically. However, according to
Porter, "there is no one type of global strategy." The
ways in which a firm decides to go global will depend on
individual circumstances and the competitive advantage
that the company derives from the approach it chooses.
"Strategies will differ in terms of which activities are
concentrated and dispersed, where activities are located,
and the nature and extent of coordination achieved.
They also differ in the extent to which companies perform activities or rely on partners."[49]

In Table 10.17, Porter offers managers questions
they can ask to help themselves in the formulation of
their global strategies.

KEY CONCEPT

GLOBAL NETWORKS LINK BUSINESSES

The global business world is enabling industries to
reinvent themselves into networks linked for specific
purposes. ABB, highlighted earlier, has a global matrix
structure that links national, regional, and local managers together. Countries and areas rationalize production, cross-sell products, share technical developments,
and transfer best practices. ABB's electrotechnical businesses gain advantage from belonging to a high-profile,
successful company with global economies and expertise, while remaining responsive to local markets.[50]

TABLE 10.17 GOING GLOBAL? STRATEGIC QUESTIONS TO ASK

- Is the industry multidomestic or global?
- Is the company based in a country with a favorable demand for the business? How can the home demand be upgraded?
- What activities in the value chain should be located in other nations to source low-cost inputs, to access foreign markets, or to tap into specialized technologies?
- Should these activities be established in-house, or with alliances or acquisitions?
- How should activities in different countries be coordinated and integrated?
- How should the company's management systems and processes be changed to facilitate better coordination and transmit the company's distinctive culture to subsidiaries?
- Are there product lines that should be based in another country? If so, which ones and where should they be located?
- Is the company gaining the maximum competitive advantage from its global presence? Are competitors doing a better job?

Source: Michael Porter, "Global Strategy: Winning in the World-Wide Marketplace," in The Portable MBA in Strategy, eds. Liam Fahey and Robert Randall (New York: John Wiley & Sons, 1994), p. 129.

As discussed in Chapter 8, information technology enables companies to create powerful global linkages, and some of the strongest can be found in the retail industry. Large retailers, like The Limited, for example, compile the day's sales from stores around the globe and then use electronic point-of-sale technologies and forecasting programs to determine the next day's cutting orders for fabric suppliers in Southeast Asia. Stock is dictated by direct, electronic connections among the customers, retailers, and manufacturers. Worldwide sourcing networks enable companies to "work with customers anywhere to create new . . . designs upon request." Overhead and direct costs can drop dramatically when operating globally, and for many manufacturers "international simultaneous development" is essential for competitiveness. Some companies use a 24-hour workday when designing: A process can start in the eastern United States, get passed on to Japanese partners, and be forwarded to Europeans before circling back to the United States.[51]

GLOBAL STRATEGIES PRESENT CHALLENGES

DANGER!

Once again, culture plays a part. Coordinating international or worldwide operations presents unique challenges. Cultural, language, and distance hurdles must be vaulted. Companies need to make sure motivations and incentives that drive individual managers and subsidiaries are aligned with the global goals of the company. Where and how information technology and other knowledge is integrated is crucial. Additionally, firms must continually upgrade and innovate the way they provide service, position their products, market themselves, and communicate in order to gain and maintain competitive advantage.[52]

KEY CONCEPT — FAR AND AWAY, BUT LOCAL COUNTS

Think global, act local has become a trite and overused aphorism, but it holds valuable truth. The vision to go global is the necessary driver that pushes the company to expand beyond safe borders, but information turned into knowledge about local, regional, and national issues helps to achieve success. Global economies of scale offer competitive advantage, but products and operations must gel with the local environment.

Acting local can refer to decisions about where to place certain activities or to how to appeal to certain markets. For example, in 1992, Premark International, Inc., maker of Tupperware, found that its "U.S. operations were caught in a steep decline. Changing demographics had reduced the number of housewives who could attend Tupperware parties, the traditional selling method." So Premark targeted women in overseas markets. As part of its marketing strategy, the company used simple but ingenious sales techniques to appeal to local buyers—in Japan, it "began selling Tupperware containers packed with nori, the seaweed used to wrap sushi, as an extra sales incentive." The Asian market now makes up 25 percent of sales, while the United States accounts for only 19 percent.[53]

Porter's diamond model (see Figure 10.1) illustrates the *location-based determinants* that spur innovation crucial to gaining competitive advantage.

Porter points to stellar performer Hewlett-Packard's strategy for leveraging locality. Although headquartered in the United States, "HP generates 54 percent of its revenues outside the U.S." It operates in 110 countries, has approximately 35,000 out of 98,000 employees working outside the United States, and bases 50 percent of its total assets outside the country. Additionally, it trades on stock markets around the world. And it "locates low-skilled manufacturing activities with high direct labor content in low-cost areas, at an estimated saving of 40 percent to 75 percent compared to U.S. locations." Electronic component manufacturing takes place in Malaysia, but PC component assembly and manufacturing happens in Singapore, while software coding and maintenance work is done in India, China, or Eastern Europe. Smart Japanese companies do the same thing. Honda, headquartered in Japan, "generates 61 percent

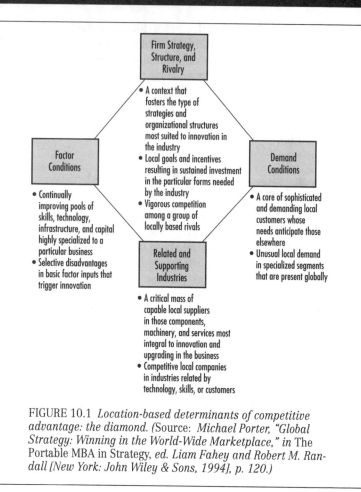

FIGURE 10.1 *Location-based determinants of competitive advantage: the diamond. (Source: Michael Porter, "Global Strategy: Winning in the World-Wide Marketplace," in* The Portable MBA in Strategy, *ed. Liam Fahey and Robert M. Randall [New York: John Wiley & Sons, 1994], p. 120.)*

of its revenues outside Japan and holds particularly strong market position in Asia and North America. Twenty-two percent of its employees and 39 percent of its total assets are based outside Japan." The company operates in 39 countries and distributes in 150.[54]

ABB has leveraged its global/local duality, and Percy Barnevik claims it is a win/win situation: Managers operate just like other small companies in their local areas, but they have the advantage of belonging to a big group. When one medium-sized plant combines with 30 others of similar size in the corporation, they "can fund research they could not afford on their own." Rather than buying from 31 different suppliers, the group can buy from several who will commit to excellence in price, quality, and service.[55]

GLOBAL STRATEGIES DEMAND LEADERSHIP

As more companies conduct business on an international basis, more demands are placed on managers. Leadership skills discussed earlier—the ability to communicate effectively on an interpersonal level, a collaborative spirit that encourages information sharing, a willingness to understand culture and its significance, an ability to develop relationships, and an ability to inspire, motivate, and negotiate—are absolute requisites. Intelligence, discipline, and courage are also needed. Slipshod approaches and feeble attempts won't work.

Success in the global market also takes time. Building trust, developing shared visions, and motivating disparate employees to work together toward goals don't happen overnight. Combining management abilities with the art of leadership is essential. In the late '80s, Whirlpool CEO David Whitman decided to go global. Like so many other large, mature U.S. businesses at the time, Whirlpool found itself with declining profit margins. As it waged a competitive war in the major appliances market, it lowered costs and improved the quality of its products, but found it was sailing in circles. Whitman decided to power up the company's engines and head across the seas, rather than diversify in American waters. In 1989, Whirlpool bought Philips N.V.'s European appliance business for $1 billion. Five years later, Whitman was quoted as saying, "The art of management is not confined to orchestrating the creation of a bold vision, a great plan, or even one set of actions that causes the organization to face up to the need for change. It must also encompass relentless follow-through, meticulous attention to detail, and the establishment of personal accountability throughout the organization."[56]

Whitman's bold move thrust the company into "the number one spot worldwide and set the pace for the appliance industry around the globe." Whirlpool now manufactures in 11 countries, sells its products in 120 locations, and has 38,000 employees working around the globe. Between 1990 and 1992, total revenues increased by almost a billion dollars.[57]

KEY CONCEPT — GLOBALIZATION INCLUDES HARD AND SOFT ISSUES

Managers must have knowledge about both hard and soft issues. In order to conduct business globally, managers require hard knowledge about the rules, regulations, and economies of countries in which they are interested as well as the roles, resources, practices, and systems of the companies they want to do business with. Information and accounting systems need to be consistent to enable comparison of figures in a meaningful way. And decision making should be based on overall global goals, and not on individual subsidiary performance.[58]

Additionally, managers must understand the soft issue of corporate culture with its below-the-waterline values and beliefs. By understanding roles and attitudes towards authority, managers can learn how much information is disclosed and what level of openness and honesty is operating. By learning about reward systems, managers learn about how success is measured, which in turn provides insight into motivation. This kind of knowledge can help in the formulation of strategy, clarifying what leverage points exist and what value-added aspects are needed. Understanding rituals also provides insight into the relevance of respect in the culture and how that respect is demonstrated. This knowledge not only provides the ability to overcome cultural disparities, but also offers the benefits of learning from doing things in different ways.[59]

Management expert and author Rosabeth Moss Kanter claims that one of the most fundamental prerequisites for global success is "direct human communication."[60] The complex web of relationships discussed in the first part of this book expands even further in a global business world. Managers will have to pay even more attention to understanding the interconnections and their own roles in weaving the strands together.

AlliedSignal, a $13 billion industrial supplier of aerospace systems, automotive parts, and chemical products, recognizes the significance of understanding markets. It created an Asian council, enabling people who are undertaking Asian initiatives to "get together, share market intelligence, and compare notes." The council provides a support network, helping people to get timely information on current market conditions.[61]

Astute global business managers must be skilled in human relations and able to bridge the gap between cultures, determining how international partners make decisions and understanding what kinds of relationships and partnerships are attractive to them.

FORD MOTOR COMPANY: RISK TAKER

Star Some companies are taking radically bold moves in their global decision-making process. Ford, the world's number two auto manufacturer, decided to go global in its production strategy and launched its Ford 2000 initiative in January 1995. It merged its European and American operations and will include Asia and South America by the end of 1995. Ford is leveraging its economies of scale to the extreme by combining all of its auto operations, hoping to trim $2 to $3 billion from its expenses.

Even though its recent record has been impressive—it "reported record earnings of $5.3 billion in 1994, up 100 percent, on record revenues of $128 billion, an 18 percent gain"—the 91-year-old company's top-heavy bureaucracy has caused it to be slow. Speed has been a big problem: Competitors get new cars to market faster and more efficiently. Toyota turns out "37 vehicles per worker to Ford's 20." Plus, competitors have had better profit margins. "Chrysler's pretax profit margin on autos, at 11.6 percent, was twice Ford's 5.4 percent."[62]

In its global restructuring effort, CEO Alexander J. Trotman has "eliminated self-contained country units and the separate vehicles, engines, and components they produce."[63] The company had six different four-cylinder engines in Europe and North America, and "currently, European and American cars have no parts in common." By buying in larger volume from a smaller number of suppliers, Ford hopes to slash spending. As well as restructuring, Ford is involving "managers from both sides of the Atlantic . . . in a massive reengineering project." Engineers and multi-functional teams are working out of "five new 'Vehicle Centers'—four in the U.S., one in Europe—each responsible for designing a different type of vehicle worldwide."[64]

Ford is facing enormous challenges with this aggressive strategic move. So far, it has made some progress: bureaucracy has been reduced and processes have speeded up. But Trotman truly has "stretch goals"—with "the will to do it," he thinks it's possible to "snare 30 percent of the North American vehicle market and 15 percent of the European market," and he wants "to land 5 percent to 10 percent of the Japanese Market."[65]

Cars designed with the new team approach won't reach the market until 1997, but it will be interesting to see how cars like the Ford Escort, which is a different vehicle in Europe than it is in the United States, will be made to appeal to both groups and be cost efficient at the same time. The question for Ford is: Will the new global strategy radiate light on new ways to operate globally, or will it suck the company into a black hole filled with red ink?

GLOBAL PARTNERING CAN PROVE PROFITABLE

Aligning with other companies around the globe not only provides access to their markets, but enables companies to utilize the technologies and skills available in a particular area. Sometimes, access to these resources is simply not available without partnering with another company that already has an established presence.

Developing relationships with a few international suppliers, as Ford and other companies are doing, can be an extremely effective strategy. Whirlpool's global strategy includes formal partnerships with Procter & Gamble in the United States and with Unilever in Brazil. Like Ford, it too is partnering with one or two suppliers, with the goal of improving processes by sharing technologies.[66]

FIAT: ITALIAN PARTNERSHIPS

Fiat, another car manufacturer trying new approaches, is linking up with its suppliers in an attempt to increase its speed. So far, its strategy of partnering has worked. By the end of 1993, exports increased 62 percent, and production increased 30 percent. Fiat's new factory, located in the southern Italian city of Melfi, sits right next door to its major supplier. In the late '80s, Fiat realized its two greatest weaknesses were time and quality. But designing better-quality cars in shorter time periods required restructuring the way the company worked and developing a better relationship with suppliers. Because Fiat bought on price, not enough attention was paid to quality and detail, and interaction with suppliers was short and sweet. Fiat needed something really enticing to lure suppliers into investing in Fiat's business, so it offered suppliers exclusive contracts. In exchange for exclusivity, suppliers had to be willing to have their designers work with Fiat designers and some suppliers had to open factories. The temptation worked: 92 percent of the parts on Fiat's latest small car, the Punto, have one supplier. Part of the 12 trillion lira Fiat annually spends to buy parts now goes into fewer pockets: The number of suppliers has been cut from 500 to 130. Fiat managers say the key to the new relationship is trust—a business miracle in Italy—and one which the skeptics are watching closely.[67]

KLM: EUROPEAN HIGH FLYER

KLM, at 75, is "Europe's fastest-growing carrier." It forged what seemed to be a risky, but has proven to be a highly successful, alliance with Northwest Airlines Inc. "Together, KLM and Northwest are the world's third-largest carrier in revenues, after American and United." Their alliance allows them to hurdle borders they couldn't clear alone and enables them to cut costs. Both airlines recorded good-sized profits in 1994. KLM has also experienced tremendous growth in Asia and Latin America. Its success is in sharp contrast to the state-subsidized airlines of other European countries. In 1991, Pieter Bouw, an insider with 28 years of service in the company, became chairman and instituted a cost-cutting, growth strategy. He increased passenger traffic by almost 50 percent, expanding flights across Europe. He paired with Northwest and developed a hub serving Africa, Asia, and the United States. The two airlines still need to standardize service to enhance their common appeal to passengers. And the two vastly different cultures of their employees will require extra attention if they are combined, but their alliance has truly demonstrated the power of global partnering.[68]

SMALL COMPANIES CAN CROSS BIG OCEANS, TOO

Small companies and entrepreneurs are also setting sail across the oceans of the world. In 1994, Arthur Andersen & Co. and the National Small Business United conducted a survey of 750 companies and found that "20 percent of companies with fewer than 500 employees exported products and services," an increase over both 1993 and 1992. And DRI/McGraw-Hill estimates "that small businesses could account for 50.8 percent of the $548 billion worth of manufactured goods that the U.S. will likely export in 1995."[69]

The North American Free Trade Agreement (NAFTA) and the General Agreement on Tariffs and Trade (GATT) have put the wind in the sails of small companies by lowering tariffs. Before NAFTA, a small ($6 million) U.S. maker of car cleaning products couldn't afford "stiff Mexican tariffs." After NAFTA, "tariffs started gradually dropping," and the company "landed contracts with almost every major retail chain in Mexico." The company's "shipments to Mexico tripled to roughly $300,000, about 20 percent of the company's total exports."[70] Doing business abroad always carries risk and the Mexican peso crisis was a disaster, but this determined company is holding on, waiting for the Mexican financial market to stabilize.

THE SMALLER THE POCKET, THE BIGGER THE CAUTION

DANGER!

Because small companies generally don't have the benefit of deeper pockets that come with bigger size, it is even more important that they understand culture, the market, and their customers. It's a good idea for small companies to use letters of credit, which can provide protection if the buyer defaults, and to allow enough time to get financing properly arranged. Conducting business outside of one's home port calls for knowledge and research. Thorough understanding of regulatory and tariffs systems is extremely important and can make the difference between profit and loss for small companies. The ISO 9000 program, run by the International Organization for Standardization, requires uniform standards on products, and if imports don't measure up they can be barred from entering countries. Costs for product adjustments and red tape can, unfortunately, add up quickly. One small computer company that "shipped a $10,000 replacement computer component to a French customer . . . was stunned when it was billed $2,500 for value-added tax."[71]

INFORMATION IS EVERYWHERE—IF YOU KNOW WHERE TO LOOK

There are numerous ways for companies, large and small, to gather information about international markets, but often smaller companies don't know where to turn. Government, private agencies, and organizations offer information, advice, and guidance.

Under the Department of Commerce, the International Trade Administration provides information on importing and exporting, international banking, and freight forwarders. It has several programs providing market research, information about distributors, and trade opportunities, including a Matchmaker Program for small- and medium-sized firms and a database of reports on countries and companies. The U.S. and Foreign Commerce Service (US&FCS) has a global network of services. Both the Commerce and State Departments staff Country Desks, where information relevant to specific countries is available. Additionally, the Trade and Development Program promotes U.S. exports and offers planning services. Economic development offices of foreign countries with offices located in the United States are additional sources, as is the International Division of the U.S. Chamber of Commerce. And overseas, most countries have American Chambers of Commerce and some have U.S. state government offices.[72]

The National Institute of Standards and Technology has information on GATT, and the American National Standards Institute provides information on standards and ISO 9000. World trade centers, world trade associations, and world trade shows are other valuable resources, but it's wise to be careful about investing in trade shows. Some of them are easily affordable; others are expensive. The cost of government-sponsored trade shows can, at first glance, seem too pricey for small firms, but going global requires ingenuity. In 1989, one computer networking company saw tremendous opportunity in Russia and "teamed up with three other small companies to pay for a $25,000 booth at a Commerce Department-sponsored trade show in Moscow." By 1994, "20 percent of the $19 million in business came from former Soviet countries."[73] Other avenues to check, which are cost free, are complementary companies in the industry. By talking to companies that have already gone global, companies can find out about industry suppliers and distributors.

END POINT

Everything is more complex in today's business world. Managers are being challenged as they never have been before—they almost need magic to foresee the multitude of changes taking place and the ramifications those changes will have. As strategic planners, anticipating seemingly constant changes, managers must decide how to stimulate desired growth, regenerate their organizations, and innovate products and services.

Managers must be excellent communicators, capable of listening to what their customers want so they can design products that provide the value customers expect. Having full knowledge of an organization's resources, competencies, and businesses and knowing how to position those businesses in a global world demands intelligence and foresight.

Operating in a global world stretches managers even more. They must have deeper knowledge and understanding of a wider range of both hard and soft issues. Information technology, as discussed in Chapter 8, is having a profound impact: As it makes the world smaller, managers must not only attempt to work in a global marketplace but in a marketspace that has virtually no boundaries.

MORE READING

Alexander, Marcus, Andrew Campbell, and Michael Goold. *Corporate-Level Strategy: Creating Value in the Multibusiness Company.* New York: John Wiley & Sons, 1994.

Bartlett, C. A., and S. Ghoshal. *Managing Across Borders: The Transnational Solution.* Boston: Harvard Business School Press, 1989.

Beer, Michael, Russet A. Eisenstat, and Bert Spector. *The Critical Path to Corporate Renewal.* Cambridge, Mass.: Harvard Business School Press, 1990.

Etzioni, A. *Modern Organizations.* Englewood Cliffs, N.J.: Prentice-Hall, 1964.

Galbraith, Jay. *Organization Design.* Reading, Mass.: Addison-Wesley, 1977.

Guillen, M. F. *Models of Management: Work, Authority, and Organizational Comparative Perspective.* Chicago: University of Chicago Press, 1994.

Guy, V., and John Mattock. *The International Business Book.* Chicago: NTC Business Books, 1995.

Hackman, J. Richard, and Greg Oldham. *Work Redesign.* Reading, Mass.: Addison-Wesley, 1980.

Hamel, Gary, and C. K. Prahalad. *Competing for the Future: Breakthrough Strategies for Seizing Control of Your Industry and Creating the Markets of Tomorrow.* Boston: Harvard Business School Press, 1994.

Hammer, Michael, and James Champy. *Reengineering the Corporation.* New York: HarperBusiness, 1993.

Hofstede, G. *Culture's Consequences: International Differences in Work-Related Values.* Newbury Park, Cal.: Sage, 1980.

Johnson, G. *Strategic Change and the Management Process.* Oxford, UK: Basil Blackwell, 1987.

Kets De Vries, M., and D. Miller. *The Neurotic Organization.* San Francisco: Jossey-Bass. 1984.

Kilmann, R. H., et al. (eds.). *Gaining Control of the Corporate Culture.* San Francisco: Jossey-Bass, 1985.

Kobayashi, Koju. *Computers and Communications: A Vision of C&C.* Cambridge, Mass.: The MIT Press, 1986.

Nadler, David A., Marc S. Gerstein, and Robert S. Shaw and Associates. *Organizational Architecture: Designs for Changing Organizations.* San Francisco: Jossey-Bass, 1992.

Ohmae, K. *Triad Power: The Coming Shape of Global Competition.* New York: The Free Press, 1985.

———. *The Borderless World: Power and Strategy in the Interlinked Economy.* New York: HarperBusiness, 1990.

Pascale, R. T., *Managing on the Edge.* New York: Simon & Schuster, 1990.

Perrow, C. *Complex Organizations.* New York: Random House, 1986.

Peters T. J., and R. H. Waterman, Jr. *In Search of Excellence: Lessons from America's Best-Run Companies.* New York: Harper & Row, 1982.

Porter, M. E. *Competitive Strategy: Techniques for Analyzing Industries and Competitors.* New York: The Free Press, 1980.

———. *Competitive Advantage: Creating and Sustaining Superior Performance.* New York: The Free Press, 1985.

——— (ed.). *Competition in Global Industries.* Boston: Harvard Business School Press, 1986.

———. *The Competitive Advantage of Nations.* New York: The Free Press, 1990.

———. "Global Strategy: Winning in the World-Wide Marketplace," in L. Fahey, and R. Randall (eds.). *The Portable MBA in Strategy.* New York: John Wiley & Sons, 1994.

Quinn, James Brian. *Intelligent Enterprise.* New York: The Free Press, 1992.

Reich, R. B. *The Work of Nations: Preparing Ourselves for 21st-Century Capitalism.* New York: Alfred A. Knopf, 1991.

Rummler, Gary A., and Alan P. Brache. *Improving Performance—How to Manage the White Space on the Organization Chart.* San Francisco: Jossey-Bass, 1990.

Schein, E. H. *Strategic Change and the Management Process.* Oxford, UK: Basil Blackwell, 1987.

Schwartz, P. *The Art of the Long View.* New York: Doubleday, 1991.

Senge, Peter. *The Fifth Discipline.* New York: Currency Doubleday, 1990.

Womack, J. P., D. T. Jones, and D. Roos. *The Machine That Changed the World: The Story of Lean Production.* New York: Harper Perennial, 1991.

Conclusion

Now comes the hard part—putting words into action. Success will be achieved when managers create environments that nourish leadership, filling the organization with creative thinkers who are willing to take risks and lead the organization forward.

Performance will improve when organizational leaders live by their belief and mission statements, providing role models for employees throughout all levels of the company. When policies and procedures accurately reflect organizational values and goals and are effectively communicated, the performance of individual employees will be enhanced and the organization as a whole will gain.

As the organization becomes more inclusive and more employees are taught to understand basic business principles, there will be greater opportunity for innovation and more accountability, which will lead to better bottom-line results.

When managers, employees, suppliers, and customers learn to work together and to develop mutually satisfying relationships, everyone within the organization and along the distribution chain will benefit. By breaking from traditional structures and envisioning new and unusual functional combinations, value has a greater potential for being added, and the organization has a better chance of operating more effectively.

Innovative approaches combined with creative strategies and information technology open the way for new products and services not even imagined today. If organizations can harness their own "soul" power, combine it with the energy available in people and machine power, and operate from principles that are inclusive and considerate of the entire system, "good" will prevail, the organization will succeed, and managers will know they have done their jobs well.

CHAPTER 1

1. Sumantra Ghoshal and Christopher A. Bartlett, "Changing the Role of Top Management: Beyond Structure to Processes," *Harvard Business Review* (January/February 1995), pp. 86–96.

2. Ibid., p. 96.

3. John P. Kotter, *A Force for Change: How Leadership Differs From Management* (New York: The Free Press, 1990), pp. 4–5.

4. "James Champy on Reengineering Management," *Business Week* Online Conference, 10 January 1995 (America Online: McGraw-Hill, 1995).

5. Kotter, pp. 7–8.

6. Janet Wylie, *Chances and Choices: How Women Can Succeed in Today's Knowledge-Based Business* (Vienna, Va.: E. B. W. Press, 1996).

7. Sally Helgesen, *The Female Advantage* (New York: Currency Doubleday, 1990), p. 29.

8. Interview with Lawrence A. Pfaff, Ed.D., human resource consultant and creator of the *Management-Leadership Practices Inventory,* the *Team Practices Inventory,* and the *Professional Communication Inventory,* Kalamazoo, Michigan.

9. "Styles of Success: Research on Gender Differences in Management Styles: Interview with Julie Weeks, Research Director of the National Foundation for Women Business Owners," *Small Business Forum* (Association of Small Business Development Centers, University of Wisconsin-Extension Small Business Development Center, 1995), pp. 52–65.

10. Ibid., p. 54.

11. Helgesen, pp. 43–60.

12. Ibid., pp. 55–59.

13. Tom Chappell, *The Soul of a Business: Managing for Profit and the Common Good* (New York: Bantam, 1993), pp. 117–119.

14. John P. Kotter and James L. Heskett, *Corporate Culture and Performance* (New York: The Free Press, 1992), p. 61.

15. Noel M. Tichy and Ram Charan, "The CEO as Coach: An Interview with AlliedSignal's Lawrence A. Bossidy," *Harvard Business Review* (March/April 1995), pp. 69–78.

16. Andrew Brown, "Top of the Bosses," *International Management* (April 1994), p. 28.

17. Jay A. Conger, "Leadership for the Year 2000," in *The New Portable MBA,* eds. Eliza G. C. Collins and Mary Anne Devanna (New York: John Wiley & Sons, 1994), p. 409.

18. Ibid., p. 410.

19. Peter Drucker, *Managing for the Future: The 1990s and Beyond* (New York: Truman Talley Books/Plume, 1993), p. 120.

20. James C. Collins and Jerry I. Porras, *Built to Last: Successful Habits of Visionary Companies* (New York: HarperBusiness, 1994), pp. 170–173.

21. Drucker, pp. 121–123.

22. David C. McClelland and David H. Burnham, "Power Is the Great Motivator," *Harvard Business Review* (January/February 1995), p. 127.

23. Ibid., pp. 126–139.

24. David C. McClelland, "Retrospective Commentary," *Harvard Business Review* (January/February 1995), pp. 138–139.

25. Peter Scott Morgan, "Ringing the Changes," *International Management* (September 1994), p. 59.

26. Christopher A. Bartlett and Sumantra Ghoshal, "Changing the Role of Top Management: Beyond Strategy to Purpose," *Harvard Business Review* (November/December 1994), pp. 81–83, and Christopher A. Bartlett and Sumantra Ghoshal, "Changing the Role of Top Management: Beyond Systems to People," *Harvard Business Review* (May/June 1995), pp. 136–137.

27. Phyllis F. Schlesinger and Leonard A. Schlesinger, "Designing Effective Organizations," in *The Portable MBA in Management,* ed. Allan R. Cohen (New York: John Wiley & Sons, 1993), pp. 246–247.

28. Bartlett and Ghoshal, "Changing the Role of Top Management: Beyond Systems to People," pp. 140–141.

29. Ibid., p. 140.

30. Ibid.

31. Bartlett and Ghoshal, "Changing the Role of Top Management: Beyond Strategy to Purpose," p. 87; The Body Shop corporate material.

32. Joshua Hyatt, "Real-World Reengineering," *Inc.* (April 1995), pp. 40–53.

33. Interview with Chuck Mitchell.

CHAPTER 2

1. John P. Kotter and James L. Heskett, *Corporate Culture and Performance* (New York: The Free Press, 1992), p. 11.

2. James C. Collins and Jerry I. Porras, *Built to Last: Successful Habits of Visionary Companies* (New York: HarperBusiness, 1994), p. 4.

3. Ibid., p. 73.

4. Lynn Sharp Paine, "Managing for Organizational Integrity," *Harvard Business Review* (March/April 1994), p. 109.

5. Collins and Porras, p. 88.

6. Robert Simons, "Control in an Age of Empowerment," *Harvard Business Review* (March/April 1995), pp. 80–88.

7. Collins and Porras, p. 62.

8. Ibid., pp. 24, 79.

9. Todd D. Jick, "Managing Change," in *The Portable MBA in Management,* ed. Allan R. Cohen (New York: John Wiley & Sons, 1993), p. 355.

10. Collins and Porras, p. 95.

11. Peter B. Vaill, "Visionary Leadership," in *The Portable MBA in Management,* ed. Allan R. Cohen (New York: John Wiley & Sons, 1993), p. 17.

12. Tom Chappell, *The Soul of a Business: Managing for Profit and the Common Good* (New York: Bantam, 1993), pp. 20–37.

13. Ibid., pp. 54–56.

14. Vaill, pp. 30–33.

15. Ibid., pp. 32–36.

16. Kotter and Heskett, pp. 68–80.

17. Alex Taylor III, "GM: Some Gain Much Pain," *Fortune* (29 May 1995), pp. 78–84.

18. Kotter and Heskett, pp. 38–57.

19. Ibid., pp. 40–41.

20. Alexander Hiam and Charles D. Schewe, *The Portable MBA in Marketing* (New York: John Wiley & Sons, 1994), pp. 27–28.

21. Kotter and Heskett, pp. 46–57.

22. Ibid.

23. Ibid.

24. Gerry Johnson, "Strategic Change: Managing Cultural Processes," *The Portable MBA in Strategy,* eds. Liam Fahey and Robert M. Randall (New York: John Wiley & Sons, 1994), p. 433.

CHAPTER 3

1. James C. Collins and Jerry I. Porras, *Built to Last: Successful Habits of Visionary Companies* (New York: HarperBusiness, 1994), p. 158.

2. Ibid., pp. 115–121.

3. Wendy Zellner, et al., "Go-Go Goliaths," and Wendy Zellner, "Southwest," *Business Week,* 13 February 1995 (America Online: McGraw-Hill, 1995).

4. Mary Anne Devanna, "Human Resource Management: Competitive Advantage through People," in *The New Portable MBA,* eds. Eliza G. C. Collins and Mary Anne Devanna (New York: John Wiley & Sons, 1994), p. 187.

5. Helen Rheem, "Performance Management," *Harvard Business Review* (May/June 1995), pp. 11–12.

6. Refina Fazio Maruca, "The Right Way to Go Global: An Interview with Whirlpool CEO David Whitwam," *Harvard Business Review* (March/April 1994), p. 140.

7. Zellner, et al., "Go-Go Goliaths."

8. Rheem, p. 12.

9. Robert Hoffman, "Ten Reasons You Should Be Using 360-Degree Feedback," *HRMagazine* (April 1995), pp. 82–85.

10. Devanna, pp. 189–190.

11. Ibid.

12. John Case, *Open-Book Management: The Coming Business Revolution* (New York: HarperCollins, 1995), p. xvii.

13. Ibid., p. xx.

14. Jay Finegan, "Everything According to Plan," *Inc.* (March 1995), pp. 78–85.

15. "Open-Book Management: Special Report," *Inc.* (June 1995), pp. 27–42.

16. David Whitford, "Before And After," *Inc.* (June 1995), pp. 44–50.

17. Case, p. xxii.

18. Ibid.

19. Ibid., p. xxi.

20. Noel M. Tichy and Ram Charan, "The CEO as Coach: An Interview with AlliedSignal's Lawrence A. Bossidy," *Harvard Business Review* (March/April 1995), pp. 69–78.

21. Christopher A. Bartlett and Sumantra Ghoshal, "Changing the Role of Top Management: Beyond Strategy to Purpose," *Harvard Business Review* (November/December 1994), p. 87.

22. Allan R. Cohen, "Managing People: The R Factor," in *The New Portable MBA,* eds. Eliza G. C. Collins and Mary Anne Devanna (New York: John Wiley & Sons, 1994), pp. 32–33.

23. R. Roosevelt Thomas, Jr., "Managing Diversity: Utilizing the Talents of the New Work Force," in *The Portable MBA in Management,* ed. Allan R. Cohen (New York: John Wiley & Sons, 1993), pp. 315–339.

24. Russell Mitchell and Michael Oneal, "Managing by Values: Is Levi Strauss' Approach Visionary or Flaky?" *Business Week,* 1 August 1994 (America Online: McGraw-Hill, 1994).

25. Robert H. Waterman, Jr., *What America Does Right* (New York: Penguin Books, 1994), pp. 153–156.

26. Mitchell and Oneal.

27. Lynn Sharp Paine, "Managing for Organizational Integrity," *Harvard Business Review* (March/April 1994), pp. 106–117.

28. Ibid., pp. 112–115.

29. Charles J. Fombrun and Drew Harris, "Managing Human Resources Strategically," in *The Portable MBA in Management,* ed. Allan R. Cohen (New York: John Wiley & Sons, 1993), pp. 254–255.

30. James B. Treece, Kathleen Kerwin, and Heidi Dawley, "Ford: Alex Trotman's Daring Global Strategy," *Business Week,* 3 April 1995 (America Online: McGraw-Hill, 1995).

31. "HR for Profit," *Investor's Business Daily,* 30 May 1995 (America Online: Investor's Business Daily, 1995).

CHAPTER 4

1. Harvey Kolodny and Torbjorn Sternberg, "Self-Managing Teams: The New Organization of Work," in *The Portable MBA in Management,* ed. Allan R. Cohen (New York: John Wiley & Sons, 1993), p. 279.

2. Ibid., p. 306.

3. Christopher Meyer, "How the Right Measures Help Teams Excel," *Harvard Business Review* (May/June 1994), p. 96.

4. D. Keith Denton, "Process Mapping Trims Cycle Time," *HRMagazine* (February 1995), p. 57.

5. Kolodny and Sternberg, p. 289.

6. Refina Fazio Maruca, "The Right Way to Go Global: An Interview with Whirlpool CEO David Whitwam," *Harvard Business Review* (March/April 1994), p. 141.

7. David L. Bradford, "Building High-Performance Teams," in *The Portable MBA in Management,* ed. Allan R. Cohen (New York: John Wiley & Sons, 1993), pp. 42–44.

8. Peter Senge, *The Fifth Discipline* (New York: Currency Doubleday, 1990), p. 235.

9. Ibid., p. 237.

10. Bradford, pp. 44–47.

11. Kolodny and Sternberg, p. 291.

12. Bradford, pp. 46–52.

13. Ibid., pp. 48–50.

14. Wendy Zellner, et al., "Go-Go Goliaths," *Business Week,* 13 February 1995 (America Online: McGraw-Hill, 1995).

15. Chris Argyris, "Good Communication that Blocks Learning," *Harvard Business Review* (July/August 1994).

16. Sumantra Ghoshal and Christopher A. Bartlett, "Changing the Role of Top Management: Beyond Structure to Processes," *Harvard Business Review* (January/February 1995), pp. 86–96.

17. Bradford, pp. 56–67.

18. Meyer, p. 95.

19. Ibid., pp. 96–97.

20. Ibid.

21. Ibid., pp. 97–101.

22. James C. Collins and Jerry I. Porras, *Built to Last: Successful Habits of Visionary Companies* (New York: HarperBusiness, 1994), p. 115.

23. Louise O'Brien and Charles Jones, "Do Rewards Really Create Loyalty?" *Harvard Business Review* (May/June 1995), pp. 75–82.

24. Frederick L. Webster, "Marketing Management: Providing Value to Customers," in *The New Portable MBA* (New York: John Wiley & Sons, 1994), pp. 158–159.

25. Tim R. Furey and Stephen G. Diorio, "Making Reengineering Strategic," *Planning Review* (July/August 1994), pp. 7–9.

26. Maruca, pp. 143–144.

27. Noel M. Tichy and Ram Charan, "The CEO as Coach: An Interview with AlliedSignal's Lawrence A. Bossidy," *Harvard Business Review* (March/April 1995), pp. 69–78.

28. Francis J. Gouillart and Frederick D. Sturdivant, "Spend a Day in the Life of Your Customers," *Harvard Business Review* (January/February 1994), pp. 116–125.

29. B. Joseph Pine II, Don Peppers, and Martha Rogers, "Do You Want to Keep Your Customers Forever?" *Harvard Business Review* (March/April 1995), pp. 103–114.

30. Ibid., p. 112.

31. Ibid.

CHAPTER 5

1. Robert C. Higgins, *Analysis for Financial Management,* 3d ed. (Burr Ridge, Ill.: Richard D. Irwin, 1992), p. 5.

2. John Leslie Livingstone, "Accounting and Management Decision Making," in *The New Portable MBA,* eds. Eliza G. C. Collins and Mary Anne Devanna (New York: John Wiley & Sons, 1994), p. 247.

3. Higgins, p. 40.

4. Ibid., pp. 38–75.

5. Ibid.

6. Livingstone, pp. 260–264.

7. Higgins, p. 54.

8. Ibid., pp. 38–75.

9. Ibid.

10. Ibid., pp. 61–64.

CHAPTER 6

1. John Leslie Livingstone and James E. Walter, "Financial Management: Optimizing the Value of the Firm," in *The New Portable MBA,* eds. Eliza G. C. Collins and Mary Anne Devanna (New York: John Wiley & Sons, 1994), p. 268.

2. Robert C. Higgins, *Analysis for Financial Management,* 3d ed. (Burr Ridge, Ill.: Richard D. Irwin, 1992), p. 346.

3. Livingstone, p. 299.

4. Higgins, p. 351.

5. Avinash K. Dixit and Robert S. Pindyck, "The Options Approach to Capital Investment," *Harvard Business Review* (May/June 1995), p. 108.

6. Livingstone, pp. 270–272.

7. Ibid.

8. Ibid.

9. Higgins, pp. 250–251.

10. Higgins, pp. 92–93.

CHAPTER 7

1. Frank Lichtenberg, "Managerial Economics: Guidelines for Choices and Decisions," in *The New Portable MBA,* eds. Eliza G. C. Collins and Mary Anne Devanna (New York: John Wiley & Sons, 1994), pp. 97–128.

2. Philip K. Y. Young and John J. McAuley, *The Portable MBA in Economics* (New York: John Wiley & Sons, 1994), pp. 8–24.

3. Ibid., p. 65.

4. "Special Report: The Rise and Fall of the Dollar," *The Boston Globe* (11 June 1995), p. A1.

5. Mitchell Zuckoff, "Crisis Control for Currencies," *The Boston Globe* (11 June 1995), p. A1.

6. Frank Connelly and Dan Weil, "Dollar soars after effort by US, allies," *The Boston Globe* (16 March 1995), p. 45.

7. Young, p. 43.

8. Ibid.

9. Ibid., pp. 43–49.

10. Ibid., p. 145.

11. "Japan's NEC will buy 20% Packard Bell Stake," *Investor's Business Daily,* 11 July 1995 (America Online: Investor's Business Daily, 1995).

12. Young, pp. 146–162.

13. Steven Levy, "How Apple Became Avis," *Newsweek* (21 August 1995), p. 42.

14. Young, p. 160.

CHAPTER 8

1. Michael J. Mandel, "The Digital Juggernaut," *Business Week,* 18 May 1994 (America Online: McGraw-Hill, 1994).

2. Neil Gross and John Carey, "In the Digital Derby, There's No Inside Lane," *Business Week,* 18 November 1994 (America Online: McGraw-Hill, 1994).

3. Peter Burrows, Linda Bernier, and Pete Engardio, "The Global Chip Payoff," *Business Week International Edition,* 7 August 1995 (America Online: McGraw-Hill, 1995).

4. Ibid.

5. Christopher Farrell, "Why the Numbers Miss the Point," *Business Week,* 31 July 1995 (America Online: McGraw-Hill, 1995).

6. Louis S. Richman, "The Big Payoff from Computers," *Fortune,* 7 March 1994, vol. 129, no. 5, p. 28 (America Online: Time, Inc., 1994).

7. Mandel.

8. Joshua D. Macht, "How Has Technology Changed the Way You Do Your Job?" *Inc.* (America Online: Inc. Technology, 1994).

9. Stratford Sherman, "When Laws of Physics Meet Law of the Jungle: Winning Ideas in Technology," *Fortune,* 15 May 1995 (America Online: Time Inc., 1995).

10. Farrell.

11. Peter Coy, "Faster, Smaller, Cheaper," *Business Week,* 18 May 1994 (America Online: McGraw-Hill, 1994).

12. Michael Meyer, "Faster and Faster," *Newsweek* (18 September 1995), p. 65.

13. Dorothy Leonard-Barton, et al., "How to Integrate Work and Deepen Expertise," *Harvard Business Review* (September/October), p. 125.

14. Burrows, Bernier, and Engardio.

15. Catherine Arnst, "Networked Corporation: Linking up is hard to do—but it's a necessity," *Business Week,* 26 June 1995 (America Online: McGraw-Hill, 1995).

16. Sumantra Ghoshal and Christopher A. Bartlett, "Changing the Role of Top Management: Beyond Structure to Processes," *Harvard Business Review* (January/February 1995), pp. 91–92.

17. Tim R. Furey and Stephen G. Diorio, "Making Reengineering Strategic," *Planning Review* (July/August 1994), p. 7.

18. Ira Sager, "The Man Who's Rebooting IBM's PC Business," *Business Week,* 24 July 1995 (America Online: McGraw-Hill, 1995).

19. Peter Burrows, "Giant Killers on the Loose," *Business Week,* 18 May 1994 (America Online: McGraw-Hill, 1994).

20. N. Venkatraman, "IT-Enabled Business Transformation: From Automation to Business Scope Redefinition," *Sloan Management Review* (Winter 1994), pp. 73–87.

21. Ibid.

22. Arnst.

23. Ira Sager, "The Great Equalizer," *Business Week,* 18 May 1994 (America Online: McGraw-Hill, 1994).

24. Philip W. Yetton, Kim D. Johnston, and Jane F. Craig, "Computer-Aided Architects: A Case Study of IT and Strategic Change," *Sloan Management Review* (Summer 1994), pp. 57–67.

25. Mary C. Lacity, Leslie P. Willcocks, and David F. Feeny, "IT Outsourcing: Maximize Flexibility and Control," *Harvard Business Review* (May/June 1995), pp. 84–93.

26. Charles B. Wang, "Multiple Choice," *Inc.* (America Online: The Goldhirsch Group, Inc., 1994).

27. Aleda V. Roth and Ann Marucheck, "The Knowledge Factory for Accelerated Learning Practices," *Planning Review* (May/June 1994), pp. 27–31.

28. Neil Gross, Peter Coy, and Otis Port, "The Technology Paradox: How Companies Can Thrive as Prices Dive," *Business Week,* 6 March 1995 (America Online: McGraw-Hill, 1995).

29. Ibid.

30. Gross and Carey.

31. Sherman.

32. Charles Stein, "Teaching Top Dogs New Tricks," *The Boston Globe* (22 August 1995), pp. 36–37.

33. Jerry Ackerman and Chris Reidy, "A Main Street Marriage, Rated G," *The Boston Globe* (1 August 1995), p. 33; Aaron Zitner, "Consumer Static Greets Warner Deal," *The Boston Globe* (23 September 1995), p. 9.

34. Aaron Zitner and Beppi Crosariol, "IBM and Lotus to Huddle on Strategy," *The Boston Globe* (13 June 1995), pp. 45–47; and Maria Shao, "Entrepreneurs Take Notes, Build Companies," *The Boston Globe* (13 June 1995), pp. 45–47.

35. Aaron Zitner, "AT&T will split into 3 companies," *The Boston Globe* (21 September 1995), p. 43.

CHAPTER 9

1. Ellen R. Hart, "Strategic Change: Reconfiguring Operational Processes to Implement Strategy," *Portable MBA in Strategy,* eds. Liam Fahey and Robert M. Randall (New York: John Wiley & Sons, 1994), pp. 358–388.

2. Elizabeth Lesly, et al., "A Bittersweet Year for Corporate America," *Business Week,* 27 March 1995 (America Online: McGraw-Hill, 1995).

3. Ibid.

4. Ibid.

5. Mauro F. Guillen, "The Age of Eclecticism: Current Organizational Trends and the Evolution of Managerial Models," *Sloan Management Review* (Fall 1994), pp. 75–85.

6. Aleda V. Roth and Ann Marucheck, "The Knowledge Factory for Accelerated Learning Practices," *Planning Review* (May/June 1994), pp. 27–31.

7. David M. Upton, "What Really Makes Factories Flexible?" *Harvard Business Review* (July/August 1995), pp. 74–84.

8. Ibid.

9. Ibid.

10. Linda G. Sprague, "Operations Management: Productivity and Quality Performance," in *The New Portable MBA,* eds. Eliza G. C. Collins and Mary Anne Devanna (New York: John Wiley & Sons, 1994), pp. 220–221.

11. Robert H. Hayes and Gary P. Pisano, "Beyond World-Class: The New Manufacturing Strategy," *Harvard Business Review* (January/February 1994), p. 84.

12. Alan David MacCormack, et al., "The New Dynamics of Global Manufacturing Site Location," *Sloan Management Review* (Summer 1994, vol. 35, no. 4), p. 72.

13. Hayes and Pisano, p. 86.

14. MacCormack, et al., p. 73.

15. Stephen Baker and James B. Treece, "New US Factory Jobs Aren't in the Factory," *Business Week,* 18 November 1994 (America Online: McGraw-Hill, 1994).

16. Elizabeth Lesly, et al., "A Bittersweet Year for Corporate America," *Business Week,* 27 March 1995 (America Online: McGraw-Hill, 1995).

17. Jerry J. Jasinowski, "Readers Report," *Business Week,* 11 September 1995 (America Online: McGraw Hill, 1995).

18. H. Kent Bowen, et al., "Development Projects: The Engine of Renewal," *Harvard Business Review* (September/October 1994), pp. 111–112.

19. Hayes and Pisano, p. 85.

20. Bowen, et al., p. 111.

21. Ira Sager, "The Man's Who's Rebooting IBM's PC Business," *Business Week,* 24 July 1995 (America Online: McGraw-Hill, 1995).

22. Dorothy Leonard-Barton, et al., "How to Integrate Work and Deepen Expertise," *Harvard Business Review* (September/October 1994), p. 124.

23. James B. Treece, "Making Samples in a Snap," *Business Week,* 16 June 1995 (America Online: McGraw-Hill, 1995).

24. Frederick L. Webster, "Marketing Management: Providing Value to Customers," in *The New Portable MBA,* eds. Eliza G. C. Collins and Mary Anne Devanna (New York: John Wiley & Sons, 1994), pp. 130–131.

25. Ibid., p. 133.

26. Daniel O. Leemon, "Marketing's Core Role in Strategic Reengineering," *Planning Review* (March/April 1995), p. 11.

27. Ibid.

28. H. Kent Bowen, et al., "Make Projects the School for Leaders," *Harvard Business Review* (September/October 1994), pp. 131–136.

29. Ibid.

30. Ibid.

31. Michael D. Hutt, et al., "Hurdle the Cross-Functional Barriers to Strategic Change," *Sloan Management Review* (Spring 1995), p. 23.

32. Peter Coy, et al., "What's the Word in the Lab? Collaborate," *Business Week,* 27 June 1995 (America Online: McGraw-Hill, 1995).

33. Ibid.

34. Stephanie Anderson Forest, "Who's Afraid of J&J and 3M?" *Business Week,* 5 December 1994 (America Online: McGraw-Hill, 1994).

35. Webster, p. 139.

36. Regis McKenna, "Real-Time Marketing," *Harvard Business Review* (July/August 1995), pp. 90–91.

37. Don Peppers and Martha Rogers, "A New Marketing Paradigm: Share of Customer, Not Market Share," *Planning Review* (March/April 1995), pp. 14–18.

38. McKenna, pp. 90–91.

39. Ibid.

40. Ibid., pp. 149–151.

41. Betsy-Ann Toffler and Jane Imber, *Dictionary of Marketing Terms* (New York: Barrons Educational Series, Inc., 1994), p. 139.

42. Alexander Hiam and Charles D. Schewe, *The Portable MBA in Marketing* (New York: John Wiley & Sons, 1992), p. 295.

43. Ibid., pp. 298–302.

44. Ibid.

45. Philip K. Y. Young and John J. McAuley, *The Portable MBA in Economics* (New York: John Wiley & Sons, 1994), pp. 185–186.

46. Webster, pp. 145–146.

47. McKenna, pp. 91–92.

48. Hart, p. 363.

49. Webster, p. 148.

50. Robert D. Buzzell and Gwen Ortmeyer, "Channel Partnerships Streamline Distribution," *Sloan Management Review* (Spring 1995), pp. 85–96.

51. Ibid.

CHAPTER 10

1. "Making Products Before They're Designed," *Investor's Business Daily,* 11 January 1995 (America Online: Investor's Business Daily, 1995).

2. Ibid.

3. Ibid.

4. James Brian Quinn, "Building the Intelligent Enterprise," in *The Portable MBA in Strategy,* eds. Liam Fahey and Robert M. Randall (New York: John Wiley & Sons, 1994), pp. 224–248.

5. C. K. Prahalad, Liam Fahey, and Robert M. Randall, "A Strategy for Growth: The Role of Core Competencies in the Corporation," in *The Portable MBA in Strategy,* eds. Liam Fahey and Robert M. Randall (New York: John Wiley & Sons, 1994), pp. 249–269.

6. Ibid., pp. 264–265.

7. Sumantra Ghoshal and Christopher A. Bartlett, "Changing the Role of Top Management: Beyond Structure to Processes," *Harvard Business Review* (January/February 1995), p. 95.

8. Prahalad, Fahey, and Randall, p. 265.

9. Ghoshal and Bartlett, pp. 91–93.

10. "How to Identify and Enhance Core Competencies: Chief Planning Officer Dialogue," *Planning Review* (November/December 1994), pp. 24–26.

11. Prahalad, Fahey, and Randall, p. 257.

12. Ibid., pp. 249–269.

13. Noel M. Tichy and Ram Charan, "The CEO as Coach: An Interview with AlliedSignal's Lawrence A. Bossidy," *Harvard Business Review* (March/April 1995), pp. 69–78.

14. Marcus Alexander, Andrew Campbell, and Michael Goold, "A New Model for Reforming the Planning Review Process," *Planning Review* (January/February 1995), pp. 13–19.

15. Gary Hamel and C. K. Prahalad, "Competing for the Future," *Harvard Business Review* (July/August 1994), pp. 122–128.

16. Robert M. Randall, "How to Reshape Your Business to Fit the Future," *Planning Review* (January/February 1995), pp. 7–11.

17. Robert Marshall and Lyle Yorks, "Planning for a Restructured, Revitalized Organization," *Sloan Management Review* (Summer 1994), pp. 81–91.

18. Bernard C. Reimann, "Gary Hamel: How to Compete for the Future," *Planning Review* (September/October 1994), pp. 39–43.

19. Hamel and Prahalad, p. 125.

20. Elisabeth Lesly, et al., "The Nimble Giants," *Business Week,* 3 March 1994 (America Online: McGraw-Hill, 1994).

21. Ibid.

22. Sumantra Ghoshal and Christopher A. Bartlett, "Changing the Role of Top Management: Beyond Strategy to Purpose," *Harvard Business Review* (November/December 1994), p. 87.

23. Carl Horowitz, "Wal-Mart: Boon or Boondoggle?" *Investor's Business Daily,* 24 May 1995 (America Online: Investor's Business Daily, 1995).

24. James C. Collins and Jerry I. Porras, *Built to Last: Successful Habits of Visionary Companies* (New York: HarperBusiness, 1994), pp. 91–114.

25. Rosabeth Moss Kanter, "Future Leaders Must be Global Managers," in *The Portable MBA in Management,* ed. Allan R. Cohen (New York: John Wiley & Sons, 1993), pp. 369–380.

26. Ibid.

27. Prahalad, Fahey, and Randall, pp. 257–261.

28. "Japan's NEC Will Buy 20% of Packard Bell Stake," *Investor's Business Daily,* 11 July 1995 (America Online: Investor's Business Daily, 1995).

29. David A. Nadler, "Collaborative Strategic Thinking," *Planning Review* (September/October 1994), pp. 30–31.

30. Tim R. Furey and Stephen G. Diorio, "Making Reengineering Strategic," *Planning Review* (July/August 1994), p. 9.

31. Paul J. H. Schoemaker, "Scenario Planning: A Tool for Strategic Thinking," *Sloan Management Review* (Winter 1995), pp. 25–40; and Charles W. Thomas, "Learning from Imagining the Years Ahead," *Planning Review* (May/June 1994), pp. 7–11.

32. Schoemaker.

33. Robert M. Fulmer, "A Model for Changing the Way Organizations Learn," *Planning Review* (May/June 1994), p. 23.

34. "Interview with Michael Hammer: The Reengineering Revolution," *Business Week* Online Conference, 26 April 1995 (America Online: McGraw-Hill, 1995).

35. Tanya Cordrey, ed., "Business Process Reengineering," *International Management* (September 1994), p. 62.

36. Michael Hammer and James Champy, *Reengineering the Corporation* (New York: HarperBusiness, 1993), p. 3.

37. Interview with Michael Hammer.

38. Hammer and Champy, *Reengineering the Corporation,* pp. 24–30.

39. "Interview with James Champy on Reengineering Management," *Business Week* Online Conference, 10 January 1995 (America Online: McGraw-Hill, 1995).

40. Online interview with Michael Hammer.

41. Ibid.

42. Online interview with James Champy.

43. Online interview with Michael Hammer.

44. Randall, p. 11.

45. Online interview with James Champy.

46. Michael Hammer, *The Reengineering Revolution* (New York: HarperBusiness, 1995).

47. Quinn, p. 238.

48. Kenichi Ohmae, "Putting Global Logic First," *Harvard Business Review* (January/February 1995), pp. 119–125.

49. Michael Porter, "Global Strategy: Winning in the World-Wide Marketplace," in *The Portable MBA in Strategy,* eds. Liam Fahey and Robert M. Randall (New York: John Wiley & Sons, 1994), pp. 108–141.

50. Alexander, Campbell, and Goold.

51. Quinn, p. 234–238.

52. Porter, p. 113.

53. Elisabeth Lesly, et al.

54. Porter, pp. 115–116.

55. Andrew Brown, "Top of the Bosses," *International Management* (April 1994), p. 28.

56. Refina Fazio Maruca, "The Right Way to Go Global: An Interview with Whirlpool CEO David Whitwam," *Harvard Business Review* (March/April 1994), pp. 135–145.

57. Ibid.

58. Kanter, pp. 369–380.

59. Ibid.

60. Ibid.

61. Tichy and Charan, pp. 69–78.

62. James B. Treece, Kathleen Kerwin, and Heidi Dawley, "Ford: Alex Trotman's daring global strategy," *Business Week,* 3 April 1995 (America Online: McGraw-Hill, 1995).

63. Paula Dwyer, et al., "Tearing Up Today's Organization Chart," *Business Week,* 18 November 1994 (America Online: McGraw-Hill, 1994).

64. Treece, Kerwin, and Dawley.

65. Ibid.

66. Maruca.

67. Tanya Cordrey and Justin Webster, "Profiting through trust," *International Management* (September 1994), pp. 38–40.

68. Stewart Toy, et al., "Flying High: Why KLM's Global Strategy Is Working," *Business Week,* 27 February 1995 (America Online: McGraw-Hill, 1995).

69. Amy Barrett, "Special Report: Small Business," *Business Week,* 17 April 1995 (America Online: McGraw-Hill, 1995).

70. Ibid.

71. Ibid.

72. Leonard M. Fuld, *The New Competitor Intelligence* (New York: John Wiley & Sons, 1995), pp. 195–266.

73. Barrett.